Wesse
shore
Culdr

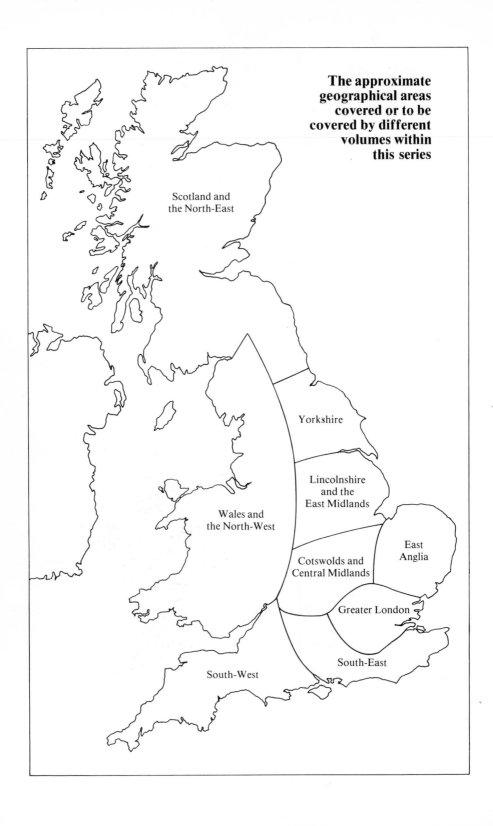

The approximate geographical areas covered or to be covered by different volumes within this series

Scotland and the North-East

Yorkshire

Lincolnshire and the East Midlands

Wales and the North-West

East Anglia

Cotswolds and Central Midlands

Greater London

South-West

South-East

ACTION STATIONS

5. Military airfields of the South-West

Chris Ashworth

PSL Patrick Stephens, Cambridge

First published November 1982
Reprinted July 1983

British Library Cataloguing in Publication Data

Ashworth, Christopher
  Action stations.
  5 : Military airfields of the South-West
  1. Great Britain. *Royal Air Force*
  2. World War, 1939-45—Aerial operations,
  British   3. Air bases—England—History
  I. Title
  940.54'43'42   D786

  ISBN 0-85059-510-X

Text photoset in 9 pt and 10 on 11 pt English Times by Manuset Limited, Baldock, Herts.
Printed in Great Britain on 100 gsm Fineblade coated cartridge, and bound, by The Garden City Press, Letchworth, Herts, for the publishers,
Patrick Stephens Limited, Bar Hill, Cambridge, CB3 8EL, England.

Contents

Introduction

Traditionally the West Country has been more concerned with seafaring than aeronautical endeavours and is probably considered by many as something of a backwater. Yet it can lay claim to the most prolific producer of pre-1914 aeroplanes, to two of the oldest active military airfields in the United Kingdom, and to a surprisingly varied amount of action by the FAA, RAF, USAAF and USN during 1939-45.

In recent years there has been an upsurge of interest in airfields stimulated by the realisation that many derelict sites are disappearing as fast as commercial interests realise their value. This interest has resulted in a proliferation of booklets listing airfield locations and sometimes giving potted histories. This book and the other volumes in the same series seek to *clothe* these bare bones by portraying the stories of the airfields and marine bases used in the south-west during the 1939-45 war, and to give an insight into the work of the units which flew from them.

For the interested spectator who is intrigued by names like Charlton Horethorne, Lulsgate Bottom, Merryfield, Upottery and all those Cornish saints, this book is intended to answer the query 'I wonder what happened there?' It should help enthusiasts by providing enough factual information to enable further investigation to start from firm ground while for ex-RAF and FAA personnel it will evoke memories and show how their small part fitted into the jigsaw—for few will have been privy to the whole story, and questions were not encouraged!

If you use the book as a guide when touring, the appropriate 1:50,000 Ordnance Survey maps will be very useful. They provide a surprising amount of information on airfield detail and even outlying sites can often be detected on them. Do remember, however, that nearly all these sites are on private land and therefore permission is needed before investigating them. Also remember that active airfields, especially military ones, may have restricted areas, and that close examination may be misunderstood. Where facilities for viewing exist or access is easy, I have recorded this in the text.

Most of the factual information in this book comes from my files built up over 40 years, or from official records at the Air Historical Branch, MoD and the Public Records Office, Kew. I acknowledge the help given by the staffs of

A Lancaster B1(FE) flies low over dispersed aircraft and a Blister hangar at Aston Down, postwar.

both organisations and those of the RAF Museum, FAA Museum and Museum of Army Flying. I have also visited every one of the sites and many private individuals have searched their memories, and in some cases their photo albums, to assist me; I am grateful to them all. I would be remiss if I did not mention in alphabetical order the particular help of Chaz Bowyer, W.G. Cornelius, R. Godden, T.H.J. Heffernan, CEng, AFRAes, J. Hewitt, J. May of the Wessex Aviation Society, M. Roberts, R. Sturtivant, D.C. Teague, K. West and P.R. White. R.N.E. Blake, BA, MRTPI, FRGS, a Senior Lecturer in Town & Country Planning at Trent Polytechnic who has a special interest in disused airfields provided invaluable assistance in locating some of the smaller grass fields used during the war. Michael J.F. Bowyer and David J. Smith, both authors of previous books in this series , have been unstinting with aid and advice, and to my old friend Bruce Robertson go my special thanks for his initial encouragement and ever-ready help. The facts and memories have come from many sources, the way I have chosen to use them is entirely my responsibility.

Photographs are of the utmost importance and I have been helped to locate suitable ones by the staffs of the Imperial War Museum and Department of the Environment. Other prints have come from private sources, the museums already mentioned, the USAAF, British Aerospace, Westland Aircraft Ltd and Osborne Studios of Falmouth.

I enjoyed researching this book and I hope it redresses the balance somewhat by showing that the south-west of England played a not inconsiderable part in the air war and contained a large number of real *Action Stations.*

R.C.B. Ashworth
Padstow,
March 1982

Glossary

AA   Anti-Aircraft.
AACU   Anti-Aircraft Co-operation Unit.
A&AEE   Aeroplane & Armament Experimental Establishment.
AASF   Advanced Air Striking Force.
ADDLs   Aerodrome Dummy Deck Landings.
ADEE   Air Defence Experimental Establishment.
ADGB   Air Defence of Great Britain.
AEF   Air Experience Flight.
AEW   Airborne Early Warning.
AFC   Air Force Cross.
AFEE   Airborne Fighting Experimental Establishment.
AFS   Advanced Flying School.
AFU   Advanced Flying Unit; (P) Pilot; (O) Observer.
AI   Airborne Interception.
AONS   Air Observer Navigation School.
ANS   Air Navigation School.
Anti-Diver   Patrol intercepting V1 flying bombs.
Anti-Rhubarb   Patrol to intercept low level intruders.
APC   Armament Practice Camp.
Armadillo   Light armoured vehicle for airfield defence.
A/S   Anti-Submarine.
ASL   Above Sea Level.
ASR   Air Sea Rescue.
ASU   Aircraft Storage Unit.
ATA   Air Transport Auxiliary.
ATTDU   Airborne Tactical Transport Development Unit.
BAT Flight   Blind Approach Training Flight.
BG   Bombardment Group (USAAF).
B&GS   Bombing & Gunnery School.
Blip   Spike or spot on radar display denoting a target.
Cab Rank   Fighter bombers on immediate call for close support to Army.

CAM (Ship)   Catapult Aircraft Merchant (Ship).
C&M   Care & Maintenance.
CFS   Central Flying School.
CH   Chain Home (radar station).
C-in-C   Commander-in-Chief.
Circus   Fighter-escorted bombing raid to attract enemy response.
CO   Commanding Officer.
Combination   Tug and glider with tow rope attached.
CU   Conversion Unit.
Darky   Emergency R/T organisation.
DFC   Distinguished Flying Cross.
DGCA   Director General of Civil Aviation.
Dicer   Low level photographic reconnaissance.
DZ   Dropping Zone.
EFTS   Elementary Flying Training School.
ELG   Emergency Landing Ground.
E&RFTS   Elementary & Reserve Flying Training School.
FAA   Fleet Air Arm.
FAW   Fleet Air Wing (USN).
FG   Fighter Group (USAAF).
FIDO   Fog Investigation & Dispersal Operation.
FIS   Flying Instructors' School.
Flak   *Fl*ieger*a*bwehr*k*annonen (German anti-aircraft gun).
FLS   Fighter Leaders' School.
FPP   Ferry Pilots Pool.
FTS   Flying Training School.
FU   Ferry Unit.
GCI   Ground Controlled Interception.
GRU   Gunnery Research Unit.
HE (bomb)   High Explosive.
IFF   Identification, Friend or Foe.
IFTU   Intensive Flying Trials Unit.
Instep   Fighter interception of German aircraft attacking shipping in SW approaches.

JG Jagdgeschwader (German fighter group).

KG Kampfgeschwader (German bomber group).

Leigh Light Trainable searchlight for A/S operations.

LG Landing Ground.

LG Lehrgeschwader (German trials unit).

Link Trainer Synthetic flight instrument trainer.

LZ Landing Zone.

Mains Mainhill type of servicing hangar used by FAA.

MAP Ministry of Aircraft Production.

MoD Ministry of Defence.

MoD(PE) Ministry of Defence (Procurement Executive).

MOTU Maritime Operational Training Unit.

MT Motor Transport.

MTB Motor Torpedo Boat.

MU Maintenance Unit.

NAAFI Navy, Army and Air Force Institute.

Nickelling Leaflet dropping.

NoBall Rocket and flying bomb sites.

OADF Overseas Air Delivery Flight.

OADU Overseas Aircraft Despatch Unit.

OAPU Overseas Aircraft Preparation Unit.

OCU Operational Conversion Unit.

Operation Cork Coastal Command A/S operation, 1944.

Operation Crossbow Offensive and defensive measures to counter V-weapon attack.

Operation Jubilee Combined operations at Dieppe, 1942.

Operation Mallard Final airborne phase of *Overlord*.

Operation Market Airborne operation at Arnhem, 1944.

Operation Neptune Amphibious phase of *Overlord*.

Operation Overlord Allied invasion of Normandy, 1944.

Operation Tonga Glider assault phase of *Overlord*.

Operation Torch Invasion of French North Africa, 1942.

OTU Operational Training Unit.

PRU Photo Reconnaissance Unit.

Q Site Flashing lights to represent airfield at night as a decoy.

RA Royal Artillery.

RAAF Royal Australian Air Force.

RAFA Royal Air Force Association.

RAT Flight Radio Aids Training Flight.

Ramrod Day bomber raid escorted by fighters.

Ranger Deep penetration flight to engage targets of opportunity.

RCAF Royal Canadian Air Force.

RFC Royal Flying Corps.

Rhubarb Low-level strike operation against targets in occupied Europe.

RLG Relief Landing Ground.

Roadstead Fighter operation against shipping.

Rodeo Fighter sweep.

RNVR Royal Naval Volunteer Reserve.

RP Rocket Projectile.

R/T Radio Telephone.

SAH School of Aircraft Handling.

SAR Search And Rescue.

SAS Special Air Service.

Schnorkel Air breathing tube for submerged submarine.

SDF Special Duty Flight.

SFTS Service Flying Training School.

SLG Satellite Landing Ground.

SofAC School of Army Co-operation.

SOE Special Operations Executive.

SofGR School of General Reconnaissance.

Sommerfeld tracking Wire mesh runway material.

Sperrbrecher German merchant ship.

Starfish Dummy fire to attract attention away from important targets.

Stopper Coastal Command patrol outside Brest harbour.

TCDU Transport Command Development Unit.

TCG Troop Carrier Group (USAAF).

TCW Troop Carrier Wing (USAAF).

Tiger Force British bombing force for operations against Japan.

TRG Tactical Reconnaissance Group (USAAF).

Turbinlite Airborne searchlight for night fighter operations.

USAAF United States Army Air Force.

USAF United States Air Force.

VHF Very High Frequency.

WD War Department.

WRNS Womens' Royal Naval Service (Wrens)

W/T Wireless telephony.

ZG Zerstoerer (German twin engined fighter).

Origins

The South-West of England means different things to different people. As far as this volume is concerned it is the land west of a line drawn between the Solent at Southampton and the Severn at Gloucester. Thus it ignores county borders by cutting Hampshire and Wiltshire in half and taking in part of Gloucestershire. It starts with Salisbury Plain and the New Forest, traverses the gentle hills and valleys of Dorset and Somerset before reaching down to the rugged moorland of Devon and Cornwall and out to the Channel and Scilly Isles. The region is not noted for its speedy reaction to new ideas but both balloons and aircraft were experimented with around the turn of the century. Not with great success, however, and the first aeronautical event of real importance was the formation of the British & Colonial Aeroplane Company at Filton, Bristol, in February 1910. By the end of 1911 the company had built well over 120 machines and its Boxkite was in service with several flying training schools, notably the very successful Bristol organisation at Larkhill on Salisbury Plain where aeroplanes had taken part in military manoeuvres the previous September.

Things were stirring but it all meant little to the average citizen until the appearance of Salmet and his Bleriot in 1912. Under the auspices of the *Daily Mail* he toured Devon and Cornwall, making visits to towns and remote villages and quickly catching the imagination of the populace. The Great War brought further activity, especially on Salisbury Plain. To the west it was almost entirely confined to anti-submarine warfare with landplane, seaplane and airship bases dotted strategically around the coasts.

Salmet and his Bleriot at Falmouth in June 1912.

After the war the military retreated and soon only the marine base at Mount Batten remained open west of the Plain. A number of civil operators, notably the Cornish Aviation Co of St Austell, did summer joyriding tours, replaced in 1931 by a flying circus. The following year Sir Alan Cobham organised a much larger circus and was a popular visitor all over the south-west from 1932 until 1935. C.W.A. Scott took over in 1936 but interest was waning and the touring circus was no longer a financial success. Scheduled passenger services were also tried, but with similar lack of success until the late 1930s when several towns opened airports, among them Bristol, Exeter and Plymouth. Three aircraft manufacturers also operated company airfields at Filton, Yate and Yeovil.

Meanwhile, the rapid expansion of the RAF during the 1930s hardly touched the region and in September 1939 there were just two flying boat bases and 13 active military airfields in the whole area. Some of the latter were little more than large grass fields. It was virgin country, soon to be defiled by the ravages of war, and not least by numerous airfields.

Below *Graham Gilmour flying his Bristol Boxkite pre-World War 1.* **Bottom** *Bristol Prier monoplane at Larkhill—Bristol's Flying School* (Bristol Aeroplane Co). **Opposite page top to bottom** *The RFC 'Concentration' at Netheravon, 1914. The aircraft of 'A', 'B' and 'C' Flights of CFS at Upavon in 1914* (via Chaz Bowyer). *The most famous World War 1 product of the Bristol company—the F2B Fighter at Filton* (Bristol Aeroplane Co). *The Cornwall Aviation Co's most famous Avro 504K—the bright red* G-EBIZ *resting before another bout of joyriding.*

Works, bricks and services

Four large airfields were under construction in the south-west at the beginning of September 1939, three for the RAF and one for the FAA. The latter, now under Admiralty control, was expanding rapidly. Its new airfield at Yeovilton was almost unique in being designed with runways, for the RAF was still stubbornly resisting laying concrete or tarmac strips across its green turf except on a few *heavy* bomber stations. Their Expansion Scheme airfields were, however, now being provided with perimeter tracks and the layout of the technical and domestic areas of these stations was excellent. Generally equipped with a number of large 'C' Type hangars, their major buildings were tastefully finished in good brick or stone and the airmens' quarters were of the very successful 'H' Block pattern. A typical example was Middle Wallop, one of the last sufficiently advanced at the beginning of the war to be finished in this form, and it remains an almost perfect example today. St Eval, which was to become the major anti-submarine base in the south-west, was hurriedly completed with wooden huts which looked incongruous against the sturdy concrete-faced hangars.

The landing area of these airfields was an average 3,300 ft (1,006 m) in diameter with a concrete or tarmac strip in front of the hangars and a watch office, the forerunner of the control tower.

With the war came a massive expansion in airfield building and the RAF quickly realised its error in persevering with grass. The new standard became a main runway at least 3,300 ft (1,006 m) long and 150 ft (46 m) wide, usually coupled with two shorter runways and connected by a perimeter track. In the south-west this meant that their location was determined more by the terrain than anything else. This is the reason for the rather strange groupings of wartime airfields in the area.

Domestic accommodation on these airfields was in almost universally wooden, or corrugated iron huts of various lengths and sizes. Many of the communal messing sites and technical buildings were in brick with cement finish know as *Maycrete*. Airfields planned during the war invariably had dispersed living sites with ablutions often yards from the sleeping huts. Essential services

Opposite page top to bottom *The pleasing design of an 'Expansion' scheme water tower—this one is at Aston Down. 'D' Type storage hangars at Aston Down. Duration-only airfields were rather haphazard in layout. These buildings, mainly of Maycrete construction, are at Babdown Farm. Maycrete buildings in better condition and still in use at Exeter Airport.*

such as heating were primitive and many airfields suffered from a chronic lack of water—through taps anyway! The sites were uncomfortable, time-wasting and very inconvenient—but it was wartime and people were adaptable.

This airfield design was adequate for fighters but proved too small for heavily loaded twin-engined aircraft. By 1942 bases operating or designed for such types were being given a main, usually south-west/north-east orientated, runway of 6,000 ft (1,828 m) and two subsidiary ones of 4,200 ft (1,280 m). The perimeter tracks now had extensive panhandle dispersals off them, and fixed electric runway and approach lighting was standard. A few utility airfields had just two runways at 90 degrees, but the FAA always had four comparatively short ones, and in the case of Henstridge used five! This may seem like naval extravagance but the reason was simple. All FAA shore bases were training stations and naval pilots were learning to fly from carriers which turned into wind for take-off and landing on. Thus there was no point in dealing with crosswinds, ADDLs were quite difficult enough to handle on their own!

There were four major Maintenance Units in the West Country and they expanded rapidly by taking in adjacent fields as open storage sites. These soon became a problem because access track were unusable in wet weather and more works services were needed to lay tarmac to enable the aircraft to be moved.

Relief and advanced landing grounds started off as grass airfields but, as the war progressed, they were often improved with steel mesh, pierced steel plank or hard runways. A few were completed as secret airfields and great pains were taken with these to eliminate any clues, even the watch office being off the LG. The same philosophy was followed with the SLGs rushed into operation for dispersal of aircraft from MUs after the French collapse. These started off as fields conveniently close to cover, usually woods or copses, but later they were developed by grading the landing strips and providing steel mesh aircraft stands. When the expected onslaught by the Luftwaffe failed to materialise they were often used as RLGs by training units. Any buildings were deliberately made to look as civilian as possible.

Q-sites, decoys laid out with lights to represent an airfield at night, were provided for all major bases open in 1941. They were usually three or four miles from the parent airfield with the intention of drawing the attention of Luftwaffe bomber crews away from the real target.

The details of airfield architecture has been very adequately covered in *Aviation Archaeology* by Bruce Robertson and other books in this series. It should suffice here to record that most stations built during the war in the south-west had Bellman or Teeside hangars supplemented by Blisters.

The 'J' and 'K' Type hangars were confined almost entirely to MUs, which also had a number of special storage units which were sometimes grass-covered for camouflage. These MUs and a number of their SLGs had transportable Robin and Super Robin hangars which could be made to look like farm buildings fairly easily. For temporary purposes portable canvas Bessoneaux hangars, first introduced during the Great War, were used throughout the 1939-

Opposite page top to bottom *The derelict Maycrete gymnasium at St Eval. This building is visible behind the PRU Spitfire on page 167. Most of the buildings at St Eval were wooden huts. Here a funeral party marches past the Station HQ towards the main gate. The last of the four mighty 'C' Type hangars at St Eval—and soon to be demolished. An Oversize Blister now in use by ECC Quarries Ltd at Warmwell. One of the two 'T2' hangars can just be seen through the trees.*

45 period and some became virtually permanent fixtures. The Admiralty used Bellman and Teeside but also had two special ones of their own, known as Mainhill and Pentads. The Mains were the same size as a Super Robin, 72 ft (22 m) by 60 ft (18.3 m) and similar in appearance, while a Pentad was a large servicing hangar, 185 ft (56 m) by 105 ft (32 m). Naval air stations were always well endowed with hangars. St Merryn, a medium-sized airfield, had one Callendar Hamilton, two Pentads, four small Teeside and 26 Mains by the end of the war.

With the almost universal introduction of R/T, the watch office was replaced by air traffic control towers. These substantial concrete buildings took various forms but were usually rectangular, two-storey, flat-roofed structures with a broad balcony on three sides. At the same time night flying aids, which at the beginning of the war were confined to an airfield identification beacon and runway flare paths, became more complex. Lead-in funnels and finally complete circuit patterns in lights known as Drem systems were installed.

Below *A purely naval hangar type—a Mainhill at the Avenger dispersal of 736 Squadron at St Merryn in March 1945 (FAA Museum).* **Bottom** *Another Mainhill, together with a common Nissen hut, in use on a trading estate at Henstridge.* **Opposite page, top to bottom** *A standard 'T2' hangar in fairly good condition at Keevil in April 1980, and still in use for storage. One of the few brick buildings at St Eval was the Operations Block—seen here in April 1981 still protected by earthworks. Another view of St Merryn with two 'T2' hangars under construction in August 1944. Amongst the other buildings is the original ATC (FAA Museum). The old St Merryn tower still stands. A Spitfire is being rebuilt in the shed in the foreground.*

Above *The much more substantial ATC tower on the other side of St Merryn—nearly complete in August 1944 (FAA Museum).*

Another unusual tower, the wooden watch office at St Eval. Note the tarred roofing felt weather protection on the top deck (via C. Luke).

Several ATC towers in the south-west were converted into dwellings. One of the more successful was the one at Zeals, now known as the Tower House.

Other types of wartime buildings are also still in use. A dispersal site at St Mawgan is the Treloy Farm Tourist Park.

The general introduction of beam approach systems during 1942 at heavy stations of Bomber, Coastal and Transport Commands brought with it a large training commitment and even quite insignificant airfields in the south-west were equipped with the aid for the use of BAT Flights. Davidstow Moor and St Eval also took part in trials of one of the first ground-controlled approach radars and the latter station was the only one in the region equipped with FIDO.

Security and defence was a constant problem. At the beginning of the war airfields were almost totally insecure. Later they were surrounded by unsightly and generally ineffective barbed wire; it was the introduction of police dogs which provided the answer though they could only cover particularly sensitive areas. A limited number of ground gunners were available but in practice most anti-aircraft defence, such as it was in 1939, was in the hands of the Army as were airfield guard posts. The equipment consisted of a few Lewis guns later supplemented by 20 mm Hispanos. In April 1941 the existing station defence personnel were gathered into squadrons and these formed the nucleus of the RAF Regiment when it was established in February 1942. By the end of the year the Regiment had taken over the defence of every airfield in the region and most had independent AA Flights manning 12 20 mm Hispano guns. Many were withdrawn during the low level attacks by the Luftwaffe on coastal towns in 1943 and again for anti-Diver operations—the threat to airfields was then small and remained so for the remainder of the war.

The effort that went into the construction of the airfields and marine bases described in this book was enormous. Under the overall control of the Air Ministry Works Department many construction firms, from giants like McAlpine, Taylor Woodrow and Wimpey to local builders, were involved in the construction of runways and the numerous buildings and services which made up a wartime airfield. Even the smaller grass fields, of which there were many in the south-west, were expensive in resources, sometimes unjustifiably so. Each was built for a purpose, some fulfilled it, others did equally important tasks, while a few were hardly employed at all. The latter were a waste of resources, effort and time—but it is easy to be wise after the event.

At war

In the whole of the area defined in this book as the South-West of England there was but one operational military base in September 1939. This was Mount Batten, from where Sunderlands were already plying their trade. Warmwell was host to 217 Squadron awaiting the opening of St Eval, and 501 rushed back to Filton, but neither of these airfields could really be called operational at that time. The comparative safety of the south-west resulted in various experimental units, notably the A&AEE, taking refuge there, and various training schools were considerably expanded in size. Plans were also made for several new airfields but once St Eval was operational little actually happened until the fall of France in June 1940.

Overnight the whole area became vulnerable to attack by the Luftwaffe and frantic efforts were made to spread the fighter defences westward. Squadrons were sent to Middle Wallop, St Eval and ex-civil airports like Exeter and these became the responsibility of 10 Group, operational at Rudloe Manor, Box, Wiltshire from July 13. Middle Wallop, Filton and St Eval were established as sector airfields to control aircraft in their areas, and led superbly by Air Vice Marshal Sir Quinton Brand, 10 Group managed to break up nearly every Luftwaffe attack despite its thinly spread forces. Tremendous efforts were made in defence of Portland naval base, a primary target for the Germans.

The occupation of NW France posed other threats, notably invasion and infiltration. During the long summer of 1940 Army Co-op Lysanders were employed to carry out dawn and dusk patrols around the coast, covering bays and inlets to check for any sign of landing. This task continued for some months during the height of the invasion scare, but gradually the units involved returned to their basic tasks during 1941.

By 1941 Sunderlands from Mount Batten were proving their solid worth and at St Eval the range of activities was constantly expanding. Spitfires of the PRU covered Brest daily while anti-submarine and anti-shipping work in the south-west approaches went remorsefully on. Attacks by the Luftwaffe on the region during 1940 had not met with much effective opposition but the 1941 *real* night fighters, in particular the Beaufighter, started to show their mettle and were active during raids on Bristol and Plymouth.

The same year saw the RAF moving slowly over to the offensive and forward airfields such as Bolt Head, Predannack, Harrowbeer and Portreath came into commission at the right time to take part in operations rejoicing in names like *Circus, Rodeo, Rhubarb* and *Ramrod*. Some of the *Circus* operations built up

87 Squadron Hurricanes spent many months in the West Country on several airfields—but never on the one in the background! It is Hullavington.

into large-scale affairs involving a number of airfields and many bomber and fighter aircraft.

Other activities included ferrying to the Middle East and ASR. After one or two night flights over occupied France direct to Malta a safer ferry route around the Iberian Peninsula into Gibraltar was devised and Portreath became the main jumping off point in the United Kingdom. It was also one of the bases for detached Flights of two Lysanders for rescue work—the small beginnings of what by the end of the war was a large and efficient organisation.

No 67 MU, formed at Taunton in October 1940, was very active as a salvage organisation clearing up the result of crashes and forced landings all over the peninsula.

Several Blenheim fighter squadrons of Coastal Command had made short detachments to the south-west for shipping strikes during 1940 and this activity increased in 1941 when they were joined by Whirlwinds of 263 Squadron. This aircraft remained in Fighter Command but must take the prize for being the most nomadic of all—it seems to have operated from every sizable airfield in the area, on all sorts of tasks.

With 1942 came consolidation of airborne forces on Salisbury Plain and a gradual take-over of airfields in the area. The Leigh-Light Wellingtons made a successful debut from Chivenor and more airfields had to be found for the Americans who started to arrive in preparation for *Bolero*, a landing in France. It was postponed in favour of Operation *Torch* but the West Country still had to find room for Douglas C-47 units, and even a number of American fighters.

The so-called *Baedecker* reprisal raids started in April 1942 with attacks on Exeter, followed by Bath, Bristol and Weston-super-Mare. They resulted in a strengthening of both night fighter and gun defences, but faded away and on August 19 *Jubilee* involved many 10 Group squadrons, mainly detached outside the area. For *Torch* several new and still incomplete airfields were pressed into service but then came a lull enlivened only by a spate of low-level attacks on

coastal towns by the Luftwaffe during January 1943, and by Exercise *Spartan* in March. This involved most of the fighter squadrons and Army Co-operation units in a 15-day close support exercise with the Army, living under field conditions in tents.

The disbandment of Army Co-operation Command and formation of the Tactical Air Force in June caused considerable upheaval, but more noticeable in the south-west were a series of heavy raids on Plymouth which continued through the summer months. In the autumn the USN became properly established at Dunkeswell and the preparatory planning for the invasion of Europe began to bear fruit with the steady build-up of airborne forces and the construction of a series of ALGs along the south coast.

During the early months of 1944 these preparations accelerated. More squadrons, both British and American, arrived in the region and were involved in training. In the main, transport units were deployed inland and fighter-bombers on New Forest airfields and coastal ALGs. On the ground the area became one enormous armed camp with thousands of troops, tanks, vehicles and stores of all kinds crammed into the coastal zone. What a target for the Luftwaffe if they had been able to take advantage of it. Strenuous efforts were made to stop them and they were only able to make isolated attacks on ports, including Weymouth, Torquay and Falmouth where landing craft were assembled. They had little success and on June 5/6 1944 the armada was on its way.

The remainder of the European war was anti-climax in the south-west, apart from anti-submarine operations which continued to the bitter end. The operational fighters and medium bombers soon vacated the ALGs for the Continent and the south-west was then used as a rest and re-equipment area, and the base for a long-range transport force.

Left *The cratered RAF Exeter on June 12 1941 after one of the worst Luftwaffe attacks (IWM).*

Right *There is no doubt about this airfield. The church tower in this photo of a 221 Squadron Wellington taking off proclaims that it is at St Eval.*

When the war against Japan ended abruptly in August 1945 many of the airfields were soon closed and abandoned. Others were retained on standby and used briefly again during the 1950s, and a very few remained operational as either military bases or civil airports.

Never again will the South-West of England see formations of 60-plus fighter-bombers, or the sky filled with straining tugs and serene gliders. It is unlikely that airfields will again be seen crammed with aircraft as Chivenor was for *Torch*, or Hurn was on D-Day. It is now just history.

What a change was wrought in the months between September 1939 and June 1944. The story of the airfields involved, from the day they opened until the 1980s or when they finally closed, is told in the next section.

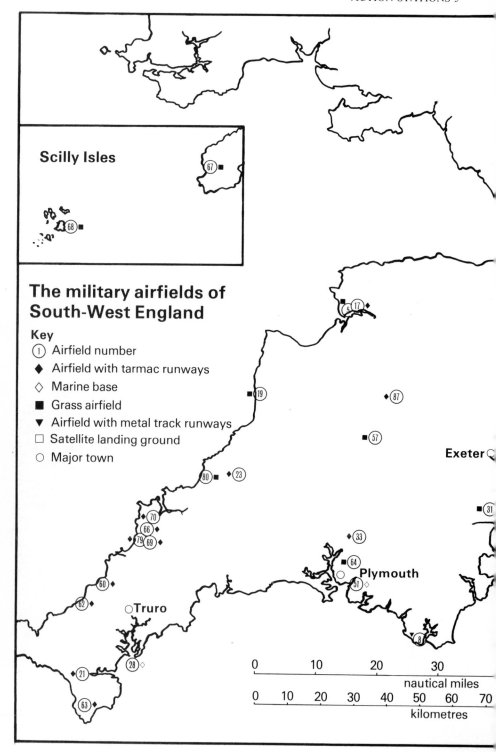

Scilly Isles

The military airfields of South-West England

Key

- ① Airfield number
- ◆ Airfield with tarmac runways
- ◇ Marine base
- ■ Grass airfield
- ▼ Airfield with metal track runways
- ☐ Satellite landing ground
- ○ Major town

Exeter

Plymouth

Truro

0   10   20   30
nautical miles

0   10   20   30   40   50   60   70
kilometres

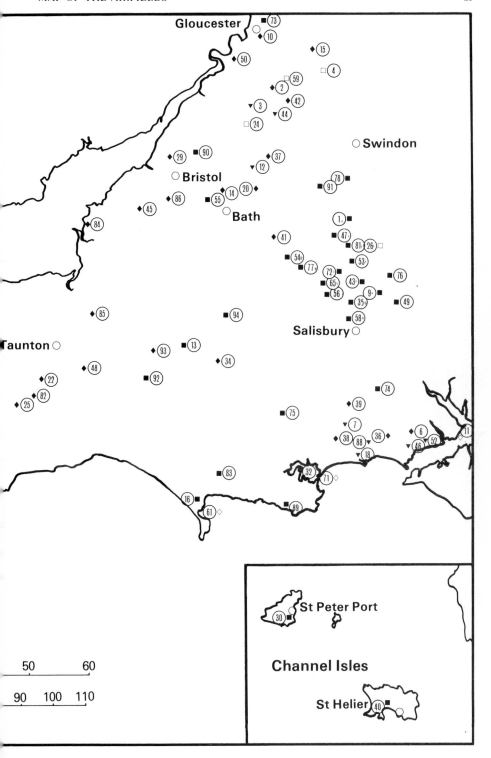

Key to airfield numbers on preceding pages

No	Name	County	No	Name	County
1	Alton Barnes	Wiltshire	48	Merryfield	Somerset
2	Aston Down	Gloucestershire	49	Middle Wallop	Hampshire
3	Babdown Farm	Gloucestershire	50	Moreton Valence	Gloucestershire
4	Barnsley Park	Gloucestershire	51	Mount Batten	Devon
5	Barnstaple	Devon	52	Needs Oar Point	Hampshire
6	Beaulieu	Hampshire	53	Netheravon	Wiltshire
7	Bisterne	Hampshire	54	New Zealand Farm	Wiltshire
8	Bolt Head	Devon	55	North Stoke	Gloucestershire/
9	Boscombe Down	Wiltshire			Avon
10	Brockworth	Gloucestershire	56	Oatlands Hill	Wiltshire
11	Calshot	Hampshire	57	Okehampton	Devon
12	Castle Combe	Wiltshire	58	Old Sarum	Wiltshire
13	Charlton		59	Overley	Gloucestershire
	Horethorne	Somerset	60	Perranporth	Cornwall
14	Charmy Down	Somerset/Avon	61	Portland	Dorset
15	Chedworth	Gloucestershire	62	Portreath	Cornwall
16	Chickerell	Dorset	63	Predannack	Cornwall
17	Chivenor	Devon	64	Roborough	Devon
18	Christchurch	Hampshire/Dorset	65	Rollestone	Wiltshire
19	Cleave	Cornwall	66	St Eval	Cornwall
20	Colerne	Wiltshire	67	St Just/Lands End	Cornwall
21	Culdrose	Cornwall	68	St Marys	Scilly Isles
22	Culmhead/		69	St Mawgan	Cornwall
	Church Stanton	Somerset	70	St Merryn	Cornwall
23	Davidstow Moor	Cornwall	71	Sandbanks	Dorset
24	Down Farm	Gloucestershire	72	Shrewton	Wiltshire
25	Dunkeswell	Devon	73	Staverton	Gloucestershire
26	Everleigh	Wiltshire	74	Stoney Cross	Hampshire
27	Exeter	Devon	75	Tarrant Rushton	Dorset
28	Falmouth	Cornwall	76	Thruxton	Wiltshire
29	Filton	Gloucestershire/	77	Tilshead	Wiltshire
		Avon	78	Townsend	Wiltshire
30	Guernsey	Channel Islands	79	Trebelzue	Cornwall
31	Haldon	Devon	80	Treligga	Cornwall
32	Hamworthy/Poole	Dorset	81	Upavon	Wiltshire
33	Harrowbeer	Devon	82	Upottery	Devon
34	Henstridge	Dorset	83	Warmwell	Dorset
35	High Post	Wiltshire	84	Weston-super-	
36	Holmsley South	Hampshire		Mare	Somerset/Avon
37	Hullavington	Wiltshire	85	Weston Zoyland	Somerset
38	Hurn	Hampshire/Dorset	86	Whitchurch	Somerset/Avon
39	Ibsley	Hampshire	87	Winkleigh	Devon
40	Jersey	Channel Islands	88	Winkton	Hampshire
41	Keevil	Wiltshire	89	Worth Matravers	Dorset
42	Kemble	Gloucestershire	90	Yate	Gloucestershire/
43	Larkhill	Wiltshire			Avon
44	Long Newnton	Gloucestershire	91	Yatesbury	Wiltshire
45	Lulsgate Bottom	Somerset	92	Yeovil	Somerset
46	Lymington	Hampshire	93	Yeovilton	Somerset
47	Manningford	Wiltshire	94	Zeals	Wiltshire

Key to symbols used on airfield maps

Local features

 Roads (important roads are numbered)

 Railway line

 Rivers and streams

 Outline of village or town built-up area

 Rocks or cliffs

 Wooded areas

 Earthworks and embankments

 Low tide line

Airfield features

 Concrete and tarmac runways and taxiways

 Steel mesh track runways and taxiways

 Aircraft dispersals

Airfield buildings

Outline of airfield domestic sites

△ 50ft   Height of ground above sea level

The airfields

Alton Barnes, Wiltshire
SU100620. 4 miles NW of Upavon

The first use of Alton Barnes was by the Central Flying School of the mid-1930s—the days of the Avro 504N. One of a number of landing grounds scattered around Wiltshire, it boasted no facilities other than a windsock. It was used by embryo instructors practising their circuit patter in comparative peace away from the main airfield at Upavon. Such landing grounds were notoriously difficult to locate from the air, but Alton Barnes was an exception. Approaching from Upavon it was only necessary to point the aircraft at the prominent white horse cut in the side of Milk Hill and, glancing down as one approached, there it was sandwiched between the Kennet & Avon canal and the Stanton St Bernard road.

A Miles Magister of the type used by 29 EFTS at Alton Barnes.

The '504s were finally replaced by Tutors in 1937 and the field was used by these powerful biplane trainers until late 1941. The threat of invasion in 1940 resulted in the construction of some concrete gun positions along the roadside, but these were no use when a German bomber dropped three bombs on the LG during the night of September 14 and the defences were then strengthened by gun positions around the perimeter.

An ever-increasing demand for instructors led to shortened courses, an inevitable decline in standards with an increase in accidents. A number of Tutors were destroyed but with the use of Alton Barnes by Oxfords and Masters the problems increased, and there were several landing crashes including a collision on June 18 1941 when both crews were killed.

At the end of 1941 Alton Barnes was transferred to 29 EFTS, Clyffe Pypard, and work to upgrade it to RLG standard

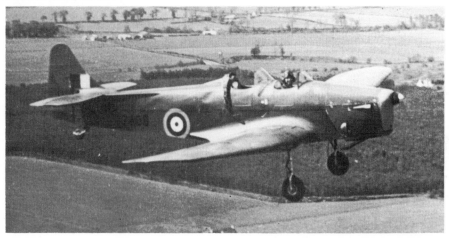

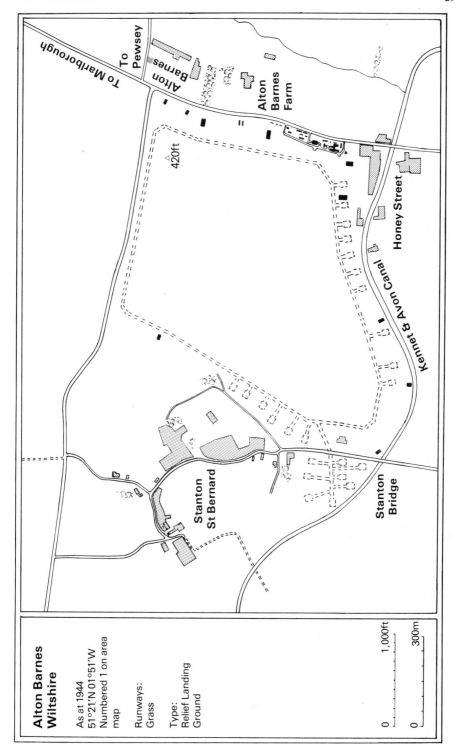

To Marlborough

To Pewsey

Alton Barnes

Alton Barnes Farm

420ft

Honey Street

Kennet & Avon Canal

Stanton St Bernard

Stanton Bridge

Alton Barnes Wiltshire

As at 1944
51°21'N 01°51'W
Numbered 1 on area map

Runways: Grass

Type: Relief Landing Ground

1,000ft

300m

0

0

The one remaining building at Alton Barnes, the gymnasium.

commenced. Nissen and Maycrete buildings were constructed alongside the Honey Street-Alton Barnes road and Blister hangars were sited around the perimeter. Night flying facilities included rendezvous lights on Milk Hill and these attracted the attention of aircraft on the nights of April 16/17 1942 when small flash bombs were dropped, narrowly missing the Armadillo vehicle guarding the gooseneck flares. The aircraft were from an OTU and the crews had mistaken the lights for a bombing range.

29 EFTS operated Tiger Moths and Magisters which soon became a familiar sight at Alton Barnes. In May 1942 the courses of RAF/RN cadet pilots changed to Army personnel on pre-glider training. At first the cadets travelled from Clyffe Pypard daily but on June 3 1942 the school was upgraded to six Flights, two of which were accommodated at Alton Barnes. The circuit became very congested and the take-off and landing free-for-all was replaced by Aldis lamp signals from an airfield controller.

The glider pilot intakes were suspended in December 1942 and RAF grading courses introduced. These were replaced by similar Fleet Air Arm courses in October 1944. Meanwhile, heavy rain over the winter of 1943-44 caused considerable difficulty with waterlogged dispersals and Sommerfeld tracking was laid in these areas and as a perimeter track. With the end of the war the task of 29 EFTS was reduced and on July 7 1945 the aircraft were flown back to Clyffe Pypard. Two

days later the RLG was closed and reverted to Care & Maintenance.

The airfield was de-requisitioned in 1947 and returned to agriculture. There is now little to see apart from the Link Trainer building and a few concrete bases near the village of Honey Street.

Aston Down, Gloucestershire

SO912010. 1½ miles SE of Chalford on A419

This airfield was planned and built as an aircraft storage unit, on the same site as the 1914-18 Minchinhampton aerodrome. The compact administrative and technical site in the north-west corner of the airfield was well and comfortably built, supplemented by eight large dome-roofed storage hangars dispersed around the station. Situated in glorious countryside, it was opened as 7 ASU on October 12 1938, becoming 20 Maintenance Unit just five days later.

First used for equipment storage, aircraft started to arrive in February 1939 and on September 6 12 Wellingtons of 214 Squadron landed from Feltwell without warning, following dispersal orders. They left the next day, however, and the MU found one of its main tasks was the preparation of Blenheims for Yugoslavia and Roumania.

Meanwhile, Fighter Command decided that Aston Down would make a good training base and formed 12 Group Pool on August 23 1939. Using Harvards, Gladiators and Blenheims, this unit gave intermediate training to pilots being posted to Group squadrons. The numbers posted in when the war started outstripped the accommodation and some officers were billeted at the George Hotel, Nailsworth, where the proprieter provided four meals a day for six shillings (30p)— how things have changed! A month later Fighter Command took over the airfield, the MU remaining as a lodger. It clung on to its buildings, however, the station HQ being established in a barrack hut until new accommodation was ready in December.

The Group Pool became 5 OTU on March 15 1940 and used Spitfires, Hurricanes, Blenheims, Defiants, Masters and Battles. One of the Spitfires shot down a Ju 88 on July 25. Further development of the station began in September and many of the new sites were ready for occupation two months later—such was the pace of wartime activity. On

A Spitfire IIB of 52 OTU at Aston Down in January 1943 (IWM).

November 1 Aston Down became 55 OTU but the task was just the same—the rapid output of new crews for Hurricane day and Blenheim night fighter squadrons.

Runway construction commenced in 1941 but progress was slow due to the weather and the number of aircraft movements. The situation improved when 55 OTU departed during February/March. Soon afterwards, on March 29, the Q site at Horsley, 3½ miles south-west of Aston Down, was bombed, but the runways were completed without hindrance from the Luftwaffe.

The Air Transport Auxiliary took over the ferrying, some of their pilots causing quite a stir, for they were women! But the best known unit at Aston Down was 52 OTU which arrived from Debden in August 1941. The Masters and Spitfires of this OTU flew hard and were involved in some spectacular accidents both on, and off, the airfield. A year later two of its six Flights moved to Chedworth but by the middle of 1943 the supply of day fighter pilots exceeded demand and 52 OTU was disbanded on August 10 when the Fighter Leader School moved in from Charmy Down. The FLS used Spitfire VBs to teach tactics to embryo squadron and flight commanders but did not stay long, going to Milfield in January 1944.

Meanwhile the MU was busy with Spitfires and Typhoons, these being superseded in 1944 by the preparation of Canadian Lancaster 10s for service, and the conversion of Albemarles for glider towing. 1311 Flight of Anson 1 ambulances arrived in May, but was replaced by 84 Group Support Unit in June. This outfit remained fully mobile, living under canvas to the south of the airfield, and was responsible for immediate replacement of aircraft for its units on the Continent. As airfields became available in France, 84 Group moved out and No 3 Tactical Exercise Unit arrived from Annan. Intended for rocket firing and other specialised ground attack training, the TEU was largely equipped with Typhoons and Hurricanes, though the latter had left by the end of August when the 'Tiffie' strength rose to 64.

Things went full circle in December 1944 when 3 TEU became 55 OTU with Typhoons, Hurricanes, Masters and Martinets on strength, a total of 134 aircraft. One of their Typhoons crashed on to a dispersal hut near B site of 20 MU on March 25 1945 and burst into flames, trapping WAAFs and airmen.

With the end of the war 55 OTU was disbanded on June 14. The MU satellites were closing down and many of the dispersal fields were handed back to their owners, resulting in over 1,000 aircraft being herded together on the airfield. In July 20 MU again took control of the station and the ATA Ferry Pool was replaced by a Tug Flight. This unit operated Whitleys and Albemarles from the ATA dispersal, and was soon joined by a reborn 2 Ferry Pool and the Harvards and Oxfords of 41 Group Pilot Training Flight.

No 83 Gliding School arrived from Moreton Valence in October 1946 but the main task of Aston Down was the reduction of the vast stock of aircraft in storage. Experiments were also carried out on cocooning, aircraft as large as the Lincoln being covered in a plastic skin and left out in the elements. Although effective in keeping the weather out it also trapped moisture in, and the airframes deteriorated almost as quickly as when left in open storage.

No 1689 (Ferry Pool Training) Flight was formed in June 1946 when 2 Ferry Pool also became 2 Home Ferry Unit. The former was absorbed in May 1952, while the latter became 187 Squadron in February 1953 and moved to Benson.

Aston Down quietly plodded along until 20 MU was closed in September 1960. The hangars were then taken over by 5 MU Kemble and in more recent years the airfield was operated as a RLG by the Central Flying School until February 1976. It is now used by the Cotswold Gliding Club. The storage facilities were taken over by the Ministry of Aviation in April 1963 and the main site remains in pristine condition as a Procurement Executive Stores Depot—definitely a round peg in a round hole.

Babdown Farm, Gloucestershire

ST845938. 3 miles W of Tetbury on A4135
Taking its name from the farm which provided most of the land, this airfield was planned in 1939 as a RLG for 9 FTS Hullavington and was first used at the end of July 1940 for night flying by the units' Harts and Audaxes. The aircraft were flown over from Hullavington in the late afternoon and handled by a small party detached from the main base who also looked after the gooseneck flarepath under the control of the duty pilot. The RLG was in use for such a session on August 3 when a German aircraft dropped a stick of HE on the flares doing no damage, but understandably reported as 'frightening'. The facilities were also used by Marylands of the OADF Kemble for training before a hazardous night flight to Malta across occupied France during November.

By 1941 Masters and Hurricanes were in use at night, but it was during the day that the second Luftwaffe visit was made. A bomber dived out of low cloud on March 26 and its gunners fired a short burst at aircraft on the ground. Again no damage was done.

No 9 SFTS became 9(P)AFU in February 1942, transferring to Castle Combe a month later while Babdown Farm was re-developed. The airfield was brought up to full RLG standard by laying two (later three) Sommerfeld track runways and by June a number of Blister hangars had been erected around the perimeter. The HQ site alongside the farm buildings was also well on the way to completion, as were the instructional and communal sites dispersed to the east at Beverston Old Broke and Broad Newell Covert.

On re-opening in August 1942 two Flights of 3 Flying Instructors School moved into the accommodation. The unit's night flying was concentrated at Babdown and the circuit was soon alive with Oxfords and Masters. It was also used by Spitfires from 52 OTU during the day and on January 26 1943 was host to three lost aircraft, an Oxford, a fully bombed-up Wellington and a Curtiss Cleveland biplane. Not many of the latter flew in this country, but one which did wore a maintenance serial issued to grounded airframes. Perhaps it was this famous (or infamous) machine.

During 1943 a Standard Beam Approach was installed on the main 3,900 ft (1,189 m) east/west runway and in June 1532 BAT Flight arrived to provide training on this aid using Oxfords. Other developments included the construction of a new maintenance site on the south-east side where three Teeside hangars were erected. 3 FIS left at the end of September and although the technical site was still incomplete 15(P)AFU moved in a month later, leaving its maintenance squadron at Andover until January 1944. By March 15(P)AFU was completely settled in and it was undoubtedly the new electric lighting on the runways which attracted a single bomber during the night of May 15. It dropped two bombs but neither did any damage, indeed throughout Babdown's short history training accidents proved much more hazardous than the attentions of the enemy. A particularly nasty one occurred on August 29 1944 when the runway controller was killed by an Oxford which landed on his caravan.

The wet weather during the autumn and winter of 1944/45 caused the runways to lift and for three months the airfield was only partially serviceable. The closure of Long Newnton increased the load on Babdown Farm, but it was not for long because the unit ceased training on May

Babdown Farm on June 29 1942 before the technical site was built. The Sommerfeld track runways and Blister hangars can be seen despite the very effective camouflage (RAF Museum).

28 and the last aircraft left on June 20 1945.

Babdown reverted to Care & Maintenance in June 1945 but the following month was taken over as a sub-site by 7 MU Quedgeley who used the hangars for storage until January 1948 when Babdown became an inactive site and was soon de-requisitioned. In 1980 the three Teeside hangars were in good condition and in use. Amongst the many derelict buildings alongside the A4135 a farming contractor uses some patched-up ones. There is plenty to look at among the other buildings on this site—but permission is needed.

Barnsley Park, Gloucestershire

SP075075. 4 miles NE of Cirencester off the A433

Among the Satellite Landing Grounds allocated to 6 MU Brize Norton was Barnsley Park, a heavily wooded estate near Cirencester. It was opened by the Ministry of Aircraft Production on June 23 1941 as No 22 SLG; intended as a temporary dispersal while the much more extensive satellite at Woburn Abbey was developed. An administrative office, guards and light AA defences were established and with aircraft landing on an adjacent field and dispersed in the parkland, 6 MU's earlier use of Watchfield aerodrome ceased in September.

No 22 SLG proved very difficult to operate, however, and in November 1941 it was reduced to Care & Maintenance for re-grading so that twin-engined aircraft of the Boston and Hudson type could use the site. The weather during the winter prevented Messrs W.G. Chivers & Son Ltd from commencing work until March 1942. On completion a test landing was made by a Gladiator but it was unsatisfactory and 22 SLG was not used again by 6 MU. After more work it was handed over to 5 MU Kemble on September 26 just as an argument between the Air Ministry and MAP developed over a proposed airfield in the area. It was therefore over a year before any aircraft arrived, three Hurricanes being dispersed in November 1943. A brick bungalow had been built as the headquarters and guard post, while other buildings were made to look like implement sheds of a farm. The number of aircraft at the SLG increased rapidly during 1944 as Kemble was swamped, but with the end of the war in Europe they were quickly returned to the main unit and in September 1945 the SLG at Barnsley Park was closed, its work complete. Some 120,000 square yards of steel meshing was lifted and disposed of early in 1946 and the area returned to agriculture.

In 1980 there was no obvious sign of the wartime site except the HQ building which has been converted into a private

Top *Looking west across Barnsley Park SLG. The landing strip can be identified by the grubbed-up hedgerows.* **Above** *The HQ and Guardroom of Barnsley Park in May 1980. It is now a private bungalow (see Overley Farm).*

bungalow—just what it was designed to look like when built nearly 40 years ago.

Barnstaple, Devon

SU505345. 3 miles W of Barnstaple

It all started in 1933 when two Sussex aviators, Bob Boyd and Tommy Nash, arrived in Barnstaple and started a joy-riding and flying instruction business, using a small field sandwiched between the railway and the Taw estuary. Amazingly they prospered and in December the Barnstaple and North Devon Flying Club was established. Two

sheds and a club house were built and the field officially opened as the North Devon Airport on June 13 1934.

Boyd and Nash then started a service to the isolated Bristol Channel island of Lundy using a six-passenger DH Dragon biplane. By the summer up to ten flights a day were being made and the company gradually increased the scope of its services. In April 1937, when the name became Lundy and Atlantic Air Lines, they were also flying regularly to Cardiff and Plymouth with Short Scions. In 1938 they took up Civil Air Guard training but Barnstaple was really put on the aviation map on May 8 1939 when Western Airways started a service from Manchester to Penzance which called at the North Devon Airport.

The airfield was requisitioned by the Air Ministry in September 1939 and passenger services ceased, the Scions being contracted for Army Co-operation flights, mainly on searchlight training. Lundy and Atlantic Air Lines also overhauled light aircraft and many Tiger and Hornet Moths, and even the odd Wicko found their way into the sheds alongside the railway track. Shortly after take-off from Barnstaple on February 13 1940, Scion *G-AETT* crashed at Heanton Hill and in May work started on the new airfield of Chivenor forcing the closure of the old airfield soon afterwards.

Subsequently the original flying field was used for dispersing aircraft as Chivenor developed, and after the war married quarters were built on the site. The original clubhouse went to Barnstaple RAFA as the Puffin Club but the Blister hangar survived for years and in 1952 still contained the remains of Scion *G-AETT*.

Top *Barnstaple, the North Devon Airport. The L-shaped field is squeezed between the River Taw and the railway. The town is off to the right* (via W. Taylor). **Above** *Idyllic pre-war scene. The Scion* G-ACUW *rests alongside DH 60X Moth* G-AAIM, *both of Lundy & Atlantic Coast Air Lines, early 1939* (via W. Taylor).

Beaulieu, Hampshire

SU350005. 4 miles NE of Lymington on B3055

The first landing ground at Beaulieu was laid out close to the village of East Boldre in 1910 when the New Forest Flying School opened. The same site was used by the RFC/RAF from 1915 to 1919 and as a civilian field from 1933 to 1938 but the Second World War base was a completely new airfield built further to the west on Hatchet Moor, and originally intended as a satellite for Thorney Island.

It was modified at a late stage to accommodate two general reconnaissance squadrons and when opened on August 8

1942 the extensive building programme necessary had not been completed. The three runways were functional but required camouflaging, while the operations room and watch office were still temporary, and most personnel found themselves in tents.

To bolster 19 Group during the renewed U-boat offensive in the Bay of Biscay, 224 Squadron moved down from Tiree, their Liberator IIIAs arriving early in September. They were soon in action, the crew of 'H' attacking a submarine on October 20. The explosion of their depth charges damaged the aircraft but it managed to make a crash landing at Predannack. Three days later came the

first attack on Beaulieu when a German bomber dived out of low cloud and dropped four bombs, but caused no casualties and little damage.

The desperate situation in the Bay, coinciding as it did with the *Torch* convoys, forced Bomber Command to lend aircraft to Coastal and one and a half squadrons were allocated to Beaulieu. 15 Halifaxes of 405 (RCAF) Squadron and five from 158 arrived on October 25. Both flew their first patrols two days later and were soon involved in anti-shipping strikes using St Eval as a forward base. The 158 Squadron detachment left for Rufforth on December 6 but 405 remained and steadily improved their reputation. A very determined attack on the surfaced *U-263* was made by the crew of *405/J* on November 27 and, despite intensive fire from the U-boat's escorts, two runs were made and the submarine damaged. On February 26 1943 Liberator *224/Z* sighted two U-boats and both were attacked, the second being badly damaged and probably sunk.

In March 405 Squadron returned to Bomber Command and 224 Squadron was joined at Beaulieu by a detachment of 1(C)OTU for Liberator conversion flying. When 311(Czech) Squadron arrived for training in May, 224 Squadron left for St Eval and with the dispersed accommodation sites now completed it was possible to dispense with the temporary billeting arrangements. Diversions sometimes overloaded the facilities and caused difficulties. During the night of August 13, for instance, five Wellingtons of 407 Squadron arrived, one of which collided with a Halifax from Homsley South just after taking off for return to Chivenor. The overlapping circuits of the two airfields were a constant hazard.

No 311 Squadron remained at Beaulieu after conversion and recommenced operations in August, 'M' being attacked by a Ju 88 on the 30th. The gunners shot it down and the Liberator returned to base, but with a dead man in the rear turret. During September 53 Squadron arrived from Thorney Island and both units were heavily engaged in Bay operations, the marauding Ju 88s continuing to be very

Left *The thin soil of the New Forest remained scarred for years after airfield construction. This is Beaulieu in August 1945* (Museum of Army Flying collection).

Right *A Sikorsky R-4 of AFEE hovers in front of the tower at Beaulieu in 1946* (Museum of Army Flying collection).

Below left *On the offensive—P-47 Thunderbolts of 365 Fighter Group, IX Air Force, line up at Beaulieu in 1944.*

troublesome. Beaulieu was able to claim its first U-boat when the crew of *53/B* sighted one by Leigh Light during the early morning of December 13. The U-boat opened fire and hit the aircraft so the searchlight was switched off and the Liberator positioned for an attack up moon. The six depth charges straddled the submarine just forward of the conning tower and after it disappeared bodies were seen in the water. The captain, Squadron Leader G. Crawford, AFC, was awarded an immediate DFC for this exploit.

No 53 Squadron left in January 1944 followed by 311 (Czech) the following month. Their replacement by Typhoon 1B squadrons had already begun, their servicing echelons arriving on January 13, followed a few days later by 257 and 263 Squadrons. Eight Typhoons of 257 took off on their first operation from Beaulieu on the 22nd—an attack on *Noball* targets on the Cherbourg Peninsula. The airfield was also used by the Ibsley Wing for several *Rodeos* during the last days of the month. A typical effort was on the 29th when two Typhoons of 266, five of 193 and eight of 257 Squadron went on a sweep to the outskirts of Paris. A Do 217 and two German training aircraft were shot down for no loss, though three Typhoons were damaged by flak.

At the end of January 257 swopped places with 486 Squadron, and the Beaulieu Wing became heavily engaged in attacks on V-1 sites. On March 1 Beaulieu was transferred to 10 Group, ADGB, in readiness for the arrival of American units. The RAF moved out and in came 365 Fighter Group, 84 Fighter Wing, IX Air Force. P-47 Thunderbolt fighter-

bombers were received later in the month and the three squadrons, 386, 387 and 388 used for bomber escort and dive bombing prior to D-Day. On D-Day + 1 the Group (together with 366 FG) put up a maximum effort over *Omaha* beachhead where American troops were taking a pounding from dug-in German defensive positions.

No 365 FG left for the Continent on June 28 and three weeks later 323 Bombardment Group, 98 Bomb Wing (453, 454, 455 and 456 Squadrons) arrived from Earls Colne during a general move south of B-26 Marauder units as the fighter bombers vacated the forward airfields. A little over a month later 323 BG also moved into France and on September 27 Beaulieu was returned to the RAF.

It remained empty until the Airborne Forces Experimental Establishment started arriving from Sherburn-in-Elmet during December. Beaulieu was ideal for AFEE operations and a very wide range of activities involving gliders, early helicopters, paratroop and freight transports was soon under way. Aircraft included the Stirling, Halifax, Lancaster, York and Dakota with Hadrian, Hotspur, Hamilcar and CG-13A gliders plus a number of experimental types. The end of the war had no immediate impact on the AFEE for there were many new aircraft to test and the momentum built up during 1944-45 ensured that there was plenty of equipment trials to carry out.

During October 1946, C Flight of 657 Squadron arrived to be converted on to helicopters, leaving in March 1947 for Andover as 1901 Flight with some of the temperamental Sikorsky Hoverflys previously on AFEE strength. By 1948 the major activity concerned Valetta and Hastings trials, including glider-towing, and it was these aircraft which provided most of the work right up to September 1950 when the AFEE was absorbed by A&AEE Boscombe Down. Beaulieu reverted to Care & Maintenance and was then allotted to the 3rd Air Force, USAF, on April 1 1953 as a standby base. It was not used for flying and the Americans returned it to the RAF two and a half years later. Beaulieu was finally disposed of in November 1959.

Most of the airfield was taken over by the Forestry Commission who broke up the runways and converted some of the building foundations into caravan parks. A piece of the old perimeter track is used as a car park for a forest nature trail.

Bisterne, Hampshire

SU155030. 1½ miles S of Ringwood on B3347

During 1943 a number of temporary airfields were surveyed and built in the south of England to provide bases for the influx of aircraft into the area expected prior to the invasion of Europe. Known as Advanced Landing Grounds, they had the minimum facilities consistent with flying operational aircraft in support of ground forces—Bisterne was one of these ALGs.

Built on low-lying pasture land just to the east of the River Avon, a steel mesh runway paralleled the B3347 road and an east/west strip lay alongside the minor road to Lakes Farm. Arrowhead-shaped hardstandings were laid along a narrow taxi-track and PSP marshalling areas were constructed on either side of the runway thresholds.

Bisterne was completed in September 1943 but not used, apart from the odd visitor, until March 1944 when the 371st Fighter Group of IX Fighter Command, USAAF, moved in direct from the United States. The ALG was extremely primitive, the domestic accommodation being in tents, many of which became swamped when it rained. All technical work was in four Blisters or the open air until a large transportable hangar was erected in the south-west corner of the airfield. Operations commenced on April 12 when the P-47s made a sweep over France without loss. It was not long before the heavy pounding from the Thunderbolts took its toll of the wire mesh runways and at the end of a week they were badly

rutted and extremely hazardous. The ALG was closed for hasty reconstruction during which the 371st operated from nearby Ibsley.

They returned to Bisterne on May 1 and were soon busy flying two missions daily attacking airfields and communications in France. A typical day was May 21 when the Group despatched 50 Thunderbolts on a sweep to the Loire river. They attacked three trains, but two aircraft were hit by the ever-dangerous German flak, and only just scraped into Warmwell. On D-Day the 371st were held until 09:00 hours when one squadron, the 404th, flew on a dive bombing mission in support of forward troops. Operations continued on close support fighter-bomber work from Bisterne until the Americans moved to the Continent on June 23.

Its work done, Bisterne was soon abandoned, and was derelict by the end of July 1944. The wire track runways were taken up and early in 1945 the site reverted to agriculture after the Royal Engineers had bulldozed the hard core foundations. There are now few traces except culverted ditches and hedges replaced by wire fences where runways and taxiways crossed them. A few pieces of runway mesh are still scattered around the local farms.

Bolt Head, Devon

SX713373. 1½ miles SW of Salcombe

One of the main operational problems with British and German day fighters in the early war years was their short endurance. While not a major fault when operating defensively, it became of great importance when engaged in bomber escort or intruder work. This was the reason for the existence of a number of rudimentary airfields with minimal facilities, but as close to the coast as possible. Built on level ground above the headland which bears its name, Bolt Head was a typical example.

It was opened in 1941 for the fighters of 10 and 11 Groups to use when escorting 2 Group bombers on raids into western France, but amongst its first users was 16 Squadron, which sent detachments of Lysanders there during May to give troops experience of chemical warfare. A permanent handling party was accommodated with the personnel of nearby Hope Cove GCI station.

The first aircraft to be permanently attached to Bolt Head were two Lysanders

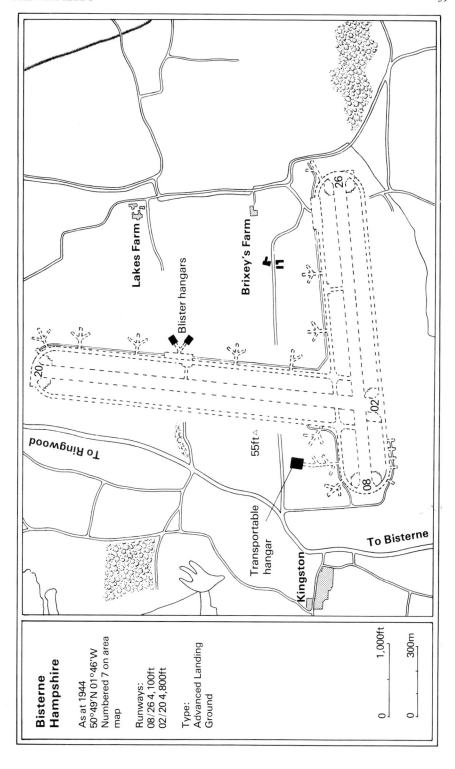

Bisterne
Hampshire

As at 1944
50°49'N 01°46'W
Numbered 7 on area
map

Runways:
08/26 4,100ft
02/20 4,800ft

Type:
Advanced Landing
Ground

Lakes Farm

Blister hangars

Brixey's Farm

To Ringwood

55ft △

Transportable
hangar

Kingston

To Bisterne

20

02

26

08

1,000ft

300m

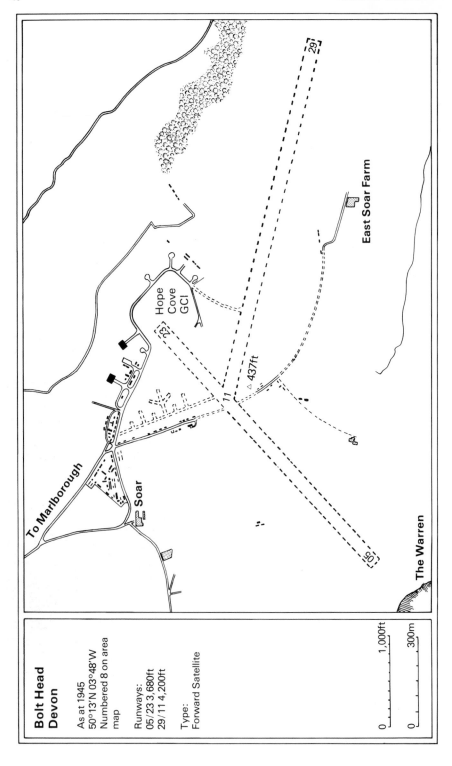

**Bolt Head
Devon**

As at 1945
50°13'N 03°48'W
Numbered 8 on area
map

Runways:
05/23 3,680ft
29/11 4,200ft

Type:
Forward Satellite

To Marlborough

Soar

Hope
Cove
GCI

East Soar Farm

The Warren

△ 437ft

29

23

11

05

1,000ft

300m

0

0

of 276 Squadron. They proved their worth on December 18 when they spotted the seven-man crew of a bomber ditched after a daylight raid on Brest, just the first of many such rescues.

During 1942 the facilities were improved. A short length of taxiway leading to two Enlarged Blister hangars and a bulk fuel storage was constructed, while barrack huts, flight and administrative offices were built alongside the existing roads. Two Sommerfeld track runways were laid originally 2,700 ft (823 m) in length, but later extended with bar and rod tracking which was also used for access tracks and the main parking area in the north-west corner of the airfield. This activity attracted the Luftwaffe, two Bf 109s diving out of the sun on March 7 just as a 317 Squadron aircraft was taking off. The Spitfire was hit but the pilot managed to land safely. Eight days later an escort of Bostons by 317 Squadron turned into tragedy when a sea mist rolled in over Devon. Short of fuel, the pilots either force-landed or baled out. Five aircraft were destroyed, the CO killed and two other pilots injured, only two Spitfires managing to land at Bolt Head.

With sufficient accommodation to support a fighter squadron, Bolt Head was upgraded to satellite status in April 1942, but was still used mainly as a

Lysander of 276 Squadron, believed at Bolt Head. Note the twin Browning guns for rear defence.

forward operating base by the Exeter Wing. Typical was the rendezvous by 302, 306 and 308 (Polish) Squadrons with 2 Group Bostons for an attack on Morlaix airfield on the 30th. As if in retaliation four low-flying Bf 109 fighter-bombers attacked next morning, peppering dispersed Spitfires with stones thrown up by the bombs' blast.

The Czechs arrived from Exeter in May to fly *Rhubarbs* over France. 310 was replaced by 257 Squadron in September, their Typhoons being used in the defensive *Anti-Rhubarb* role, gaining victories on November 3 when two Fw 190s were overtaken 35 miles west of Guernsey. Both were shot down by the devastating fire provided by the Typhoons' guns. Meanwhile, the strength of the fighter forces on *Rhubarbs* was increasing and the planning required meticulous co-ordination. Typical was an attack by 12 Bostons of 88 Squadron on St Malo during July 3. The bombers used Exeter and escort was provided by the Ibsley, Portreath and Exeter Wings, plus squadrons operating from Tangmere, totalling nearly 100 aircraft. Eight squadrons, two from Bolt Head, joined up with the Bostons over the airfield and flew low level until 30 miles from the French coast. They then climbed to 8,000 ft (2,438 m), bombed and, turning for Start Point, descended back to sea level. Some of the fighters provided close escort while the remainder carried out sweeps over nearby German fighter airfields—a triumph of careful timing.

A practice rescue but much like the real thing. A Walrus of 276 Squadron off the South Coast.

An operation that went very wrong was a raid on Morlaix by 18 B-17s of the 97th Bombardment Group escorted by Spitfires of 133 (Eagle), 401 and 412 Squadrons operating from Bolt Head. The Wing was to take off, climb to 2,500 ft (762 m) and meet up with the Fortresses over the Channel. Unfortunately the met forecast was incorrect and the expected headwind was a strong tailwind. The B-17s were not seen, so after some fuel-consuming orbits the fighters set off in pursuit. The bombers flew much further south than intended, turned round and met the Spitfires. One of the 133's 12 Spitfires developed engine trouble and another was assigned to accompany it back. After flying for half an hour they started to let down for Bolt Head. But they were still over France and one was shot down, the other, out of fuel, just made the English coast and crash-landed. Worried about their fuel situation after 2¼ hours' flying, the other ten descended in formation and found themselves over a coastline with a city off to the right. They thought it was Plymouth—unfortunately it was Brest! All ten were either shot down or lost through fuel shortage. The other squadrons just got into Bolt Head, and the B-17s jettisoned their bombs harmlessly into the sea. The raid was an unmitigated disaster, especially for 133

Squadron which three days later transferred to the USAAF.

In September 610 Squadron moved in from Perranporth for *Anti-Rhubarb* operations, but there was little enemy activity so the squadron turned to *Rhubarbs* themselves. During one operation they beat off an attack on the dinghies of a B-17 crew, and while at Bolt Head claimed four Bf 110s during one ten-day period.

Bolt Head was host to 141 Airfield (234 and 266 Squadrons) in March 1944. The Typhoons of 266 were replaced in April by 41 Squadron flying the rare Spitfire XIIs which had been modified for bombing and proved excellent for *Rhubarbs*. Intended for this role during D-Day, they were rushed to West Malling when the V-1 offensive began—the Griffon-powered XIIs were among the few fighters able to catch the 'doodle-bugs'.

Over the invasion period B Flight of 276 ASR Squadron was at Bolt Head with Walruses and Spitfires and the strength of the station reached a new peak with the return of 610 Squadron whose new Spitfire XIVs attacked pre-invasion targets. They soon moved to Culmhead and were replaced by the 'Tiffies' of 263 Squadron for attacks on coastal shipping and radar sites in France.

In August 276 Squadron moved on to the Continent and was replaced by 275, similarly equipped with Spitfires and Walruses. Mosquitoes of 151 Squadron now used Bolt Head occasionally, but the war had moved away, and it was reduced to Care & Maintenance on April 25 1945.

Several parenting changes occurred during 1945-46 and Bolt Head was little used though a Wellington XIII suffered an undercarriage collapse on May 1 1946 and the strip was not finally closed until the following year. It has now reverted to farmland though a few buildings and a strip of access track remain alongside the National Trust property known as the Warren.

Boscombe Down, Wiltshire

SU182398. 1½ miles SE of Amesbury

Two days after their arrival at Boscombe Down on August 14 1940, Red Section of 249 Squadron (Flight Lieutenant James Nicolson leading Squadron Leader Eric King and Pilot Officer M.A. King) was scrambled to patrol an area bounded by Poole, Ringwood and Salisbury. An attack on Gosport by 12 Ju 88s and 18 Bf 110s had developed and Red Section spotted the bombers. While turning into the attack they were bounced by Bf 109s, and all three Hurricanes were hit.

Squadron Leader King broke away and managed to get back to Boscombe. Pilot Officer King baled out of his blazing aircraft while Nicolson, his Hurricane on fire, continued his attack on a Bf 110. With flames burning his hands and face he was forced out of the cockpit and came down close to King. To add insult to injury they were both fired on by an RA detachment and some Local Defence Volunteers who mistook them for enemy parachutists. King's parachute disintegrated, probably due to damage in the burning aircraft, and he plunged to the ground. Nicolson landed safely in great pain from burns and peppered with gunshot, but was rushed to hospital and made a complete recovery. He later received the Victoria Cross for this exploit—the only such award to a pilot of Fighter Command.

Boscombe Down first opened in 1917 as a flying training unit, No 6 Training Depot Station forming in October to fly Avro 504K, BE 2E, DH 4 and DH 9

Boscombe Down seen from the south-east in 1944, just before the construction of runways started (MoD(PE) A&AEE).

aircraft. Two hangars and rows of bell tents were the only buildings but plans were made to extend the facilities and at the end of the war two more TDSs arrived. In 1919 second bays were being added to the main hangars and there were numerous wooden huts and a large number of canvas Bessoneaux hangars on the base. But these were very uncertain times and the station closed before the end of the year.

The land was acquired again in 1927 and work started on a permanent station, built to accommodate two bomber squadrons as part of the Wessex Bombing Area. The station re-opened in 1930 and the Virginias of 9 Squadron arrived from Manston in November, and were joined by 10 Squadron with Hinaidis the following April. The two squadrons occupied Boscombe until the mid-1930s when the formation of new squadrons caused a general reshuffle.

In February 1937 Boscombe was briefly handed over to Coastal Command to house 217 and 224 (GR) Squadrons equipped with Ansons. But the airfield soon returned to Bomber Command, first with 4 Group, and from April 1938 in 1 Group. The residents at the outbreak of war were the Battles of 88 and 218 Squadrons but they went immediately to France and were replaced by the Aeroplane and Armament Experimental Establishment. This unit had started to leave its comfortable, but vulnerable,·

home at Martlesham Heath on September 1 and was completely installed two weeks later.

Boscombe Down was far from ideal as a test establishment, especially one with a rapidly increasing task. There were no runways, or gun butts and the only ranges were the nearby Army ones on Salisbury Plain—and naturally the Army had first call on these. Domestic and technical accommodation was just not equipped to cope with some 40 experimental aircraft and large numbers of civilian and service boffins (as the research staff were soon called).

To make things even more difficult a detachment of 58 Squadron Whitley IIIs arrived from Linton-on-Ouse in September to carry out anti-submarine patrols over the English Channel and the first winter of the war was the worst in living memory. Everything at Boscombe rapidly iced up and remained that way for days on end.

No 58 Squadron left in February 1940 and the airfield was extended and improved. The first stop butts were built and a large weapons range developed in Lyme Bay. Bombing ranges were also established on Crichel Down, Dorset, and Ashley Walk in the New Forest, and several new departments and sub-units were formed. One of the latter was the Beam Approach Development Unit which came into existence in May 1940, became the Wireless Interception Development

As in most photographs at Boscombe Down, the background is as interesting as the subject. On the left is the Officers' Mess and behind the tail of the Spitfire F XIV are the First World War hangars (IWM).

Unit in October and 109 Squadron two months later. Meanwhile the original two squadrons forming the A&AEE were subdivided. Armament Testing Squadron gained small divisions dealing with navigation and radio, while Performance Testing was divided into Flights, A for fighters, B for bombers and C for all multi-seat single-engined types including naval aircraft.

As already outlined, the desperate situation after the fall of France resulted in 249 Squadron arriving in August. They were replaced by 56 Squadron in September but as the pressure from the Luftwaffe decreased they left in November and were succeeded by the Bomber Development Unit and the Handling Squadron, both allied units of the A&AEE. A special High-Altitude Research Flight was formed in 1941, about the same time as there was a sudden increase in the number of aircraft on strength as new types flooded in from America.

Surprisingly, Boscombe escaped any attack during 1940 when so many airfields in the south were raided. Late in 1941, however, there were attacks in the area nearly every night and the A&AEE suffered five light raids, one of which resulted in the destruction of one aircraft—fortunately a low priority trials machine.

An Intensive Flying Development Flight was formed in 1942, followed by the Test Pilots Training Flight in May 1943. The latter became the Empire Test

Pilots School in 1944 and moved to Cranfield the following year.

The A&AEE got through a tremendous amount of work during the war. In addition to the ever-increasing test work on new prototypes, armament trials and intensive flying tests to assess in-service problems, every 100th heavy bomber from the shadow factories was put through a test sequence to ensure that the standard achieved by the main factory was maintained by the subcontractors. Inevitably there were accidents, such as the experimental Lancaster which collided with an Oxford while in the circuit at Boscombe. Some were tragic, but others merely comic, like the demonstration of rocket-assisted take-off being given to a number of VIPs including the Minister of Aircraft Production. There were many red faces following the activation of the rockets—for the aircraft did not move, but the rockets roared over the heads of the assembled spectators.

Late in 1944 McAlpines moved in to commence construction of the first runway at Boscombe, but it was not completed until long after the early jet aircraft had left their mark on the grass. Just before the end of the war there were 176 aircraft on the strength of the Establishment, and it was some time before there was much reduction for momentum built up during the war took time to dissipate.

A civil aircraft test section was formed and all the early airliners of this period,

The weighbridge hangar which has dominated the Boscombe scene since completion in 1955. It dwarfs the prototype Shackleton 3 (Crown copyright).

such as the Viking and Tudor, carried out their Certificate of Airworthiness trials at Boscombe. In 1951 the Airborne Experimental Establishment joined A&AEE from Beaulieu and in 1954 the airfield was completely rebuilt and the imposing weighbridge hangar, which now dominates the scene, was constructed. This hangar has a clear span of 250 ft (76 m) and was built to accommodate the Brabazon. That airliner never reached Boscombe but the hangar with its intricate weighing equipment has proved its value many times.

In January 1968 the EPTS returned to Boscombe, and with the RAF Handling Squadron also back in its early wartime home, the wheel had turned full circle. During the 1960s and '70s the station changed little in appearance, but in 1979 a new spate of construction work started when the airfield was assigned as a NATO dispersal base and began to sprout hardened shelters of the type which deface Upper Heyford. A month-long detachment of F-111Ds from America during 1980 suggests that these shelters are intended for such deployments, but the main work of the station continues to be trials work, as clearly defined by the A&AEE's motto *Probe Probare* (Properly to Test).

In spite of all the buildings constructed in the 1930s, and the rebuild after the war, one of the original 1919 two-bay hangars still remains. Occupied by a variety of units over the years, it currently houses the Establishment archives. Understandably in view of its work the station is never open to the public, and has only put on one major display for invited guests since the war. This was on March 19 1971 in celebration of 50 years of test flying by the A&AEE. A surprisingly good view of the airfield can, however, be obtained from a lay-by on the A303 which passes to the north of the station while traversing Beacon Hill.

Broadfield Down (Lulsgate Bottom), Somerset

See Lulsgate Bottom

Brockworth (Hucclecote), Gloucestershire

SO882160. ½ mile S of Brockworth on A417

This factory airfield had its origins in 1915 when H.H. Martyn & Co Ltd of Chelten-ham, engaged in sub-contract work for the Aircraft Manufacturing Co, used a field at Hucclecote for flight testing. The firm was re-organised in 1917 and the aircraft division acquired by the Gloucestershire Aircraft Company in June. Initially the aircraft were towed from the Sunningend factory in Cheltenham to Hucclecote behind Ford lorries but later the Air Board built an Aircraft Acceptance Park on the field specially for the firm's products. The AAP consisted of five hangars for aircraft assembly and 21 large storage sheds and was nearly complete when the Armistice was declared. In 1919 the AAP was disbanded and the RAF withdrew, though the Air Board retained ownership of the assembly sheds.

Wholesale cancellations left the Cheltenham company in a difficult position for, though limited production of the Bristol F2B and Nieuport Nighthawk continued, they were dependent on sub-contract work and had no design team. They decided to remain in the aircraft industry, however, and in November 1920 the production rights of the Nighthawk were acquired and a design team formed.

The company rented hangar space from the Air Board but on becoming Gloster Aircraft Co Ltd in November 1926 decided to purchase the airfield, hangars and offices. The gradual move from Cheltenham was finally completed in 1930. However, orders were insufficient for financial survival and in May 1934 the firm was taken over by Hawker Aircraft Co Ltd, then looking for more production capacity to build their highly successful Hart variants. Substantial additions to the available space at Hucclecote were made between 1934-37, the new factory being built on the eastern side of the airfield. Further expansion on the new site followed when a Ministry shadow factory for Hurricane production was authorised, work starting in August 1938. When completed in November 1940 there was over 24 acres of factory space available.

The factory was camouflaged soon after the war started, followed by the painting of hedgerows on the airfield surface which proved remarkably effective. The first Gloster-built Hurricane was completed on October 27 1939, production reaching a peak a year later when 160 were delivered to the Air Ministry. This was despite a daylight raid by one aircraft, which hit a machine shop with a single large bomb and caused

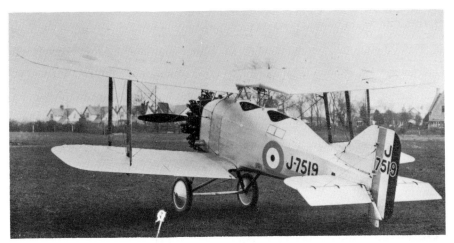

Above *A Grebe two-seater at Hucclecote in 1924. The houses in the background have remained throughout the airfield's active operation. It closed as Brockworth in 1960* (British Aerospace). **Below** *Brockworth on June 18 1959 showing the single runway built during the war* (DoE).

considerable damage and some injuries. The factory was an obvious target for the Luftwaffe and it was the primary target for the Ju 88s of KG51 on October 21. They failed to locate Hucclecote, however, and attacked Old Sarum instead.

To prevent slowing of production deliveries due to waterlogging of the airfield, a single runway was built between the two factory areas during the autumn of 1941 and completed in the following spring. Typhoons had replaced Hurricanes on production lines before the

next raid made on April 4 1942. No damage was suffered by the factory, but one bomb fell in the bus park just as the day shift were leaving, killing 13 and injuring many more.

Peak production of the Typhoon was reached in December 1942 when 130 were delivered, and when the final aircraft was completed in November 1945 3,330 had been built at Hucclecote. But Gloster was also responsible for some original design work. In February 1940 the firm received a contract for two prototypes of a revolutionary machine, the E28/39. Built

to prove the practicality of the gas turbine, the aircraft started taxying tests at Brockworth in April 1941 and even achieved short hops before being taken to Cranwell where a longer runway and comparative isolation provided the safety and security necessary. It was followed by the Meteor, and it was this aircraft that kept the company afloat in the early post-war years.

The boundary line between Brockworth and Hucclecote ran down the middle of the airfield and, while the original factory was definitely in the latter parish, much of the newer assembly sheds were in Brockworth. Gradually the airfield became generally known as Brockworth and was officially so named in the post-war period.

With the advent of the Meteor the short runway and difficult approach over houses in the prevailing sou' westerlies, Gloster was forced to transfer nearly all flight testing to Moreton Valence. Many production aircraft, Meteors and later Javelins, took off from Brockworth but landed at Moreton Valence to complete their test programme before delivery. Others were sent to Moreton Valence as major components and assembled there before flight test. This work continued until April 8 1960 when the last Javelin was flown out by Dicky Martin, Gloster's chief test pilot, and the factory went over to the production of specialised non-aeronautical products such as road tankers and refuellers, and even vending machines. It was not enough to keep the firm viable however, and in April 1964 Hawker-Siddeley sold the Hucclecote factory to Gloucester Trading Estates Ltd.

To commemorate the pioneer Gloster E28/39 a plaque was unveiled by Sir Arnold Hall in May 1979 on the spot where it was finally assembled at Hucclecote. The original assembly sheds can still be distinguished on the estate, and the name of the aircraft firm lives on in Brockworth—for the name of a pub is 'The Gloster Flying Machine'.

Calshot, Hampshire (Marine)
SU489205. 2 miles SE of Fawley

One of the more unusual military flying bases in appearance, Calshot was also one of the first in the country, having been opened by the Royal Naval Air Service on March 29 1913. Built on a strip of land projecting into the Solent, it took its name from its central feature, Calshot Castle. The original station consisted of three sheds capable of housing 12 seaplanes, and a few coastguard cottages used as accommodation.

Calshot's main function was experimental but in August 1914 it took on a training task, and with RNAS Dover and a number of smaller stations, became responsible for Channel patrols, using seaplanes and, later, flying boats. With the formation of the RAF in April 1918 Calshot became the HQ of 10 Group and the flying units became 345 and 346 Flights using Felixstowe F flying boats, and 410 Flight with seaplanes. These Flights were combined to form 240 Squadron and in the last three months of the war the unit sighted 13 submarines, of which eight were attacked.

The station survived the end of the war to become the School of Naval Co-operation and Aerial Navigation, a long-winded but self-explanatory title. Re-organised as RAF Base, Calshot, on February 5 1922, No 480 (Coastal Reconnaissance) Flight was established with Felixstowe boats, replaced in August 1922 by wooden-hulled Southamptons.

The number of hangars on the Spit gradually increased and the domestic site at Eaglehurst, about 1¼ miles from the castle, also expanded. A narrow-gauge railway built in 1917 to carry stores down to the technical site was retained as the 'Calshot Express', some of the trucks being fitted with rough wooden seats and used to transport airmen between the two

Calshot Spit sticking out into the Solent—a jumble of hangars and flying boats (via C. Bowyer).

Sunderlands of 201/230 Squadrons and 235 OCU in 1948. Calshot Castle provides a unique base for air traffic control (via C. Bowyer).

sites. Between the wars the training units were often renamed but their roles remained roughly the same.

The station became well-known in the late 1920s for the activities of the RAF High Speed Flight formed for the Schneider Trophy competitions. Each competition year between 1927 and 1931 the Flight carried out several months of training at Calshot, culminating in the outright winning of the Trophy on September 13 1931. A fortnight later Flight Lieutenant Stainforth set up a new World Speed Record of 407.5 mph (655 km/h) in the Supermarine S.6B—a speed not exceeded for two years.

Still with Southamptons, 480 Flight became 201 Squadron on January 1 1929 and until the formation of 240 in March 1937 was the sole operational unit on the station. During the Munich crisis both squadrons moved to their war stations and at Calshot machine-gun posts and shelter trenches were constructed. A sign of the seriousness of the situation was the removal of the civilian bathing huts along the Spit—Calshot was preparing for war.

Both operational units left on August 11 1939 and Calshot entered the war with just the Flying Boat Training Squadron (FBTS) on strength. Originally formed on October 1 1931, the FBTS was now using the magnificent Stranraer and Singapore biplane flying boats for the training of crews in the art of seamanship as well as airmanship. Calshot itself remained responsible for the major servicing of the boats of 201, 209 and 240 Squadrons, was a holding unit for aircraft spares, and carried out all marine craft servicing and

training. To cope with the increase in personnel more huts were built at Eaglehurst in October 1939, covering even the previously sacrosanct grass square.

Operation *Dynamo*, the Dunkirk evacuation, resulted in five seaplane tenders being sent to Dover, and they succeeded in rescuing 500 men before being withdrawn for repairs. Calshot now found itself very much in the front line and the Flying Boat Training Squadron was hurriedly despatched to Stranraer on June 23. Surprisingly, the Luftwaffe did not show much interest in the station though Luftflotte 3 dropped bombs on the Spit during August 27 and a night raid was attempted on the 30th. The barrage balloons over the hangars and the gradually increasing anti-aircraft defences, which now included 3-inch guns, probably saved the unit from opportunity raids. The guns certainly achieved one success, shooting down a He 111 on September 24.

Meanwhile three He 115 floatplanes appeared among the Sunderlands, Stranraers and Singapores. Arriving from Norway in June 1940, they were converted for clandestine work, two of them leaving in October 1941 for Malta. The third, *BV184*, was retained for trials, some of which could be hazardous—it was no fun flying a distinctively shaped German aircraft over the Channel! A fuel consumption test on April 23 1942 proved this, for while on its way back to Calshot from Lands End it was attacked by two Spitfires. They sheered off following recognition signals, but Verey lights did not deter naval vessels which continued to

Eaglehurst—the domestic site for Calshot. Seen here in 1934 it was extended during the war by building on the square! (via C. Bowyer).

fire at the He 115 until it was out of sight. Despite this unwelcome attention the floatplane got back safely, but soon left for Wig Bay.

The Marine Training School transferred to Galloway in May 1942, and the facilities at Calshot were then used for a succession of ASR marine craft units. The aircraft repair organisation became No 6 Flying Boat Servicing Unit in September 1943 and then concentrated on Sunderlands, no less than 22 being flown in during April 1944 for repair and modification.

At the beginning of 1944 Calshot had replaced Hamworthy as a weather diversion for flying boats, but it was not used operationally during the war. It was a different story for marine craft. The ASR launches were constantly on call and in May 1944 a mobile rescue unit consisting of 14 high-speed launches was formed at Calshot. At first light on D-Day six of them sailed to appointed positions alongside Fighter Direction Tenders off the beachhead, ready to move off as soon as a fighter pilot initiated a Mayday call.

It was not until March 1946 that an operational unit returned to Calshot and fittingly it was 201 Squadron which brought their Sunderland Vs in from Pembroke Dock. A month later they were joined by 230 Squadron, and apart from the time they spent on the Berlin Airlift, both stayed until early 1949. Meanwhile 4(C)OTU arrived from Alness in 1947, becoming 235 OCU in July. The Sunderland training unit then soldiered on at Calshot until October 1953 when it moved to Pembroke Dock, leaving the Spit to the marine craft.

On October 17 Calshot was transferred from Coastal to Maintenance Command and became 238 MU. Servicing of marine craft was the MU's task, to which were added a Bomb Disposal Flight and Explosive Training Unit in 1956.

Apart from the retirement of the 'Calshot Express' in 1947—the engine went to Wales for use on a local line at Tallyn—Calshot outwardly changed little after the war. The Sunderlands parked untidily in the confused hangar area around the castle had left by the early 1950s but were replaced by two of the elegant but ill-fated Saro Princess flying boats, sitting sadly in their protective cocoons. They remained after the RAF station finally closed in May 1961.

Since then the Officers' Mess at Eaglehurst has become the 'Owl and Crescent' Hotel and the hutted accommodation has been used as a camp for refugees from the Tristan de Cuna volcano disaster. The Spit is now a yacht marina while the castle and hangars are used by a County Council Activity Centre. Despite the passage of 20 years the Spit retains its RAF *feel* and it is hard to believe that you will not come face to face with a beautiful silver flying boat round the next corner. A place full of good memories for Calshot was always a happy station.

Castle Combe, Wiltshire

ST854767. ½ mile SE of village

Close by the picturesque village of Castle Combe is a motor racing circuit which during the season erupts spasmodically into noisy action. A glance is enough to discern its origins for the control centre is on top of a wartime tower, backed by a variety of WD buildings which formed part of the main airfield technical site. The race circuit uses the tarmac perimeter track which might have been designed for the job—even to a ready-made chicane.

Operated as a landing ground for Harts and Audaxes of 9 FTS Hullavington, this small grass airfield was upgraded in May 1941 to RLG status for the same unit, now re-designated as 9 SFTS. Used for day and night circuit flying by Master 1 and Hurricane aircraft, during the summer months Castle Combe proved very satisfactory, but with the onset of winter it was a different story. The grass surface soon became waterlogged and completely unusable for long periods.

On February 14 1942 the SFTS became 9(P)AFU and was given a new commitment—the training of Fleet Air Arm pilots on Masters, Hurricanes, Swordfish and Albacores—though in practice RAF pilots also continued training at Castle Combe. During 1942 work started to make Castle Combe fully self-supporting and it was transferred to 3 FIS when 9(P)AFU moved to Errol in Scotland. The FIS arrived from Hullavington on August 8 and commenced flying immediately but poor weather and the inevitable waterlogging caused delays, the courses during the winter having to be extended in duration.

In fact, conditions were so bad that from December until early March 1943 the staff and students had to travel daily to Hullavington, Colerne and Charmy Down for flying. After the laying of two Sommerfeld track runways, construction of the perimeter track, and the erection of a Teeside and seven Blister hangars, the airfield was again usable. With both Masters and Oxfords in use by the FIS, flying was in full swing by May but any chance of a settled existence for 3 FIS was rudely shattered when representatives of 15(P)AFU Babdown Farm, arrived to inspect the airfield and declared themselves interested. 3 FIS moved to Lulsgate Bottom at the beginning of October, and after more waterlogging had been dealt with the first of the AFU's Oxfords arrived in November. Because of the poor state of Long Newnton another Flight moved in during January but Castle Combe was only the lesser of two evils. The AFU was still struggling to catch up its backlog when a Stirling carrying five magnetic mines force-landed on March 13. Two of the mines exploded causing serious damage to the ground instructional buildings. It was three days before training could restart using temporary accommodation.

Despite the use of foam slag and re-grading of the runways, trouble continued to be experienced with the Sommerfeld tracking throughout 1944 and it was not until March 1945 that the airfield became fully serviceable. This was just in time to cope with the extra load produced by the closure of the Long Newnton satellite, but with the end of the war in Europe, 15(P)-AFU ceased flying and Castle Combe was transferred to Care & Maintenance in May, parented by Babdown Farm.

The station was completely unoccupied until July 1946 when it was taken over by

A typical dispersed domestic site—No 3 at Castle Combe in August 1942. To the north-west of the airfield (845778), it was later extended and still exists (RAF Museum).

The control tower and part of the technical site at Castle Combe are now used for motor racing activities.

27 Group for use by No 2 (Polish) Resettlement Unit. They occupied the huts until June 1948 when Castle Combe became an inactive site and was disposed of in September.

Cattewater (Mount Batten), Devon

See Mount Batten

Charlton Horethorne, Somerset

ST643244. 2 miles NW of Charlton Horethorne

On a west-facing escarpment, the attractively named Charlton Horethorne was anything but a pleasant place to fly from. It would have made a good gliding site with excellent ridge soaring, but it was intended as a secret satellite for Exeter. Great efforts were made to prevent its identification as an airfield, both during construction and on completion. Hedges, ditches and trees were all retained wherever possible, and paths were made inconspicuous in colour and followed the lines of natural features. The living sites were widely dispersed to the east of the airfield and carefully camouflaged. Even the watch office was sited off the airfield itself and there were no hangars or dispersals.

An officer was despatched from Exeter in August 1941 to supervise development but before Charlton Horethorne was completed it was no longer needed by the RAF. When officially opened on May 26 1942 it was destined for use by RNAS Yeovilton and the airfield was first used by the Navy on July 10.

No 790 Squadron, the flying unit for

the Air Direction School, moved into Charlton Horethorne using Fulmars, later replaced by Oxfords and Ansons for the basic training of GCI operators, and Wildcats and Fireflies for the advanced stages of the course. The Wildcats of 893 Squadron arrived from St Merryn in September but left after a month and were replaced by Fulmars of 879 Squadron. This unit was also little more than a visitor, going to Old Sarum in November when the airfield was transferred from 10 Group to Admiralty control. The last RAF personnel left in January 1943 when Charlton Horethorne commissioned as HMS *Heron II*, a satellite of Yeovilton which ran the ground courses of the Air Direction School.

Interception training was also given to operational squadrons, the Seafires of 884, 887 and 897 using the facilities during 1943. At the same time the Admiralty started to improve the very rudimentary airfield. A number of Blister hangars were added to the original 10 Group aircraft blast pens, and work started on a number of larger hangars, air traffic control, an aircraft storage section and additional living quarters. The usual naval layout of five runways were graded and mown, though they remained grass, and there were no taxiways as such.

By the autumn of 1943 the last operational squadron had left and as accommodation became available, 780 Squadron, the pilot refresher training unit, arrived from Eastleigh with its Tiger Moth, Proctor, Harvard and Swordfish aircraft, followed by 794 Squadron in December. The latter operated as an Air Target Towing Unit flying Defiants and Martinets and continued dragging drogues about the country until disbanded in June 1944.

Meanwhile, a most unusual naval unit, the Travelling Research Unit (765 Squadron) was formed in March 1944. Equipped with Wellingtons, it moved around the country on recording duties but was based at Charlton Horethorne. 790 Squadron went to Culmhead in August but returned little over a month later when 10 Group decided to reduce that fighter base to inactive status. 780 Squadron left for Lee-on-Solent in November 1944, the original unit, 790, moved to Zeals on April 1 1945 leaving the airfield ready for hand-over to the RAF.

Charlton Horethorne was used by 42 Group, Maintenance Command, as one of the many ammunition storage sites of 11 MU Chilmark. It was cleared at the end of 1947 and transferred to Old Sarum in June 1948 who held it as an inactive site until it was de-requisitioned and returned to farmland. There is now virtually no sign of the airfield west of the minor road between Blackford and Corton Denham, but a number of Nissen and Maycrete buildings on the old dispersal area to the east are occupied by Charlton Hill Farm.

Charmy Down, Somerset (now Avon)

ST764700. 3 miles N of Bath on A46

On a plateau in the hills above Bath, Charmy Down is practically impossible to see from the roads around it, all of which lie in valleys. The airfield was built during 1940 complete with three runways and a connecting track off which were a large number of double blast pens. It opened in November as a satellite of Colerne and was used in the defence of Bristol and Bath. A detachment of black-painted Hurricanes of 87 Squadron moved in from Colerne for night fighting, the remainder of the unit following in December as accommodation in widely dispersed sites to the north-west (either side of the A46) became available.

It was quiet during the winter of 1940/41 but with the spring came increased but fruitless activity trying to intercept Luftwaffe bombers raiding Bristol Channel ports and towns. The Hurricane was virtually useless at night unless the target was silhouetted against cloud and it was pure chance if the fighter was in the right place at the right time. A

Charlton Horethorne on October 3 1944. No longer secret, the airfield now has Blister hangars, blast pens and mown grass runways (FAA Museum).

few intruder sorties were made in the Caen area but it was not until May that the first success came whilst flying from Charmy Down—a Do 17 shot down by the CO.

No 87 was joined in August 1941 by 125 Squadron working up on Defiant night fighters, and 263 Squadron similarly employed ironing out the bugs in the Whirlwind. Neither became operational at Charmy Down, though the latter provided a nucleus for 137 Squadron which formed on September 20 and a month later had one Flight at readiness on this tricky aircraft. They lost their CO after a collision on October 28 and a couple of days later another pilot flew into the sea. The squadron reverted to non-op status until moved to Coltishall in November.

By now Blister hangars were dispersed around the perimeter and a single Bellman was being built on the Holts Down Lane technical site. Amongst the more promising night interception solutions being tried was the Helmore Turbinlite, and in January 1942 a small number of Havocs fitted with this device arrived to co-operate with 87 Squadron. The Havocs were to illuminate the target with this powerful light while a Hurricane flying in formation shot down the enemy bomber. This idea was fraught with difficulties, but the first patrol by a 1454 Flight Havoc and 87 Squadron Hurricane combination was flown on March 24. But despite increased operations in the summer the Havocs at Charmy Down had no success and were withdrawn in January 1943 in common with other Turbinlite units.

Nos 234, 245, 417 (RCAF) and 421 (RCAF) Squadrons spent short work-up periods at Charmy Down during 1941-43, and in September 1942 two bomber squadrons, Nos 88 and 107, were attached. 88 sent six Bostons to a 10 Group *Ramrod* to Le Havre on the 8th, and seven days later 107 carried out the most successful Boston operation of the month, setting a 12,000 ton ship on fire in Cherbourg docks.

With the departure of the operational squadrons during February 1943, the Fighter Leaders School moved in from Chedworth. Equipped with 36 Spitfire Vs and operated as part of 52 OTU, the school gave short, sharp tactics courses to Flight and Squadron Commanders. 88 Squadron spent some time in April and June at Charmy Down practising tactics with the FLS. On completion of their last visit their stores and rather reluctant groundcrew were flown back to Swanton Morley in two Horsas towed by Whitleys of 297 Squadron—all part of a scheme to keep glider and tug pilots in practice! Charmy Down suited the FLS very well but during 1943 the airfield was provisionally allocated to the USAAF and with space available at Aston Down the unit moved there during August.

There was considerable delay before the Americans took over and for a short period during the autumn Charmy Down was used to house over 2,000 RAF Regiment personnel. It was finally transferred to the IXth Air Force in February 1944 and used during the build-up for D-Day as a Tactical Air Depot. The

Left *Charmy Down taken by 58 Squadron on September 26 1958* (DoE).

Right *The brick tower at Charmy Down was used for some time as a house but is now derelict like the many other buildings on the airfield* (D.J. Smith).

Below *Mosquito II of 264 Squadron at Charmy Down in April 1943.*

USAAF remained in possession until October 1944 when the airfield went to 23 Group, Flying Training Command, as a satellite for South Cerney.

Because of waterlogging at Castle Combe, 15(P)AFU used Charmy Down, joined by B Flight of 3(P)AFU in November when their Oxfords arrived from Bibury. It proved difficult for these units to operate properly because Colerne would not allow them to night fly locally and its distance from South Cerney meant a lot of wasted transit flying. With the end of hostilities in Europe 3(P)AFU quickly withdrew from Charmy Down and the airfield reverted to Care & Maintenance under South Cerney control. In January 1946 it was transferred to 54 Group and used by 92 Gliding School for ATC flying and as a Personnel Re-settlement Centre for Australians, finally closing down in October 1946. The majority of the communal sites were transferred to the Ministry of Health in September 1947 and

the airfield de-requisitioned two years later, leaving the VHF transmitter in Air Ministry hands for use by Colerne. Since then the hangars have been removed, and most of the runways broken up. The ATC tower, on the north-western side of the field, was renovated as a private house, but the remainder of the buildings are derelict—a melancholy sight.

Chedworth, Gloucestershire

SP042131. 1½ miles NW of Chedworth village

Chedworth was opened in April 1942 as one of the 'crossbow' utility airfields planned during the early war years. In addition to the airfield site, with its two runways, two Blister hangars and extensive dispersals, a number of domestic sites were built to the north-west, some of them deep in Withington woods. A satellite of Aston Down, it was used by

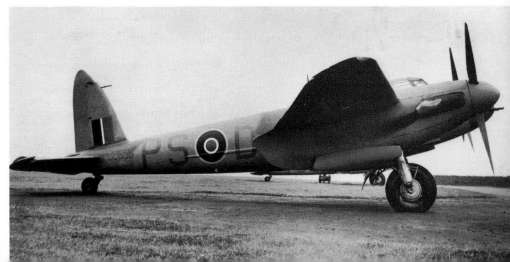

Chedworth on October 30 1967. Two Blister hangars and a number of huts are still in use for agriculture (DoE).

the Spitfires of 52 OTU, aircraft being detached there permanently as accommodation and technical facilities became available. In December 1942 Fighter Command's *Banquet Fighter Apple* scheme was put into effect. This required the senior courses during their last three weeks to be formed into 552 Squadron and be available for operational scrambles, practice interceptions, GCI and searchlight co-operation under the control of Colerne.

This did not last long, however, for on January 15 1943 the Fighter Leader School was formed at Chedworth as an offshoot of 52 OTU, with half the latter's aircraft and personnel. Operational pilots were given a three-week course in tactics, including 25 hours' flying at Chedworth, but the first course was hardly under way when the FLS was moved to Charmy Down. Chedworth was then used by Oxfords of 3(P)AFU South Cerney while their base was waterlogged, followed by aircraft of 6(P)AFU which ran a detachment until October 1943.

Chedworth now became a satellite of Honiley and a combined 60/63 OTU air gunnery squadron moved in with ten Mosquito 2s and two Martinets. They operated until January 1944 after which the airfield was deserted until March when 3(P)AFU returned for night flying, the close proximity of Down Ampney, Fairford, Broadwell and Blakehill Farm

having made South Cerney too hazardous.

During June and July 1944 the IXth Air Force, USAAF, HQ Squadron and the 125th Liaison Squadron, used the airfield for communications work with L-5 Sentinels and other light aircraft. On July 17 No 3 Tactical Exercise Unit was moved into Aston Down and C Squadron was detached to Chedworth with its Mustangs. The TEU became part of a re-formed 55 OTU in December with Chedworth remaining as its satellite. This OTU was used for fighter-bomber training and flying was intensive, the unit having 120 aircraft, mainly Typhoons, spread between Aston Down and Chedworth by early 1945.

The end of the war in Europe brought an immediate end to Typhoon training and the satellite was closed down in May, Chedworth reverting to Care & Maintenance. It remained inactive until December 3 1945 when it was transferred to the Admiralty, who probably used it for storage.

The grass areas were soon returned to farming use and a minor road across the airfield from Chedworth village to Withington was re-opened, while another one used part of the perimeter track. The Central Flying School used the airfield as a practice forced landing field for many years, joined by a civilian gliding club in the late 1960s. In the 1970s it fell into disuse though Wessex 2s of 72 Squadron

Chickerell landing ground in April 1929 when 447 Flight was in camp. Similar in appearance during the war though more houses had been built to the right of the public house at the road junction.

operated from part of the airfield during exercises in April 1977.

Both Blister hangars were still in use for agricultural purposes in 1980 and part of the domestic site was occupied by an organisation called Worksavers. Most of the sites are still in existence but derelict and the whole area looks rather sad and neglected.

Chickerell, Dorset

SY655796. 1½ miles NW of Weymouth

Chickerell had a long, intermittent and rather elusive career for it does not feature on official maps of the 1939-45 period. It was originally established in 1918 as one of a series of small aerodromes strategically positioned around the coastline of Britain for use by short-range anti-submarine aircraft. D Flight of 253 Squadron was operating three DH 6 patrol aircraft by the end of June 1918, but a re-organisation in August brought 513 Flight of 241 Squadron to Chickerell.

The squadron faded away in December 1918 but Chickerell was earmarked as one of an ambitious chain of civil aerodromes planned during the immediate post-war period. For a short time Handley Page Air Transport flew 0/400s from Cricklewood to Weymouth (Chickerell) as part of their network of services but these were not a financial success and the route was soon abandoned.

From 1927 to 1930 Chickerell was used as a temporary RAF base for Fleet Air Arm units exercising with ships from Portland. The fixed facilities consisted merely of a landing circle and windsock on a roughly square grass field, each unit setting up its own tentage. In the early 1930s Chickerell was used as playing fields but Sir Alan Cobham appeared regularly with his Circus and in 1937 the Air Ministry leased it as a forward base for armament training on the Chesil Bank ranges. It was used both for emergency landings and for re-arming aircraft of No 6 Armament Training School, continuing in operation throughout the many name changes of that unit. The hutted camp on the east side, first opened during 1918, was used by the handling parties and Chickerell was retained throughout the 1939-45 war, aircraft up to the size of Blenheims being flown from the 2,400-ft (731-m) grass strip.

In addition to RAF units, Chickerell also played host to 793 Squadron, FAA, during 1939-40 and to the Rocs, Masters, Martinets and Defiants of 794 Squadron, Yeovilton, in the spring of 1943. When 14

Sikorsky S-55 WW339 on trials at Chickerell while attached to 705 Squadron early in 1953.

and 17 Armament Practice Camps closed at Warmwell in November 1945 Chickerell had already been virtually taken over by the Admiralty for communication flights to Portland and for a detachment of 771 Squadron on range duties. Early in 1953 they were joined by Dragonfly helicopters of 705 Squadron for a short time but with the withdrawal of 771 in August 1955 Chickerell fell into disuse and was finally de-requisitioned in 1959. Today much of the old landing ground is covered by housing and industrial estates. There is little evidence of its former use.

Chivenor, Devon

SS492344. 5 miles W of Barnstaple

During the early hours of June 4 1942 the 1,076-ton Italian submarine *Luigi Torelli* was traversing the Bay of Biscay on the surface recharging her batteries. Suddenly the lookouts were blinded by a brilliant white light. The officer of the watch ordered a hard turn to port. The light went out and the Italians heard an aircraft go overhead. Aboard the 172 Squadron Wellington, the crew had caught a glimpse of the submarine, but too late to attack. Disappointed, the pilot turned back towards the sighting position and the crew were surprised to re-locate the contact on radar, and delighted when the puzzled

Italians helped by firing recognition signals. At 250 ft (76 m) and ¾ mile, the light was again switched on and the beam slowly raised on to the submarine. At 50 ft (15 m) the pilot, Squadron Leader Greswell, released his 250-lb (113-kg) depth charges. It was a perfect straddle, but though the submarine was badly damaged she was able to limp into Bordeaux. It was the first time the Leigh Light had been used operationally—and it was to become virtually synonymous with the name of Chivenor.

The contractors moved on to the site of the old North Devon Airport during May 1940 and started work laying three 3,000-ft (914-m) runways on fields just to the west of the original grass aerodrome. Reopened as RAF Chivenor on October 1, it was a typical wartime airfield with four 'T2' and four Bellman hangars and extensive hutted accommodation. First occupied by 3(C)OTU with Blenheims, Ansons and Beauforts for training new Coastal crews, it was also used during 1941 by 252 and 272 Squadrons for their conversion to Beaufighters.

No 3 OTU left in July but was immediately replaced by 5(C)OTU which carried out similar training. Navigation was one of the skills learnt by pupils on the courses, and it must have been of some comfort to discover that the Germans also suffered from being 'uncertain of their position' sometimes. While night flying was underway on November 26 a strange aircraft joined the

A late war photograph of Chivenor with over 50 Wellingtons on the extensive dispersals. The remains of the North Devon airport are to the right (J. Rounce).

circuit and landed. Much to everyone's amazement it was seen to be a Ju 88 in full Luftwaffe markings. It was stopped by a MT vehicle, though not before a Defence Company had fired at it. The crew, on a shipping search over the Irish Sea, thought they had crossed the Channel and landed in France. The virtually undamaged Ju 88A-5 was flown to Farnborough and later joined 1426 Flight, the enemy aircraft circus, which toured airfields giving recognition training to personnel. When the Flight visited Chivenor in November 1942 the Ju 88A-5 *EE205* accompanied it, and in a strange way got its revenge for the capture of its compatriot. During an affiliation exercise with Beaufighters of 235 Squadron, one of the latter stalled while attempting to keep on the '88's tail and crashed into the river Taw.

Though detachments were deployed it was not until 1942 that complete squadrons were based at Chivenor. The first was 172, formed in February to work up on the new Leigh Light with 16 Wellington GR VIIIs. Increasing U-boat activity in the Bay of Biscay forced desperate measures on the C-in-C Coastal and he gratefully added the obsolescent Whitleys of 51 and 77 Squadrons to his thinly-spread forces. They joined 172 Squadron in April but relief for the over-crowded airfield was provided when 5

OTU left the following month and Chivenor proclaimed its operational status by transferring to 19 Group, where it was to remain for the rest of the war.

With the Ju 88s causing heavy losses over the Bay, 235 Squadron brought its Beaufighters to combat them. But the Whitleys, which had been useful in keeping the submariners' heads down, left in October so that Chivenor could provide refuelling facilities for aircraft flying to Gibraltar and North Africa for Operation *Torch*. The peak load reached was 88 aircraft, a tremendous strain on the unit.

The coastal strike squadrons never stayed anywhere very long, constantly rushing about the country plugging holes, and 235 Squadron was soon away. In January 1943 404 (RCAF) Squadron arrived to take on the Ju 88s, but only stayed a couple of months. Meanwhile 172 Squadron received Wellington GR XIIs (Leigh Light) fitted with ASV Mk III which the U-boat receivers could not detect. The result was disastrous from the German viewpoint. *U-665* was the first victim, destroyed on February 22, and in March alone 12 sightings resulted in seven attacks by the squadron. They were joined by Chivenor's first four-engined aircraft when the Fortress IIs of 59 Squadron arrived in February, but the airfield was not really large enough and their stay was brief. Instead two more Wellington

The technical and part of the domestic area of Chivenor in the 1960s, though hardly changed from wartime days (via W. Taylor).

squadrons, 407 (RCAF) and 547, moved in. 547 left in June and was replaced by 612 Squadron which made the last operational flight by a Coastal Whitley on June 5 and then converted to Leigh Light Wellingtons. Chivenor could justly claim to be the home of the night anti-submarine forces.

Nos 407 and 612 Squadrons were hurriedly moved to St Eval in November when Chivenor's runways began to break up, but they were back in December. After some shuffling of units early in 1944, during which 304 (Polish) arrived from Predannack, Chivenor fielded four Wellington (LL) squadrons in time for the spring U-boat offensive. In May 1944 the submarines began to concentrate in Biscay ports in readiness to attack the expected Allied invasion and sightings were few. On May 5, however, *304/N* homed on to a large contact which split on the radar screen at the last moment, and in the glare of the searchlight the crew was surprised to see two U-boats. Despite heavy flak the Wellington pressed home its attack and one submarine was believed sunk.

For D-Day, Coastal Command was given the task of helping to seal the Channel against U-boats and a sustained 'maximum effort' was mounted by the Chivenor squadrons. Few sightings were made, but the attack ratio was very high, crews taking every opportunity such as on the night of June 18 when a surfaced submarine was seen in the moonlight. The pilot of *304/A* swung his aircraft round and straddled the *U-441* with six 250-lb depth charges. It disappeared in a mass of spray and sank with no survivors.

August 27 was a night for heroes. The crew of *172/B* picked up a U-boat on radar, confirmed by Leigh Light. At half a mile range flak set fire to the aircraft's port engine and, as the depth charges were dropped, the starboard engine was hit. The Wellington was ditched and four of the crew survived, but had only one small dinghy between them. The navigator, Flying Officer R.B. Gray, helped his wounded pilot into it then found another survivor and got him into the dinghy as well. Gray and the fourth survivor clung to the outside. With the dawn Gray was found to be dead, and the reason became obvious—his leg had been shot away, but he had not mentioned it. Fifteen hours after the ditching a 10 (RAAF) Squadron Sunderland landed in the open sea and picked up the three survivors. Gray received the George Cross posthumously for 'magnificent courage and unselfish heroism enabling the lives of his comrades to be saved at the cost of his own'.

With the Biscay ports in Allied hands, the U-boats moved away and by October the original Leigh Light Wellington squadrons had all left Chivenor. They were replaced by 179 Squadron from Predannack, and two from the Middle East. 407 Squadron returned in November and all four worked up on Wellington GR

XIVs (LL). With these aircraft they flew long and generally fruitless patrols over the English Channel, sometimes in terrible weather. In February 1945 Chivenor was under a foot of snow and it took all available station personnel to clear the main runway. After one aircraft had taken off, a thaw set in and the airfield was flooded! The runways had been slightly extended during 1944 and a large number of new dispersals built, some on the original North Devon Airport. But the U-boat war was now out of range of Wellingtons and the squadrons were soon moved or disbanded.

The first year of peace was one of order and counter order. A Strike Wing (248 and 254 Squadrons) briefly occupied Chivenor, followed by meteorological squadrons, but by April 1 1946 No 21 Aircrew Holding Unit was in sole occupation—and six years of association with Coastal Command was at an end. The station was taken over by Fighter Command on October 1 1946, but not as an operational base. It was used for anti-aircraft co-operation work, the home of 691 Squadron flying Spitfire XVIs, Oxfords and Martinets.

Eleven months later 203 AFS arrived from Keevil, remaining until 1950 when Chivenor was taken over by Transport Command for No 1 Overseas Ferry Unit. The location was too far west for peace-time operations, however, and the airfield reverted to Fighter Command. 229 OCU arrived from Leuchars on March 28 and thus commenced 24 years' association between Chivenor and this unit. Starting with Meteor T7s and Vampire FB5s, the OCU worked its way through Sabres to the Hunter, an aircraft that will always be associated with the North Devon airfield. Extensive alterations were made to runways and perimeter tracks and a large hardstanding laid in front of the hangars. But the Air Ministry was strangely reluctant to consider Chivenor as a permanent station, and the wartime wooden huts remained in use as accommodation for single personnel.

Chivenor proved ideal for fighter training, having a good weather factor and easy access to excellent air-to-air and air-to-ground ranges. The type of aircraft and flying naturally led to some accidents and in June 1957 the rescue facilities were very much improved by the arrival of E Flight of 275 Squadron equipped with two Sycamore HR 14 helicopters. Despite

Below *A Wellington GR XIV of 36 Squadron at Chivenor in 1944* (via Chaz Bowyer).
Bottom *The rebuilt tower at Chivenor is visible over the nose of Hawk T 1 XX254 of 2 TWU/63 Squadron in May 1981* (A.S. Thomas).

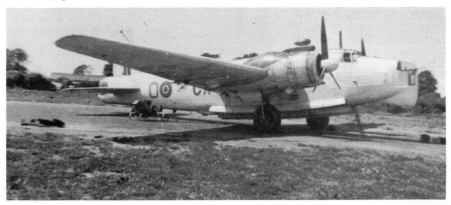

performance limitations these choppers performed 18 months' valuable service in the Bristol Channel area before replaced by the much more effective Whirlwind 4s of 22 Squadron. They were soon in demand to rescue sailors, rock climbers and the more foolhardy summer visitors to North Devon. It was the numerous rescues, some extremely hazardous, plus the general goodwill built up over the 34 years of the airfield's existence, that led to the station being granted the Honarary Freedom of Barnstaple on April 17 1974. This was just in time for, after several official announcements of closure, and rumoured moves of the OCU, it finally happened in September 1974, when the Hunters flew away to Brawdy.

It was not the end for Chivenor, however, for 22 Squadron (now flying the turbine-powered Whirlwind HAR 10) remained in a small enclave on the airfield. Chivenor was also used by 624 Gliding School for the ATC and was made available by MoD to civil aircraft in 1975. In April 1976, 22 Squadron moved to the northern end of the hardstanding where they occupied one of the hangars.

A variety of schemes for the airfield were proposed, some practical, others grandiose, but all came to naught for in the spring of 1978 MoD announced that an increased requirement for weapon training meant that a second Tactical Weapons Unit would be needed. It was formed at Lossiemouth, but a major redeployment meant that it would have to move in 1980—and Chivenor was chosen.

During 1979-80 the airfield was completely rebuilt. The main runway was relaid and a secondary one built for emergencies. The temporary wartime buildings still in use when 229 OCU left were replaced by permanent brick structures, and an additional hangar was brought all the way from East Anglia. In August 1980 the first Hawks for 2 TWU arrived and Chivenor built up to full strength again during 1981. Hopefully the very popular Open Day will be re-introduced in the near future.

Christchurch, Hampshire (now Dorset)

SZ185932. ½ mile NE of Christchurch

Christchurch opened in 1935 as a small flying club field on meadowland alongside the river Mude and soon attracted summer scheduled services by a number of small airlines. All found it very difficult to make their routes viable and it was not until 1939 that Great Western & Southern Air Lines started to make their services pay.

In September 1939 the airfield closed but the siting of the Air Ministry Research Establishment at Swanage started a search for a suitable location for its associated Special Duties Flight, then at St Athan. Christchurch was selected and authority for its requisition given on April 21 1940, together with instructions to site a Bellman hangar. Six days later the unit started to move in its Battles, Blenheims, Ansons and Harrows.

The capitulation of France put Christchurch in the front line and heavy air raids were expected. Particular anxiety was felt about the vulnerability of parked aircraft and in July an emergency landing ground was established at Sway, 6½ miles to the east. Ten aircraft were sent there in August but the scheme was not a success because continual changes to experimental equipment meant that many aircraft had to be kept at Christchurch. During September one of the pilots, Flight Lieutenant D.L. Rayment, made a name for himself by twice engaging the enemy. On the 12th he intercepted a Ju 88 while flying a trials Blenheim and a week later used Hurricane *L1562* to shoot down another Ju 88 off St Catherine's Point.

The Air Ministry had long wanted to move the AACU from Gosport and in October H Flight arrived at Christchurch, its Battles joining those of an expanding Special Duty Flight in operations for the ADEE Swanage. By the end of October there were 30 aircraft on station strength and accommodation for both equipment and personnel was a problem, even though much property was requisitioned in the area.

During 1940 work on a shadow factory alongside the western boundary of the airfield went ahead and at the end of the year it was taken over by Airspeed Ltd for Oxford production. The first of three 'disappearing' pillbox gun positions (which retracted into the ground) was completed by the Kent Construction Co at the end of January 1941, and twin dispersal pens were also under construction. Plans were made to move the SDF to Hurn but its opening was delayed and the unit was still based here when Sway ELG was bombed on April 9, followed a month later by an attack on Christchurch by a He 111. It dropped 13 bombs from low level resulting in damage

Viewed from the south-east in October 1941, Christchurch has been camouflaged by extending housing estate roads. Most of the aircraft are dispersed near the woods on the banks of the River Mude (IWM).

to local houses and RAF huts on the airfield. Two days later another He 111 attacked early in the morning, but this time the defences opened fire and claimed hits.

These events hastened the camouflaging of the airfield and Airspeed factory, connecting roads being simulated by white chippings. The results were so good that a visiting Hampden circled the field but did not land because the pilot thought the available area too small. Meanwhile there was a stir on April 30 when a Bucker 131 Jungmann biplane landed. It had been stolen by two ex-French Air Force pilots from Caen airfield and flown at low level across the Channel. It was dismantled and sent to London. Another unusual visitor was a Boeing 247 which arrived for trials on 10 cm AI radar in August 1941.

During the same month the SDF did move to Hurn and became Telecommunications Flying Unit, leaving a small

detachment at Christchurch until November. On August 1 the airfield was transferred to 10 Group as Hurn's satellite but, with the AACU detachment disbanded, Christchurch was now used almost exclusively by Airspeed who were expanding their activities rapidly. During February 1942 the first of 695 Christchurch-assembled Horsas was towed off the small grass field by a Whitley, and in 1943 the company received a contract for the conversion of Spitfires into Seafires. Most of them were ferried in by ATA pilots though some had to be collected from Holmsley South when weather conditions were difficult. The weather also made test flying problematical on occasions but things improved following the laying of a 4,800-ft (1,463-m) wire mesh runway during the year. This was part of a programme to provide a series of advanced landing grounds along the south coast for British and American fighter

A wire-mesh runway being laid by the 833rd Engineer Aviation Battalion at Christchurch in 1943. It was to the south-east of the original airfield (USAF).

squadrons, but it was used by Airspeed until the arrival of the 405th FG, 84th FW, IXth Tactical Air Command, USAAF, in April 1944.

Using tented accommodation for the personnel and working on aircraft in the open, the Americans roughed it at Christchurch. They went operational on their P-47D Thunderbolts on April 11 and were quickly engaged in softening-up enemy forces and communications in France. There were several accidents with P-47s. One day three crashed on take-off, and bombs had a habit of dropping off while the aircraft bounced over the rough runway. One bomb-carrying Thunderbolt crashed on the bungalows just outside the airfield and his load exploded causing widespread damage and 19 deaths.

When the Americans left for the Continent on June 30, the end of the war being by now in sight, Airspeed decided that Christchurch was easier to develop than Portsmouth and started expanding the facilities during that autumn of 1944. Design and drawing offices, research laboratories and a technical block were constructed, and the design team moved in during September to concentrate their efforts on the AS 57, later the Ambassador.

The Air Ministry transferred control of the airfield to Ibsley when Hurn became a civil airport in November 1944. Shuffled around Transport Command, but not used except for communications flights, Christchurch was finally taken over by the MAP as a factory airfield on January 10 1946. During this year assembly of the prototype Ambassador started and the

Horsa II RN310 *at Christchurch in August 1944* (IWM).

aircraft made its first flight from the grass strip on July 10 1947. The Airspeed company was also given the task of developing the Vampire trainer and a tarmac runway was laid at Christchurch during 1950 to allow the testing of the prototype. In June 1951 Airspeed was completely absorbed by de Havilland and with a strengthened design team developed the Venom for naval use and completed an 80 per cent re-design of the DH 110 to produce the Sea Vixen.

Aircraft production ceased at Christchurch in 1962 and the airfield finally closed five years later. Housing estates then started to encroach from the southwest, while the MoD Signals Research Establishment took over buildings at the north-eastern end of the airfield. The de Havilland works were taken over by industrial concerns and in 1979 the main airfield site was sold to Barratts Development Ltd for an extension of the industrial estate. An association with aviation is retained by road names on the estate such as *de Havilland Way* and *Ambassador Close*, and there are still a few ex-WD buildings scattered about, including a pillbox in a small copse.

Church Stanton (Culmhead), Somerset
See Culmhead

Cleave, Cornwall
SS205125. 4 miles N of Bude

Cleave was planned as a landing ground for summer anti-aircraft co-operation camps. Work started on the clifftop site in February 1939 and it was occupied by G and V Flights of No 1 AACU in May.

They lived in tents alongside Bessoneaux hangars erected on the south side of the airfield, but already plans to enlarge the station had been made and work started in October.

G Flight used Wallaces for target towing for the Royal Artillery AA Practice Camps at Cleave and Watchet, while V Flight had Queen Bees for pilotless operation. The catapult and crane were ready late in June 1939 when the first pilotless flights were made using this cumbersome equipment. The following month take-offs from the grass were tried successfully, and the catapult was abandoned.

In September D Flight arrived for air-to-air firing and all three units steadily increased their operations. Barrack blocks, messes and two Bellman hangars were completed by the end of July 1940 and Cleave began to look and feel like an RAF station. It was not long before the Luftwaffe took some interest, two Ju 88s dropping 12 bombs on August 26 damaging two Wallace aircraft and injuring a civilian. A 1,100-lb (500-kg) bomb hit one of the Bellmans on October 2, but fortunately failed to explode.

By now six AACU Flights were in occupation and more accommodation was being built. Henleys had largely replaced the Wallaces and were in use on the Cleave, St Agnes and Penhale ranges, while the Queen Bees flew for live gunnery practice over the sea. During the winter waterlogging was a constant problem and a couple of Beauforts which landed on the 2,700-ft (823-m) runway in March 1941 were lucky to get down safely. Although Cleave was 400-ft (122-m) above sea level,

Perched on the cliffs north of Bude is the grass airfield of Cleave, September 1942 (RAF Museum).

the thin soil and impervious rock made absorption and drainage of water very slow, and flying was often interrupted. Despite this, diversions by operational aircraft were common early in 1942 and included Spitfires, Whirlwinds and even a Mosquito.

On November 24 the AACU was re-organised, the Henley-equipped units becoming 1602, 1603 and 1604 Flights while V became 1618 Flight. In January 1943 things were enlivened by the arrival of the first WAAFs, and four months later by a USAAF B-17 which landed without difficulty. But it was lightly loaded for it had just flown direct from North Africa in 13 hours. Its VIP passengers, led by Major General Edwards, US Army, were probably relieved to reach *terra firma* but not overly impressed by the navigation!

With the disbandment of Army Co-operation Command in June, Cleave was taken over by Fighter Command but retained its AACU role. On December 1 the three Henley Flights became 639 Squadron and, with the Queen Bee too slow to provide anything remotely like a realistic target, 1618 Flight was disbanded. The large Army camp on the northern perimeter, now partially occupied by American servicemen on AA gunnery courses, even attracted full US Army stage shows, one of which had both Bob Hope and the Glenn Miller band appearing on the same bill! It also attracted senior British Army staff officers who visited in March 1944 to study Cleave's suitability as the post-war School of AA Defence..

The unit's closure came very suddenly on May 16 1945 when it was reduced to Care & Maintenance. Three days later all except the C & M party had been posted and the airfield was closed completely in November.

It was the end of Cleave as an RAF unit but in more recent years it has been taken over as a Combined Signals Organisation Station with the name of Morwenstow. Nearly all the old buildings have been removed, to be replaced by modern brick accommodation dominated by two large dish aerials which can be seen for miles. The few cottages which comprised Cleave village disappeared when the airfield was enlarged, and all that now remains of the name is *Cleave Crescent*, a small enclave of Ministry married quarters alongside the minor road built on the eastern perimeter track of the wartime airfield.

Colerne, Wiltshire

ST803715. 4 miles NE of Bath on Fosse Way

Colerne was very quiet on D-Day, the war seemed far away—but all this changed with the arrival of 147 Wing, 85 Group, 2nd Tactical Air Force, during July. The Wing's three Mosquito NF XIII squadrons roamed nightly over France with great success, though undoubtedly the highlight was the sortie by Flight Lieutenant G.E. Jameson, DFC, with his navigator, Flying Officer N.E. Crookes, on July 29/30. Flying *MM466* of 488 (RNZAF) Squadron on standby patrol between Caen and Lisieux, they despatched three Ju 88s and a Do 217 in the space of 20 minutes—and used only 90 shells from each of their 20 mm cannon!

Perched on a plateau, Colerne was one of the last Expansion Scheme airfields to be completed. Laid out as a maintenance unit, it was still under construction in September 1939 and many of the planned buildings were not completed, while others were modified. It was opened by 41 Group on January 1 1940 in a partially completed state, 39 MU being formed on May 18 as an aircraft storage unit. The MU was the sole occupant until September when Fighter Command decided to form a 10 Group Sector HQ at Colerne. The runways were still incomplete, however, and heavy rain made the airfield unusable until

November 27 when 87 Squadron arrived with their black night fighter Hurricanes. But they did not stay long, moving to the Charmy Down satellite as soon as possible. Colerne was then used for training new fighter squadrons.

With the runways completed at last, the first fully operational unit arrived in April 1941. This was 600 Squadron, equipped with a mixed force of Blenheim 1 and Beaufighter II night fighters which they used to mount patrols covering Bristol and the south-west generally. They scored regularly, bringing down a Ju 88 and an He 111 before the end of the month, and two He 111s on May 7. The next night a Ju 88 was damaged, but on May 9/10 a Beaufighter was shot down—by another British night fighter. It was difficult to tell friend from foe in the pitch dark and without IFF. The slow replacement of the ill-equipped Blenheim was a problem, but when engineless Beaufighter airframes started to arrive from Filton for storage, the reason became clear. They were completed by a working party when engines became available in March 1942.

A BOAC repair facility moved into Colerne in 1941 and used some of the new hangars to the north of the airfield. With part of the Fosse Way as an access track they were soon producing two aircraft a day, and later undertook the assembly of fighter aircraft before RAF personnel took over the work in March 1942. As 218 MU the unit changed from assembly to secret special installations in August. At first this meant AI radar, but later the work included all sorts of one-off modifications to many different types of aircraft.

Meanwhile, a Polish Hurricane squadron, 316, had spent a couple of months at Colerne during the summer of 1941 on convoy patrols, but little happened until they escorted Hampdens on Operation *Sunrise* and were able to claim a Bf 109E. The following month they carried out a few sweeps before moving to Church Stanton. A string of other squadrons spent short periods on the airfield and 263 tried its Whirlwinds on night flying but soon gave up. 125 Squadron, however, managed to gain its first probable on April 26 1942 using its Defiants whilst awaiting conversion to Beaufighters IIFs.

After much frustration with Defiants, 264 Squadron received Mosquito IIs in May 1942 which were soon operational, damaging a Do 217 over Weston-super-

A night fighter Hurricane of 87 Squadron lands at Colerne in May 1941.

Mare. A Ju 88 was destroyed in July but there was little action and in December they started day patrols over the Bay of Biscay and occasional *Rangers* over France. The weather was appalling that winter and at one stage 12 of their Mosquitoes were being repaired after water soakage in the wooden wings and fuselages.

More unusual visitors were P-38F Lightnings of the 27th Fighter Squadron, 1st Fighter Group, XIIth Air Force, USAAF, which spent nearly two months at Colerne before flying out to North Africa on November 6 via Chivenor and Portreath. Training activities continued into 1943, with 184 Squadron working up using Hurricane IID tank-busters, and 183 converting on to Typhoons. The Mosquitoes of 151 Squadron carried out night intruder operations over France until August when they left for Middle Wallop. Re-equipped with Mosquito NF XIIIs, 151 returned in November and after claiming an Me 410, had an He 177 confirmed during the night of January 21/22 1944 when one of these four-engined monsters was shot down near Hindhead.

Following a very successful night when three Ju 188s and an '88 were claimed, 151 Squadron moved to Predannack in March and was replaced by a detachment of 219 Squadron flying Mosquito NF XVIIs. On March 27 a Ju 88 of 3/KG54 fell to the Colerne detachment, one of eight bombers shot down that night. The Mosquitoes had all gone by early May leaving the airfield to the two MUs and 286 Squadron, the latter having moved in

on the 20th, joined three days later by a detachment from 587 Squadron. Both units had a mixture of Oxfords, Hurricanes and Martinets, used to provide a variety of training targets for Army gunners.

During June 1944, 39 MU worked flat out to prepare aircraft in readiness for anticipated heavy invasion losses, but the tempo had moderated by the time that Mosquitoes of 147 Wing appeared in July. 604 Squadron soon left for the Continent but 410 and 488 Squadrons were to remain until the autumn, a crew of 410 achieving the first success with the powerful but troublesome Mosquito XXX during the night of August 19/20 when they shot down two Ju 88s. 604 returned briefly in November and was joined by 264 Squadron on shipping reconnaissance over the western approaches. They both left in December and Colerne entered a new era as the first permanent Meteor base. 616, now re-equipped with Meteor IIIs, arrived in January 1945 but left for East Anglia later in the month, and was replaced by 1335 Conversion Unit which flew Oxfords and early Meteor variants. Its first job was to train 504 Squadron which was joined by 74 Squadron in May to form the first jet fighter Wing in the RAF. 1335 CU went to Molesworth in August, the Wing staying until September 1946 when all fighter units left Colerne and it was transferred to 41 Group, Maintenance Command, with 39 and 218 MUs still in residence.

Apart from test flying and ferrying, the airfield was little used for the next five years. 218 MU was disbanded in February

Colerne on September 26 1958. The extensions to the original wartime configuration can easily be seen (DoE).

1948 but replaced in May by 49 MU which arrived from Lasham and was retained when the original Colerne MU, No 39, was closed in October 1953. Two Flights of 662 Squadron, an Auxiliary unit flying Auster AOPs, were formed in February 1949, but it was not until Fighter Command returned during June 1952 that the station regained some of its former glory. Their unit was 238 OCU, responsible for basic night fighter training of navigators using Brigands. It received Meteor NF 12s in 1956 before leaving for North Luffenham at the beginning of 1957.

Colerne was taken over by Transport Command and in January 24 Squadron moved in its Hastings from Abingdon. 511 Squadron arrived from Lyneham in May 1957 and in a move to retain older numbers became 36 Squadron on September 1 1958. They were joined by 114 Squadron and operating as a Wing the three squadrons flew all over the world on the famous Transport Command routes and all sorts of special flights.

No 49 MU continued to use the storage hangars at the northern end of the airfield until 1962 when it too disbanded, having spent its last years on modification work on aircraft such as the Shackleton.

No 114 Squadron disbanded in September 1961 but the others converted to the Lockheed Hercules during 1967-68 and moved to Lyneham. Meanwhile Colerne became the main engineering base for the Hercules in April 1967 and saw the re-formation of 48 Squadron during October of the same year. 48 soon left for the Far East but Colerne continued as an engineering base until there was sufficient room at Lyneham for both squadron and technical organisations.

Colerne was among the airfields listed as 'no longer required' in the 1975 Defence White Paper and it was closed on March 31 1976. The thriving museum, formed in 1964, had officially closed a few days earlier, all the aircraft having been sent to other museums or scrapped.

The station was taken over by the Army as Azimghir Barracks and in 1980 was the home of the Junior Leaders Regiment, RCT. The airfield was initially retained on reserve and has been kept in good condition. Recently, however, MoD has been selling the land on the runway approaches and it is presumably no longer considered as an emergency base. A good general view of the airfield can be obtained from the Fosse Way which forms part of its western boundary.

Culdrose, Cornwall

SW675258. 2 miles SE of Helston on A3083

Scramble! booms the tannoy in the squadron ready room—the crew sprints to the aircraft and is airborne in 90 seconds—a performance repeated 122 times in just one year. This would not be a bad record for a fighter squadron during the war—but this was 1976! They were not fighter ops but search and rescue missions, a task for which Culdrose has been justly renowned since 1970, and which resulted in the rescue of 875 persons up to March 1982.

Many military airfields have been completely rebuilt since the 1939-45 War, but Culdrose is unique in being the only one opened in the United Kingdom on a site not previously used for flying. Its gestation period was long, the initial survey having been completed in 1943 and the 700-acre site purchased by the Admiralty in February 1944 and provisionally given the name RNAS Helston (HMS *Chough*) after the Cornish bird. Later their Lords of the Admiralty changed their minds and when the station was commissioned on April 17 1947 it was as RNAS Culdrose (HMS *Seahawk*).

Changes had been made to the original plans but Culdrose was still largely a hutted camp when it opened though the hangarage was extensive, consisting of 17 Pentad and six Mainhill hangars. The unit's main task was to house the Naval Night Fighter School and its first squadron, 780, specialised on instrument flying training, using Oxfords and Harvards. The station also performed the usual secondary role of FAA shore bases, that of providing a home for disembarked front-line squadrons. One of the first was 807 Squadron which arrived in August, re-armed with Sea Furies, but left for Eglinton on September 29.

To prepare for the introduction of the Sea Hornet, the Fleet's first real night fighter, 792 Squadron was formed on January 15 1948 with Firefly NF 1 and AI-fitted Ansons, followed by 762 which arrived from Ford in May to provide twin conversion flying. It was 1949 before the Sea Hornet materialised and 809 Squadron formed at Culdrose. A

The domestic site at Culdrose in 1973 while the station was being rebuilt. Most of the prefabricated huts have now been replaced (FAA Museum).

prolonged work-up followed, for the unit not only had to evolve operational night fighter tactics but also to train in the secondary strike fighter role. After deck practice on *Illustrious* 809 Squadron embarked on *Vengeance* on May 18 1951. But the aircraft were not suitable for operation from Light Fleet Carriers and four days later they were back at Culdrose, where they remained until sent to Hal Far in January 1952.

Meanwhile, the training organisation had been revamped, Culdrose becoming No 1 Naval Air Fighter School in February 1950. 736 Squadron arrived from St Merryn and with a re-formed 738 it provided the School with 60 Sea Furies and about 12 Seafires. The day of the piston-engined fighter was drawing to a close, however, for the Naval Jet Evaluation and Training Unit (702 Squadron) had been at Culdrose since April 1949. It was merged with 736 Squadron in August 1952 and the phase-out of the Sea Fury was well under way.

On October 1 1951 a new and very significant unit arrived on the scene. This was 778 Squadron equipped with Skyraiders for trials in the AEW role. With the trials successfully completed, 778 disbanded on July 6 1952, re-forming the next day as 849 Squadron which consisted of a shore-based HQ Flight and four self-

contained Flights embarked on carriers as required. After eight years' outstanding success the Skyraider was replaced by the Gannet AEW 3 when 700 G Flight became 849 Squadron A Flight on February 1 1960. The unit stayed at Culdrose until December 15 1964 when a mass formation of eight AEW 3s and six Gannet T5s left for Brawdy.

But 849 Squadron had been just a small enclave on the station and elsewhere big changes were afoot. In the autumn of 1953 the long planned shuffle code-named *Solitaire* took place, resulting in the Fighter School moving to Lossiemouth and Firefly-equipped units from St Merryn (796 Squadron) and Lossiemouth (766 Squadron) arriving at Culdrose to form the Naval Observer and Air Signals School. They were joined by 750's Sea Princes in March 1954 and HMS *Seahawk* then settled down to its new task of producing naval observers for anti-submarine and all-weather fighter squadrons. Further extensions were made to the married quarters estate on the outskirts of Helston and during 1953-55 more accommodation was built on the station, including a new site for the Air Torpedo Development Unit, which was transferred from Gosport.

No 766 Squadron was disbanded in November 1954 but its place was soon taken by a re-formed 765 Squadron which operated as a pool for piston-engined trained pilots. The first Gannet squadrons were formed at Lee and Eglinton but 825

recommissioned at Culdrose on July 4 1955, closely followed by 816 and 817 Squadrons of the Royal Australian Navy. They embarked on HMAS *Melbourne* in March 1965 for the long journey home— the first of an extensive list of overseas air arms to receive training at Culdrose. As Fireflies were replaced by Gannets in front-line units, 765 Squadron slowly faded away and was disbanded in March 1957.

Another specialised unit arrived in the shape of 751 Squadron, equipped with Avengers and Sea Venoms, and engaged on trials of electronic equipment. It became 831 Squadron in May 1958 and continued to operate Sea Venoms, Gannets replacing the Avengers early in 1959. The squadron spent a lot of time on detachment, but with the move of 750 Squadron and the Observer School to Hal Far in October 1959, it maintained the fixed wing presence alongside 849 until leaving for Watton in 1963.

Culdrose had been chosen as the main helicopter training base for the Royal Navy and the takeover was soon under way with the Hillers, Whirlwinds and Dragonflies of 705 Squadron arriving from Lee in January 1958. Other training units moved in during 1959, the largest of which was the School of Aircraft Handling. This school trains ratings in the intricate business of moving aircraft about the restricted spaces available on carrier decks and in hangars. Over the years the SAH has operated a very cosmopolitan

Sea Otter RD920 *outside the main technical hangars at Culdrose.*

selection of aircraft, many of which have been happily snapped up by museums when at the end of their useful lives.

No 700H Squadron arrived in April 1960 as the Intensive Flying Trials Unit for the Wessex 1, and at last the Navy had a really operational anti-submarine helicopter. In January 1962 it became 706 Squadron and remained at Culdrose as the training unit. As new front-line Wessex squadrons were formed they used Culdrose as their shore base, resulting in a renewed building programme on the station. New helicopters were also being introduced at a rapid rate, 700W being formed with the Wasp in June and 700V with the twin-engined Commando Wessex HU 5 in December 1963. Both were re-commissioned as front-line squadrons during the following spring and the aircraft were brought into the Culdrose training set-up later in 1964. The Wasp joined 706 and the Wessex HU 5 equipped a reformed 707 Squadron.

Culdrose now settled down to almost five years of little change amongst the resident squadrons and their aircraft. With some 65 helicopters on strength, increased to about 110 when front-line squadrons were disembarked, the station could justly claim to be the largest helicopter base in Europe.

The Station Flight originally established to provide a local rescue and communications service gradually expanded its operations as more efficient helicopters became available. One of the early off-base rescues was made on March 18 1965 when, in bad weather and at night, a successful search was made for eight soldiers on a canoeing exercise.

The anti-submarine helicopters were also becoming more effective, the Wessex 3 entering service at Culdrose in 1967, followed by the outstanding Sea King 2½ years later. 706 Squadron received its Sea Kings in November 1969 and the remaining Wessex 3s were soon transferred to Portland. Two operational Sea King squadrons, 824 and 826, commissioned at Culdrose in 1970, coinciding with a £3½-million rebuilding programme on the airfield. This was finally completed in May 1972 with the opening of the Duke of Cornwall Building which now houses the Helicopter Ground School, the Engineering School and the Royal Naval Observer School. The latter unit had returned to Culdrose, complete with 750 Squadron and its Sea Princes in

1972, after its sojourn in the Mediterranean and northern Scotland.

On completion of the work on the airfield the contractors transferred their attention to the administrative and living quarters on the other side of the A3083 and started a £4½-million transformation, which swept away the wartime huts and replaced them with modern multi-storey living blocks, a social centre, wardroom and CPOs' Mess. The social centre contains clubs for ratings and WRNS, a heated swimming pool, cinema, theatre, shops and gym.

Meanwhile, Sea King training was being given at Culdrose to aircrew of foreign air arms which had purchased the aircraft from Westland. The first were Indian Navy crews who completed their work-up during the summer of 1971, followed by the Royal Norwegian Air Force for whom the Royal Navy set up a special training unit in July 1972. When the Federal German Navy also requested assistance it was decided to form the Royal Navy Foreign Training Unit and over the years this has resulted in Sea Kings of many different colours flying from Culdrose. When the unit finally closed down in November 1976, crews from India, Norway, West Germany, Pakistan, Australia, Egypt and Belgium had used the facilities. Several of the trainee crews took part in real rescues, the most notable after the sinking of the 480-ton *Merc Enterprise* in appalling weather on January 16 1974. A combined force of five Sea Kings from 706, 824 and the German squadron took part and 11 survivors and five bodies were recovered by the helicopters and the Russian trawler *Leningrad*. International co-operation at its best.

By now the Sea Kings of 706 Squadron were regularly making rescues 200 miles out into the Atlantic while the arrival of 771 Squadron in September 1974 upgraded the inshore rescue facilities. This unit's basic task was to provide aircraft for the Aircrewman School, give operational training in SAR techniques, and pilot conversion on the Wessex. But it also provided three aircraft as a SAR Flight providing a dawn-to-dusk standby for 365 days a year, while the Sea Kings cover the night and long-range missions.

The RAF had long recognised the outstanding qualities of the Sea King for SAR duties, but it was not until the late 1970s that they were allowed to start replacing their ageing Whirlwinds. Like the foreign air arms before them, they took advantage of the naval training facilities at Culdrose. In February 1978 the first of their bright yellow HAR 3 Sea Kings arrived and soon became a familiar sight around the Lizard Peninsula. With the main conversion task complete, the number of RAF Sea Kings at Culdrose has been reduced to two, which now operate as part of 706 Squadron.

There have been no recent changes in the task of units at Culdrose, but a certain amount of upgrading of equipment. The Sea Kings have become Mk 2s, the Wessex of 771 Squadron are now twin-engined Mk 5s and the aged Sea Princes of 750 Squadron have been replaced by Jetstreams—modern aircraft to fit the very modern image of the station.

Apart from the annual Air Day when a full scale air display is mounted, Culdrose is worth a visit during a family outing, especially on a weekday. Flying can be viewed from a free enclosure at the eastern end of the airfield near the junction of the B3291 and B3293, while nearer Helston is the Cornwall Aero Park. This is run by ex-naval personnel and has benefitted from its close affinity with the Air Station. In addition to the museum, the Aero Park has restaurant and play facilities for all ages.

Culmhead (Church Stanton), Somerset

ST208154. 5 miles SE of Wellington

Fighters joining the Culmhead circuit on April 20 1944 caused little interest, but no-one overlooked the sudden influx of naval uniforms. They caused quite a stir in the nearby villages of Tricky Warren and Church Stanton, for this small compact airfield was high up in the Somerset hills, well away from the sea. Led by Lieutenant Commander N.G. 'Buster' Hallett, DSC, RN, 24 Naval Fighter Wing had been specially formed for D-Day and had come to Culmhead to work-up with 10 Group, RAF—their task to support Typhoons with their Seafire IIIs. During the next three weeks they flew 400 sorties over France and saw not one enemy aircraft, but plenty of action for when no Typhoon operations were scheduled they went on *Rodeos*. Eight aircraft visited St Nazaire on May 7 but, when escorting Typhoons, fuel was always a problem and during a strike on a damaged destroyer four days later the Seafires were forced to hold off during the actual attack. The last full

Wing sorties were flown on May 12, when the Typhoons bombed a merchant ship off St Malo, scoring two hits, while the eight Seafires of 887 and 894 Squadrons shot up shipping and then went on to strafe the wireless station at Cherbourg. No 24 Wing had received its baptism of fire and it had been fairly cheap—one aircraft from each squadron was lost while at Culmhead.

Originally intended as an emergency landing ground and dispersal, Church Stanton was actually a typical three-runway day fighter base when opened on August 1 1941. Double blast pens were dispersed around the airfield, together with ten Blister hangars. The accommodation sites were to the north-west, with messing and administrative areas close to Widcombe House. Later a Teeside hangar was built on the north-west side of the airfield.

For almost a year the exclusive home of No 2 Polish Fighter Wing, Church Stanton became known as *the* Polish airfield. The amount of Luftwaffe activity over the south-west at this time was small and, although intended for the defence of Bristol and Exeter, the squadrons (302 and 316) were used mainly on convoy patrols. The Poles found this very dull work and welcomed the introduction of Channel sweeps and the occasional escort of bombers raiding the Brest peninsula. 316 was replaced by 306 Squadron in December but it was April 1942 before the first opposition was met.

On February 15 1942 a detachment of the RAE Farnborough, called euphemistically the Research Flight, arrived at Church Stanton. They deliberately flew their Battle and Wellington aircraft into cables suspended from barrage balloons to test types of balloon cable cutters. This was a dangerous business, as was quickly demonstrated by the CO, when he had to bale out of Wellington *P9210* on March 24 after the controls were damaged by the cable.

Czechs replaced the Poles in June 1942, 313 Squadron, later joined by 312 to form a Wing, remaining for a year during which they enlivened their hated convoy patrols with *Ramrods* and *Rhubarbs*. In November the poachers became game-keepers when the Wing began *Anti-Rhubarb* patrols against German fighter-bombers making hit and run raids. The Czechs left in June 1943 and were replaced by 66 and 504 Squadrons which used their Spitfire Vs for deck landing

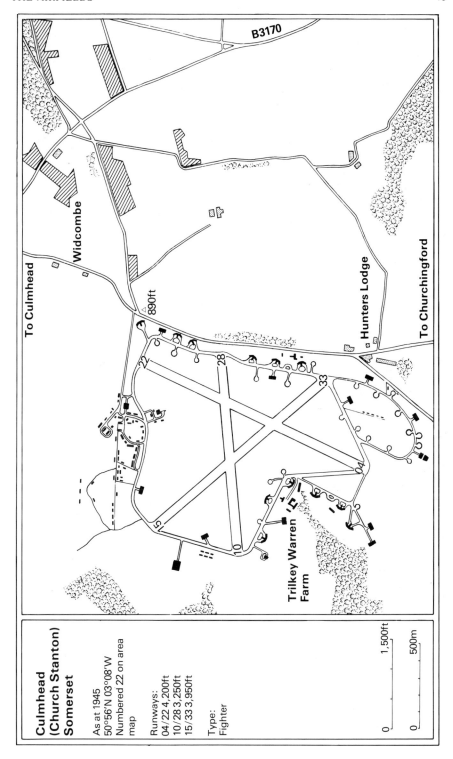

**Culmhead
(Church Stanton)
Somerset**

As at 1945
50°56'N 03°08'W
Numbered 22 on area
map

Runways:
04/22 4,200ft
10/28 3,250ft
15/33 3,950ft

Type:
Fighter

B3170

To Culmhead

Widcombe

890ft

22

28

33

04

15

10

Hunters Lodge

To Churchingford

Trilkey Warren
Farm

1,500ft

500m

0

0

Top *Spitfire HF VII of 131 Squadron at Culmhead in 1944.* **Above** *610 Squadron operated their new Spitfire F XIVs from Culmhead in 1944 (IWM).*

practice and low-level bombing training. The object of this was not revealed, though it led to plenty of rumours.

On December 22 1943 the airfield was renamed Culmhead to reduce the risk of confusion between the numerous stations now using 'Church' as a prefix. 131 and 165 Squadrons, flying Spitfire IXs, were now operating, many of their sweeps being flown from forward airfields in the south-east under the control of 11 Group. In April 1944, 610 Squadron and 24 Naval Fighter Wing arrived as replacements, and more rapid changes brought 126, 131 and 616 Squadrons together at Culmhead over the D-Day period, when they flew armed recce and *Rhubarbs* ahead of the troops in France. On June 6 they strafed aircraft, locomotives and German transport on the Brest peninsula. A week later, as their Spitfires were landing on improvised strips in France, came the electrifying news that 616 was to become the first Allied operational unit to fly jet-propelled

aircraft. The isolated position of Culmhead, so often cursed by the personnel stationed there, now allowed training to go ahead in secret using two Meteors which arrived in July. By the end of the month they had left for Manston, where a very surprised ATC cadet heard and saw one as it came in low over the beach early in August. That cadet was me—on a flying visit during a summer camp at Bircham Newton.

Meanwhile, the move of the USAAF into Weston Zoyland had forced the dispersal of its AACU and 286 and 587 Squadrons arrived at Culmhead with their very mixed bag of Hurricanes, Martinets and Oxfords. 286 did not stay long, but 587 was joined by the Oxfords and Fireflies of 790 (Naval Fighter Direction School) Squadron in August.

With no units left at Culmhead, 10 Group was anxious to reduce it to Care & Maintenance. On September 22, 587 Squadron was transferred back to Weston

Zoyland and 790 to Charlton Horethorne and the airfield made inactive in October 1944. On December 10 Culmhead was transferred to 23 Group as a satellite of Stoke Orchard and a detachment of No 3 Glider Training School moved in with Master II and Hotspur gliders. 3 GTS went to Exeter in January 1945, but Culmhead remained a RLG until the main unit was transferred to Wellesbourne Mountford in July. It then reverted to Care & Maintenance.

Taken over by Maintenance Command in August, the airfield was used by 67 MU for a few months. It also housed a number of Mobile Dental Surgeries, self-contained units on trailers, until August 1946 when Culmhead was closed.

'Tricky Warren', as the locals call it, is now covered in W/T masts and aerials, and has a large modern brick building in the centre of the old airfield. A sign at the entrance near Widcombe Bird Gardens proclaims it as a unit of the Composite Signals Organisation. All the larger wartime buildings have been removed but there is still evidence of its former use in the form of derelict Maycrete and similar domestic accommodation visible from the road—closer study is obviously discouraged!

Davidstow Moor, Cornwall

SX150850. 2 miles NE of Camelford off A39

The name itself suggests isolation and bleakness, and at 970 ft (296 m) Davidstow Moor was both the highest operational airfield in the United Kingdom, and a miserable place on anything but a sunny day. Open to Atlantic gales, it suffered from rapid changes of weather and persistent low cloud. A difficult airfield from which to mount operations, it was rarely used for anything other than a relief base.

Davidstow Moor opened on October 1 1942 before the accommodation was ready or the water supply laid on, though the three runways and 50 panhandle dispersals were complete. Its premature opening was due to Operation *Torch* when every airfield in the south-west was in demand. On October 12 the few locals witnessed the arrival of a 98-vehicle convoy carrying a large number of Americans and much equipment. Then nothing happened until

Davidstow Moor photographed by 543 Squadron on June 13 1967. The minor roads and heavily forested area around the dispersals can be plainly seen (DoE).

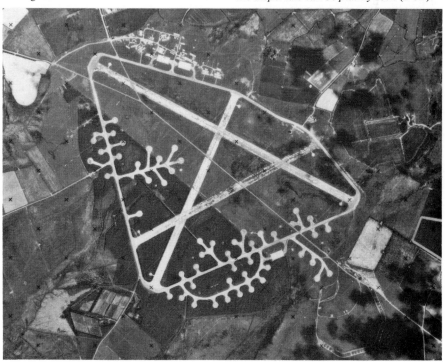

November 8 when 18 Liberators of the 44th and 93rd Bombardment Groups flew in. Bombed up and refuelled, they set off the following day to join B-17s in an attack on U-boat pens at St Nazaire in support of *Torch*. The aircraft crossed the Channel at low level, then climbed to 18,000 ft (5,538 m) before turning for the target. Flak was intense and it was a very bedraggled collection of aircraft which returned to Davidstow. Similar missions to the U-boat pens were flown later in the month by VIIIth Air Force B-17s, and even Airacobras were to be seen at Davidstow during December.

The first British aircraft to visit were two Henleys of 1603 Flight following waterlogging of Cleave during December, but with the departure of the Americans a number of 53 Squadron Hudsons arrived in January 1943 and stayed a month, joined by three similar aircraft from 279 Squadron. The latter were for rescue work and carried airborne lifeboats.

Detachments from other anti-submarine units, 304 (Polish) and 612 Squadrons among them, followed, but none stayed long and the major event during the spring of 1943 was the secret return of the VIIIth AF Liberators, 45 from the 44th and 93rd Groups arriving on May 16. Early next morning 39 B-24s took off and flew a 700 mile (1,126 km) arc out into the Atlantic before turning in to attack the port of Bordeaux from 22,000 ft (6,769 m). The ruse worked, for they met only light opposition and observed direct hits on a long pier, lock gates and the Matford aero engine works. One Liberator had to abandon the attack, but the only casualties were two crewmen injured, and one lost when he was sucked out of a waist gun position after his parachute opened accidentally.

Full control of the airfield was now taken over by 19 Group and in June 1943 the Wellingtons of 304 (Polish) and 547 Squadrons moved in for anti-submarine operations over the Bay of Biscay. 304 Squadron was equipped with the Mk XIII on arrival, which coincided with the change of U-boat tactic—they started crossing the Bay in packs and stayed on the surface to fight it out with aircraft. They made a dangerous foe for the Wellingtons and neither squadron had much success. In August 547 Squadron started flare dropping during A/S patrols, joined by 304 Squadron the following month. But it was obvious that the Leigh Light was much more effective and as soon as Wellington XIVs became available the Polish unit was withdrawn for specialist training. Their XIIIs were handed over to 547 which left in October, to be followed with ill-concealed satisfaction by 304 Squadron in December.

The poor weather factor at Davidstow Moor prompted the Air Ministry to allocate the secret and still rather rudimentary American ground controlled approach (GCA) radar to the airfield in August 1943. Trials started the following month, but the very reason for its existence prevented it being calibrated properly and it was soon transferred to St Eval.

As soon as 304 Squadron left for Predannack, a detachment of 280 Squadron arrived and air-sea rescue was Davidstow's pre-occupation for the next few months. They were soon able to notch up a success for on January 8 1944 Warwick *280/E*, escorted by six Beaufighters, dropped a lifeboat to a Mosquito crew 95 miles south-west of Brest. Half-an-hour later the two

Beaufighter TF X of 404 Squadron RCAF at Davidstow Moor in 1944.

survivors were under way and heading for home.

The Warwicks were joined by 269 Squadron from Reykjavik during January, this unit converting to the SAR role with Hudsons, Spitfires and Walruses, before moving to Lagens, Azores, in March. The Hudsons flew out via Gibraltar, while the Spitfires and Walruses, joined by Martinets, were transported on HMS *Premier*, flying off the carrier near the island.

On March 11 nine Wellingtons of 172, 304 and 612 Squadrons used Davidstow to mount a concentrated anti-submarine patrol. All landed back at their home base of Chivenor except *612/R* which was lost, and *612/C* which just made Portreath short of fuel after attacking a U-boat well out into the Bay. This seemed to remind the Command of Davidstow's declared purpose for, on April 7, 524 Squadron was re-formed (having previously operated Martin Mariner flying boats) as another Wellington XIV unit. A fortnight later it absorbed the Wellington Flight of 415 Squadron and then fielded 16 aircraft. Further reinforcements came with the arrival of the Wick Strike Wing (144 and 404 Squadron Beaufighters) on May 12, and they joined 524 in working-up for the anti-shipping role as 154 (GR) Wing. On the afternoon of D-Day, the German High Command ordered three heavy destroyers to leave Bordeaux to intercept Allied invasion shipping. Promptly reported by the ever vigilant PRU, 144 and 404 Squadrons were launched into the attack. The ships were found off Belle Island and all were damaged and forced into Brest. Two days later they were intercepted by an Allied destroyer force off the Brest peninsula. One was sunk, one driven on to the rocks and the survivor returned to Brest. A subsequent RP and bombing attack by 144 and 404 disposed of the beached vessel and, with only one destroyer and a torpedo boat available, the Germans gave up any attempts to force the Channel Stop.

With the immediate threat over, 154 (GR) Wing moved to Strubby, but 404 and 236 Squadron as its partner, hastily returned in August to take part in strikes on German naval forces. Both squadrons used 25-lb 'J' type rockets as their main armament and it proved a devastating one. In a series of attacks between August 6 and 26 they destroyed or badly damaged minesweepers, a floating dock, armed trawlers, two *Speerbrecker*, and the only destroyers available to the Germans in the Bay of Biscay. The latter were caught by 20 Beaufighters in the mouth of the Gironde River, north of Bordeaux, and in a beam attack both vessels were hit and set on fire. Flak, however, was intense and only three Beaufighters came through unscathed. Three had to land in France and one was ditched but all the crews were rescued.

This was the swan song of the Strike Wings in the Bay and virtually the end of Davidstow as an operational station for it reverted to Care & Maintenance on September 20 1944. From July the RAF Regiment had been using it as a training camp and their numbers built up to eight squadrons in November. They started to run down the camp in 1945 and finally left for North Witham on October 5. The Admiralty considered using the airfield but wisely turned it down and Davidstow Moor closed in December 1945.

Since then the southern part of the airfield has been taken over as a Forestry

Many of the buildings on the northern side of Davidstow Moor are still in use by various organisations. The air raid shelters are used by the sheep.

Commission plantation and in April 1959 a Tiger Moth of Crop Culture Ltd spent some time flying from the airfield on forest spraying experiments. One of the runways and the perimeter track were used in the early 1950s for motor racing, but later two C-class roads were built across the airfield. Both 41 Commando (in 1968) and 845 Squadron (in July 1973) have operated helicopters from the airfield and more recently it has been used by powered gliders. A radio station now occupies the western part of the site while some of the original buildings are used by the Milk Marketing Board. The roads crossing the old airfield provide good views of the typical wartime ATC tower and many other derelict brick and Maycrete buildings litter the area. There is still a fair chance of being able to locate a particular hut in a domestic site, though the three 'T2' hangars have long since gone. I fear that few will be very nostalgic over Davidstow Moor though—it was unloved by most.

In 1981 a plan to build 1,299-ft (366-m) long airships at Davidstow was floated by Mr Boothroyd of Bournemouth. The scheme envisaged the construction of a large 300-ft (91-m) high inflatable hangar on a 70-acre site on the airfield. By March 1982 no planning application had been submitted but it was still claimed that the project was going ahead. Time will tell.

Down Farm, Gloucestershire

ST855906. 3 miles SW of Tetbury off A433

Designated No 23 Satellite Landing Ground, Down Farm proved to be one of the most successful aircraft dispersal/storage locations. Chosen by 10 MU, Hullavington, in 1940, the SLG made use of woods in Westonbirt Park and a landing strip on the farm.

The CO of 10 MU made an inspection in March 1941 which resulted in the planned opening on April 1 being put back. However, the weather improved and after a successful test landing it opened on the 15th of the month when four Defiants were picketed out, joined later by three Hampdens. In common with other SLGs, the small handling party at Down Farm had trouble with intruders and an airman guard was provided from August 1941, later replaced by an Army detachment, and in July 1942 by guard dogs. Additional dispersals in Westonbirt

Park had been authorised early in 1942 together with a secondary runway, but work stopped when the Air Ministry dropped a bombshell—they proposed to develop the site into a full-scale airfield for the USAAF. The Ministry of Aircraft Production protested vigorously because Down Farm was already proving one of their best dispersals and in November the airfield project was dropped.

Following ample evidence that heavy rain had little effect on the grass strip or the dispersals, Down Farm was cleared for use by four-engined aircraft, and arrangements made for the provision of Sommerfeld Track hardstandings capable of supporting Stirlings. These were under construction by the autumn of 1943 when 110 aircraft were in residence. Further aircraft arrived in 1944, and with the need for camouflage relaxed 23 SLG began to be used for circuit training by Oxfords of 15 (P) AFU from October. Night flying by means of a sodium flare path was started in March 1945, but with Babdown Farm back in commission the AFU ceased using Down Farm as a RLG early in the following month.

The end of the war in Europe brought a temporary increase in the number of aircraft in storage at Down Farm, peaking in July when it reached 182. During the autumn there was a significant reduction, and in January 1946 the decision to clear the site was made. All the aircraft had left by the end of January, leaving a working party to tidy up and remove 147 tons of steel mesh tracking. The land was handed back to its owners in February 1946 and there is now no obvious sign of the Farm's wartime usage, though some outlying buildings are probably camouflaged WD huts, and it is possible that other evidence remains in the woods.

Dunkeswell, Devon

ST134078. 4 miles N of Honiton

For 18 months the United States Navy flew PB4Y-1 Liberators from Dunkeswell—the only operations from the base in three years of war. It was built by Wimpey during 1941-42 as a standard three-runway airfield high in the hills above Honiton. During construction it was on the books of 10 Group, Fighter Command, but in May 1942 was transferred to Coastal, under whose direction it was given the basic facilities required to operate three maritime squadrons.

Unfortunately it was not ready during the autumn of 1942 when the Command was stretched to the limit, and afterwards 19 Group had no use for it until the formation by the United States Navy of Fleet Air Wing 7 in mid-1943 for Bay of Biscay operations. The headquarters of the Wing was established in Plymouth on August 21, and Dunkeswell became its main operational base.

Dunkeswell was opened up for the Americans in July 1943 and the RAF initially provided most of the ground personnel. During August the temporary anti-submarine squadrons of the USAAF, the 4th and 19th Squadrons of 479 Bomb Group, arrived from St Eval, but a month later they were replaced by VP103, the first USN unit to complete training with the RAF. VP105 and 110 followed in October and FAW7 gradually built up the scale of their operations. The airfield grew into a major base with large panhandle dispersals, five 'T2' and two US Navy canvas hangars. Large dispersed accommodation sites were to the south-east in wooded countryside. But what the Americans made of Dunkeswell and the surrounding villages it is difficult to imagine. Even today it is an area strangely cut off from the rest of Devon. Forty years ago it must have appeared a dream

world of tiny thatched cottages clinging to steep hillsides or nestling in valleys around a village duckpond.

The Liberators first used were gradually replaced by the PB4Y-1, a specialised anti-submarine version for the US Navy. Painted white underneath and light blue on top, these Liberators had the ball turret replaced by a retractable radar scanner. Some of them also carried a Leigh Light beneath the starboard wing.

The winter of 1943-44 was particularly severe in the West Country and the US Navy squadrons found it difficult to maintain operations, hampered by a shortage of ground staff and equipment. The short aircrew tour length of 300 hours or 30 sorties, combined with their training methods (they had no RAF OTU equivalent, but were converted on the squadrons) undoubtedly led to the small number of sightings converted into successful submarine attacks.

In March 1944 Dunkeswell was handed over to FAW7 and all remaining RAF personnel were posted away. An unusual incident occurred a few days later when a visiting Whitley of 24 OTU was written off following an accidental burst of gunfire from a parked Liberator. By May the three squadrons were capable of flying 18 aircraft a day though shortage of crews

Dunkeswell being built in September 1943—viewed from the west. The hangars on the east side near the village and the extensive dispersals on the west have still to be constructed (RAF Museum).

meant that each had to fly every other day to achieve this high rate. The intensive operations over the D-Day period resulted in many sightings by Dunkeswell aircraft and the first operational U-boat use of the *schnorkel* tube was reported. On June 22 no less than eight contacts and four attacks were claimed.

A special air unit was formed in July to carry out attacks on V-1 and V-2 launching sites using war-weary PB4Y-1s converted into assault drones. Under *Project Anvil* the first conversion was flown across the Atlantic to Dunkeswell where Lieutenant Joseph Kennedy, USN, was serving with VP110. He volunteered to fly the aircraft on its trials and left with it for Fersfield on July 30. Unfortunately the Liberator blew up on its armed sortie before the crew had parachuted to safety, and the elder brother of the future President Kennedy was killed.

Other aircraft at Dunkeswell included a detachment of PBY-5A Catalinas, two Vultee Vengeances and a single NAF N3N biplane trainer. Six Seafire IIs were supplied to the Americans in August. They retained their British markings but were fitted with American VHF R/T and used for air combat training for the patrol squadron crews.

With western France in Allied hands the activity in the Bay of Biscay declined rapidly and there were few sightings between the autumn of 1944 and the spring of 1945. On April 25 the crew of a VP103 aircraft sighted a *schnorkel* and dropped one of the first homing torpedoes over 80 yards (73 m) away. Such weapons were very erratic, however, and it was three long minutes before the torpedo exploded, nine times longer than the theoretical time to cover the distance. Their job almost complete, the crews of FAW7 kept up their sortie rate throughout April and into May, and were rewarded with the first surrender of a U-boat after the cessation of hostilities when *U-249* raised a black flag off the Scilly Isles on May 9 1945.

The run-down commenced immediately, the Liberators leaving for the States in June. The HQ of FAW7 moved from Plymouth to Dunkeswell on July 11, and to the USA at the end of the month. On August 6 Dunkeswell was transferred to 46 Group, Transport Command, and No 3 Overseas Aircraft Preparation Unit moved in from Llandow to become 16 Ferry Unit when it absorbed 11 FU from Talbenny. Used for ferrying aircraft to the Middle East and for foreign air forces, one of its major customers was the French Air Force which received large numbers of aircraft from British stocks, ranging from Tiger Moths to Halifaxes. 16 Ferry Unit operated until March 1946, the airfield reverting to Care & Maintenance the following month. It was obviously still in use, however, for a Lancaster III of 1 FU aborted take-off and finished up on its belly on May 7. It was scrapped on site, and Dunkeswell was then unused until September when it

A B-24 of the 479th Anti-Submarine Group, USAAF, at Dunkeswell in August 1943. Lieutenant Hill and his crew pose in front of their aircraft (USAF).

Dispersed site south of Dunkeswell village, still almost complete in April 1980.

became a sub-site of 265 MU Grove, and then an equipment disposal depot for 267 MU until December 1948.

After the RAF relinquished the airfield in February 1949 it was used by the Devon and Somerset Gliding Club for a number of years before they moved to the nearby North Hill site. A minor road was built across the eastern end of the main runway but the remainder of the original airfield was purchased by Westward Aviation Ltd and subsequently leased to Dunkeswell Aero Club on its formation in 1967. The Aero Club built a new club house and flying control and has been joined by the Royal Marine Sports Parachute and Dunkeswell International Skydiving Clubs in recent years. In 1976 the accident feared by such clubs occurred, a parachute wrapped itself around the tailplane of their Cessna 185 leaving a marine dangling behind the aircraft. After an agonising 25 minutes he managed to free himself using an emergency release and parachuted to safety on his reserve pack.

Part of the original technical site is used as a trading estate by a number of organisations, and two of the 'T2' hangars are in use for storage. An annual Air Day is held by the clubs, usually in June, and is well worth a visit.

Everleigh, Wiltshire

SU186556. 4 miles E of Upavon

Everleigh was another of those elusive places which spent most of the war as a Satellite Landing Ground, in other words, a Maintenance Unit dispersal area. It differed from most, however, in having started as a relief landing ground for the Central Flying School.

Situated just north of the village of Everleigh, it was a large comparatively flat grass field almost surrounded by trees, and was used for circuit training and as a practice forced landing ground by the Masters of CFS during 1940-41. One aircraft, *N7426*, was turned over on landing by an unfortunate student on May 13 1941, but by this time the field had been earmarked by 15 MU Wroughton as a suitable location for a SLG. The attraction was the good natural camouflage for dispersed aircraft provided by the surrounding woods; in particular Everleigh Ashes.

It was opened as 31 SLG on November 22 1941 when a party of men from Wroughton arrived to take over the Detachment HQ and Guard Hut from the contractors. The NW/SE grass strip was completed in December and with a 20-man Defence Flight travelling daily from Upavon the SLG was ready to receive aircraft—one arrived during the month. Bad weather delayed work on the aircraft hides and hardcore approach tracks, but by April 1942 there were 14 aircraft at the site.

During the same month an airborne exercise was staged on the landing ground for the Prime Minister and a strong contingent of Dominion and allied observers. The demonstration was to start with a Whitley dropping paratroops, followed by eight Hotspur troop-carrying gliders. The Whitley arrived on time, but failed to drop on the first run, and when it

Nothing obvious remains of Everleigh SLG—but this farm shed on the edge of the Ashes may be the Super Robin hangar erected in 1943.

1944 when 87 were in residence. By the end of the war this number had been reduced to 17, and in November the site was cleared and closed down soon afterwards.

The same area of downland is now occasionally used by the Army as a landing ground for liaison aircraft and helicopters exercising with troops, and is currently called Everleigh Down.

Exeter, Devon

SY002938. 1 mile E of Clyst Honiton alongside A30

During the night of May 12/13 1941 Exeter was attacked by a strong force of Luftwaffe bombers. Many incendaries and HE bombs fell on the airfield and a large portion of the RAF camp went up in flames. Both the officers' and sergeants' messes were destroyed and much equipment lost, including one Defiant, but amazingly there were no casualties. 307 (Polish) Squadron, the first night fighter unit in the south-west, had arrived just a fortnight earlier, but the Sector Control was caught out by this surprise attack and the only Defiant to get airborne went on the crew's own initiative. Dodging the bomb craters, two sergeants took off and claimed a He 111. This was typical of the Poles, but their indiscipline earned them a mild reproof, while the mechanic who started the engine and guided the aircraft to the runway got a richly deserved Polish Cross of Valour!

Built on a site to the east of the city, Exeter Airport was opened for flying on May 31 1937. The following month Jersey Airways commenced flights from the Channel Islands which connected with the Plymouth to Bristol schedules of Railway Air Services. The terminal building was completed in 1938 and the Airport formally opened on July 30 by the Air Minister, Sir Kingsley Wood. The aerodrome was operated on behalf of the local authority by the Straight Corporation which also ran the Aero Club, and gained the contract for No 37 E&RFTS which formed on July 3 1939. Equipped with Tiger Moths and intended for reservist training, the E&RFTS was overtaken by events and closed down at the beginning of September.

did so the Hotspurs could already be seen commencing their spectacular dives from 8,000 ft (2,438 m). Faced with a field dotted with running paratroops, the glider pilots had difficulty in choosing a clear landing run. One paratrooper was hit and killed by a Hotspur which then cartwheeled into the hedge and split open, fortunately without further casualties, while another, unable to find a clear path, swerved off into a steep bank. The escorting officers did their best to draw attention to the neat grouping of the remaining six Hotspurs and their quickly deploying troops, but Mr Churchill was not easily mollified by such tactics. It was not the first, nor the last, incident experienced by the fast-growing airborne forces.

A new NE/SW grass strip was completed by the contractors in May and the SLG could now accommodate 37 aircraft. The 24 currently on site were very varied in type and included Blenheims, Hurricanes, Lysanders, Oxfords, Spitfires, Wellingtons and Hotspurs.

On September 30 1942, 31 SLG was transferred to 33 MU Lyneham and the security guard was changed, five dogs and their handlers replacing 20 men. New access tracks were cut in Everleigh Ashes and Hog Down Wood and the maintenance of the aircraft was now in the hands of a MAP working party, the only RAF personnel being two officers, a sergeant and the dog handlers.

A Super Robin hangar was erected in 1943 and following an inspection it was decided that Everleigh was fit for use by four-engined aircraft. In December it became one of several SLGs used by 10 MU for the storage of Stirlings, the number of aircraft reaching a peak in July

With the outbreak of war Exeter became a sub-station for the National Air Communications organisation. Amongst the machnes dispersed there were Handley Page HP 42 and Short S17/L passenger biplanes, but these ancient warriors were soon out of action following accidents. The fuselage of *Syrinx* ended up as an office at Exeter.

The NAC was followed to Exeter by another evacuee, an off-shoot of the RAE Farnborough known only as '02 Detachment. It was a strange name for a strange unit for among its several experimental tasks was the deliberate flying of aircraft, including Battles, Harrows and the Fairey P4/34, into wires suspended from barrage balloons, to test the efficiency of cable cutters being developed for bombers. The detachment arrived on September 14 1939 and remained until the remote satellite of Church Stanton became available in February 1942. It was joined at Exeter by the Gunnery Research Unit which formed on June 3 1940 from a nucleus provided by A Flight, Armament Testing Squadron, A&AEE. The GRU was to remain for nearly four years testing guns and turrets on a large variety of aircraft.

The fall of France forced Fighter Command to spread its forces further west and 213 Squadron brought its Hurricanes to Exeter in June, followed by 87 Squadron on July 6 1940, the day the airfield officially became RAF Exeter. It was developed by 10 Group into one of its main fighter stations. Hangars were built on the north and south sides of the airfield together with large dispersed accommodation sites and aircraft pens, while the airfield itself was extended to the east and north-west and runway construction commenced. The first contact with the enemy by the Exeter-based squadrons was on August 11 when a large force, estimated at 165 aircraft, headed for Portland. Fourteen Hurricanes were scrambled and arrived over Portland at the same time as the main force of Ju 88s and He 111s. They shot down two '88s before getting mixed up with the fighter escort, claiming three Bf 109Es and two Bf 110s damaged for the loss of four Hurricanes. It was the start of a period of intensive operations, with nearly all interceptions during August and September being in the Portland area.

No 610 Squadron replaced 213 during September but the pace slackened and they had few contacts—though one on December 12 resulted in the claim of a He 111 by Flight Lieutenant Straight, the pre-war operator of Exeter Airport! An unusual and exciting shape appeared in November when 263 Squadron brought in their Whirlwinds and it was from Exeter that they started *Chameleon* patrols, searching for E-boats positioned in the Channel to pick up ditched Luftwaffe bomber crews after night raids on the West Country.

Exeter from the north-west in September 1942. The A30 runs across the foreground while on the far side is the main technical site (now the terminal area) (RAF Museum).

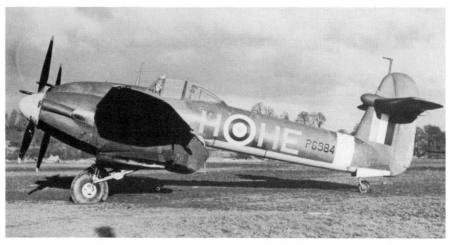

Whirlwind of 263 Squadron at Exeter in January 1941 (IWM).

In 1941 a succession of Hurricane and Spitfire squadrons spent short periods at Exeter, usually carrying out convoy patrols and sector recces while officially resting. The airfield was visited five times by the Luftwaffe during the early part of the year, the worst raid being on April 5 when a low-level attack by three bombers wrecked the main hangar, damaged 16 aircraft and burnt out a Wellington. The arrival of 307 Squadron on April 26 meant that day and night defence for the area was available for the first time, but in practice the Poles had little contact with the enemy until November when a sudden burst of activity enabled them to claim two destroyed, one probable and two damaged. In the meantime No 2 Polish Fighter Wing had been formed and 317 Squadron (with 302 and 316 at Church Stanton) arrived in July for the express purpose of defending the City of Exeter and south coast ports.

Exeter UAS was formed during August 1941 with Tiger Moths and operated until 1943 when courses for art graduates were suspended—an interesting reflection on the qualities thought necessary for a pilot! On February 12 1942 the airfield was attacked by three Do 217s and in April the so-called *Baedecker* reprisal raids began with 40 bombers from KG2 (Do 217s), KG106 (Ju 88s) and 1/KG100 (He 111s) aiming for Exeter on the 23rd. The night was cloudy and only one aircraft hit the target, but the next night they came again and caused a lot of damage. 307 managed some interceptions on this and other

nights during April/May, destroying three Ju 88s and damaging another.

A different sort of night specialist arrived in May in the form of 247 Squadron which carried out intruder operations on Luftwaffe bases in France and in August also started night *Roadsteads.* Typhoons were based from September when 257 Squadron arrived to commence *Anti-Rhubarbs* to try and catch the coastal raiders, and towards the end of the year a detachment of Turbinlite Havocs from 536 Squadron spent some time at Exeter.

No 307 Squadron left in April 1943 after two years at Exeter, easily the longest time for any of the operational squadrons. They swopped places at Fairwood Common with 125 Squadron which added ASR patrols to its night fighter work. While at Exeter they had one good night, shooting down four enemy bombers during a raid on Plymouth, before moving to Valley in November on exchange with 406 (RCAF) Squadron. Both flew the dependable Beaufighter VIF, but like the day fighters they saw little action because Luftwaffe activity was very spasmodic.

Exeter had occasionally been used as a forward operating base for 2 Group bomber operations in 1942 and this increased during 1943 when the Americans joined in with A-20Bs, P-38s and P-47s. Even the Fleet Air Arm took part, the black-painted Swordfish of 834 Squadron flying night anti-E-boat patrols from Torbay to the Lizard during February/April. They had great difficulty in identifying the E-boats even when located on radar but the Admiralty were desperately anxious about the threat posed by these powerful craft, and the newly formed 816 Squadron also tried its luck from May until August. Their only success was in June when groups of E-boats were attacked off the Channel Islands.

No 406 Squadron spent the early months of 1944 trying to prevent the Luftwaffe reconnoitring the area to pinpoint troop concentrations and equipment stockpiles, but in April all the RAF residents were suddenly moved out and the airfield handed over to the USAAF as Station 463. On April 15 the four squadrons of the 440th TCG, 50 TCW, brought their 45 C-47s and a number of CG-4A Hadrian gliders to Exeter, and started intensive exercises working up for D-Day. In the early hours of June 6 they joined other TCGs carrying paratroopers to Normandy, losing three aircraft in the initial phase of *Neptune-Bigot*.

After operating an ambulance service from France, the Americans left Exeter on November 20 and A Flight of 275 Squadron moved their six Walruses in from Bolt Head. They left for Harrowbeer in January 1945 when the station transferred to 23 (Training) Group and No 3 Glider Training School arrived, equipped with Master II tugs and Hotspur gliders. The ASR presence was maintained, however, by a detachment from 282 Squadron St Eval which remained until July when Exeter returned to Fighter Command, this time as part of 11 Group with Cleave and Bolt Head as satellites. The Oxfords, Hurricanes and Vengeances of 691 Squadron moved in for towing operations, followed by 329 (French) Squadron whose Spitfires were much in evidence until the unit disbanded in November.

Throughout all these changes the Sector Operations Room continued to function from Poltimore House, three miles to the north of the airfield. 222 Squadron (Meteors) and 151 (Mosquito XXXs) arrived in June 1946 but the Sector was suddenly disbanded on July 1 and the squadrons dispersed. When 691 Squadron left in October 1946 the station was closed down.

Exeter was transferred to the Ministry of Civil Aviation on January 1 1947 and opened for civil operations. When Heston closed, Chrislea Aircraft Ltd moved in and started small-scale production of Super Ace and Skyjeep light aircraft. The Aero Club also resumed operations but in the difficult post-war era there was no rush to provide passenger services and it was with relief that the airport authorities saw the formation of 10 RFS in May 1949 and 3 CAACU in March 1951. The former flew Tiger Moths, Chipmunks and Ansons, but with the reduction of reserve forces was disbanded during June 1954. The latter started calibration and target-towing for the Navy and Army with Spitfires and Beaufighters, later receiving Mosquitoes, Vampires, Meteors and, uniquely for a CAACU, even a few Hunters before it too was disbanded at the end of 1971. The last RAF unit, and the only one still remaining, was 4 Air

A C-47A of the USAAF taxies past the signals square at Exeter in the spring of 1945 (via H. Holmes).

Experience Flight which formed in 1958 with two Chipmunks to give flights to ATC cadets of the Cornwall, Devon, Dorset and Wilts Wing and eleven school CCF units.

Meanwhile, Jersey Airlines restarted scheduled services to the Channel Islands in 1952. Ten years later they became British United (CI) and having worked their way through the British Island Airways title are now Air UK. Other airlines have operated through the airport for varying lengths of time, usually with little success, but since the Devon County Council took over responsibility in April 1974 the situation has settled down and the airfield has survived the loss of the major service units.

Apart from a runway extension and modifications to the civil terminal, Exeter Airport has changed little since the war. A very large number of ex-RAF buildings are still in use by the airport authorities, flying club, aircraft servicing firms and an adjacent trading estate. In common with all CAA-approved airports, access to the airport parking areas is strictly controlled but there is a small public viewing enclosure alongside the terminal giving a good view of arrivals and departures.

Falmouth, Cornwall

SW815334. In outer harbour, north of town

The natural harbour of Falmouth was one of many sites considered during both World Wars as a flying boat base. Ideally placed for Atlantic operations, it suffered from poor approaches into the prevailing wind and was only used occasionally by small detachments of seaplanes during the 1914-18 conflict. Squadron cruises by flying boats in the inter-war years used moorings between Trefusis Point and the village of Flushing, and it was earmarked as an emergency base during the 1930s.

As soon as war was declared 204 Squadron found itself overwhelmed with commitments as it tried to carry out both anti-submarine patrols and merchant ship escorts from Mount Batten. A detachment of three London flying boats from 240 Squadron was therefore sent from Invergordon. On September 20 1939 they were moved to Falmouth and started convoy escorts, these continuing until October 4. The Londons were then relieved by three 209 Squadron Stranraers which had arrived on October 1. These good-looking, but antiquated, biplanes continued the work for another month before rejoining their squadron which had moved to Oban while they were away. During the detachment one Stranraer, *K7294*, crashed near Falmouth on November 3 but their operations were otherwise uneventful.

A Care & Maintenance party remained at Falmouth and the moorings were occasionally used by Sunderlands from Mount Batten and Pembroke Dock. During one such visit a 204 Squadron aircraft, *N9021: KG-G*, was damaged when being towed off mud by a power boat in March 1940, and movements were few because of the poor facilities. From February 1941 the C&M party was administered by Mount Batten, but the base finally closed down on December 1 1942 when other diversions became available.

A Sunderland 1 aground off Flushing. Falmouth town is in the background.

Filton, Gloucestershire (now Avon)

ST595802. 4 miles N of Bristol, alongside A38

Filton from the south-east on August 25 1942. The A38 runs across the foreground with the main factory area alongside (RAF Museum).

Following reconnaissance which showed that there were no fighters at Filton, the Luftwaffe mounted a major attack on the Bristol Aeroplane and Engine Company works on September 25 1940. 58 He 111s of the three Gruppen making up Kampfgeschwader 55 *Greifen* crossed the south coast, apparently making for Yeovil. 10 Group ordered three fighter squadrons to the area, but the bombers passed well to the east and reached Filton unopposed half an hour later, led in by markers dropped by Bf 110s of ERPR GR210. The He 111s dropped some 100 tons of bombs on the factories causing 238 casualties amongst the workers and another 107 in the general area. Production was halted, eight Beaufighters were completely destroyed and another 12 aircraft badly damaged.

Fighter Command reacted quickly, 17 Hurricanes of 504 Squadron arriving at Filton the following day. It looked like a case of shutting the stable door after the horse had bolted, but in fact the Germans mistakedly thought little damage had been done at Filton and returned on the 27th. 30 He 111s of KG55 preceded by 19 Bf 110s of ERPR GR210 and covered by 27 Bf 110s of III/ZG26 were despatched. The main force was intercepted over Dorset and Somerset but ERPR GR210 forced their way through and were set upon by 504 Squadron losing three of their number over the Bristol area, including their commanding officer.

Aviation had come to Filton in February 1910 when the British & Colonial Aeroplane Co Ltd was formed and leased premises from the Bristol Tramways Company at their northern depot. By November Bristol Boxkites were in production and in March 1911 a War Office order was received. Land to the north of the two iron sheds was acquired as an airfield and in August Filton House was added to the factory to provide general offices as the works expanded. Following the declaration of war in August 1914 enormous expansion took place and there were over 3,000 on the payroll at the Armistice. The Royal Flying Corps also made use of the airfield from December 1915 to work-up new squadrons before they left for France.

The South West Aircraft Acceptance Park was formed on the airfield to process aircraft completed by factories in the area, 18 large hangars being built for the unit. After the war activities at Filton were much reduced, though the company was awarded a contract to run a Reserve School for the RAF. This opened on May 15 1923, instruction being given on a variety of Bristol types until 1933 when Tiger Moths were standardised. Even more significant was the formation of 501 (County of Gloucester) Squadron on June 14 1929. This special reserve squadron started flying in Avro 504Ns and received its first operational aircraft, a DH9A, in March 1930. The same year work started

Beaufighter If V8322 *newly completed at Filton* (Bristol Aeroplane Co).

on the alteration of existing buildings, and the erection of new accommodation sufficient for one regular and one cadre squadron on the RAF site to the north of the airfield. The Reserve School became 2 E&RFTS In 1937 but was still operated by the Bristol company on behalf of the Air Ministry.

Production expanded rapidly following the adoption of the Blenheim as a standard light bomber, and with output now more than squadron pilots could deal with, a Ferry Flight was formed in January 1939, later becoming No 2 Ferry Pilots Pool.

At the end of 1938 501 Squadron became a fighter unit and was at Manston on summer camp in September 1939 when embodied into the RAF for the duration of the emergency. The Hurricanes immediately returned to Filton but there was little action—the first scramble not being until November 11 and even then there was no contact with the enemy. Two weeks later 501 left for Tangmere, being replaced by the newly formed 263 Squadron, equipped with Gladiators. Again there was little for the pilots to do, and their first interception nearly ended in tragedy when they fired at a Blenheim—fortunately they missed!

No 263 Squadron left hurriedly for their Norwegian adventure in April 1940 and Filton remained largely defenceless apart from its balloon barrage, until the sudden arrival of 504 Squadron in September. In the meantime the ferry organisation had become 4 (C) RAF Ferry Pool, 8 AACU had been based for a few months and in August No 2 EFTS moved to Staverton, because of increasing problems with the balloon barrage.

Naturally the Luftwaffe was interested in Filton, for in addition to aircraft production it was also the main source of Bristol engines. The first night raid on the city occurred on June 24 1940 without damage at Filton, and day attacks during July and early August were equally ineffective. Further night attacks during August did cause some damage and casualties, however, and work was interrupted most days by warnings of raids. The company started its own warning system to cut down this disruption and on September 25 the scheme worked well, all employees being in shelters when the attack came. Unfortunately two shelters received direct hits killing 72 outright and injuring 166, of whom 19 subsequently died.

No 504 Squadron left for Exeter in December and was replaced by 501. Again it was a slack period and they spent most of their time on convoy patrols before being replaced by the Whirlwinds of 263 Squadron in April 1941. They also undertook convoy patrols enlivened by low-level attacks on French airfields and anti-tank trials. 263 left for Charmy Down in August 1941, the last operational squadron based at Filton during the war.

Work now started on the construction of two tarmac runways and in December 1941 Filton was transferred from 10 to 44 Group in readiness for its new role as an Overseas Aircraft Preparation Unit. The Beaufort/Beaufighter task was taken over from Kemble while its previous Blenheim commitment was retained.

Taken on September 26 1958, this photograph clearly shows the Brabazon hangars and the extended runway which cuts two roads (DoE).

The last major night attack on Bristol developed on April 11 1942, the Luftwaffe hitting the main Filton works with one bomb which demolished the wind tunnel and an office building, but caused no casualties.

The OAPU became No 2 Aircraft Preparation Unit in December 1942 and in place of detachments 528 Squadron was formed with Blenheims in June 1943 for radar calibration. It stayed until May 1944 after which Filton was left to its ferry and flight test organisations. The decision to build the mighty Brabazon airliner provided the next change in the appearance of the airfield. It was decided that the runway would have to be extended, although this involved the demolition of the majority of Charlton village and the closing of a dual carriageway road. There was local opposition and the decision to go ahead was finally made by the Cabinet. Work commenced in March 1946 on the 8,150 ft (2,484 m) specially widened runway, and at the same time the Bristol company built large extensions to the main works, together with a completely new assembly hall for the Brabazon.

On August 7 1946 the airfield was transferred to the Ministry of Supply, while the RAF enclave was taken over by 62 Group, Reserve Command, on the demise of 44 Group. Bristol UAS was again active, and 501 Squadron had reformed as an Auxiliary Air Force unit during the previous May. They were joined by 12 RFS in 1948, this unit flying Tiger Moths and Ansons, operated by the

Bristol Aeroplane Company in a similar fashion to the pre-war school. With the cutback in reserve forces 12 RFS was disbanded in March 1953, followed by 501 Squadron in February 1957, but the UAS joined by No 3 AEF in 1958 soldiered on with Chipmunks.

Currently Filton is a British Aerospace factory airfield, which is also used by Rolls Royce (Bristol) for test flying. The Bristol UAS Bulldogs and AEF Chipmunks operate as lodgers. A good view can be obtained from Cribbs Causeway to the west of the airfield, but British Aerospace also have Open Days from time to time when a closer look at the buildings and activities in general can be obtained.

Folly Gate (Okehampton), Devon
See Okehampton

Ford Farm (Old Sarum), Wiltshire
See Old Sarum

Guernsey, Channel Islands
3 miles WSW of St Peter Port

After 16 years of flying boat operations an airport was built on Guernsey and opened by Sir Kingsley Wood, Secretary of State for Air, on May 1 1939. Guernsey Airways began new services to Alderney, Jersey, Southampton and London four days later. Guernsey was an obvious forward base for Anson squadrons expected to patrol the English Channel in time of war, and in August a Care &

Maintenance party arrived from 16 Group, Coastal Command.

Civil flying ceased on the declaration of war and A Flight of 48 Squadron moved its five Ansons in on September 6. The only accommodation was at Fort George, St Peter Port, so some airmen had to sleep in the hangar with the aircrew at Happy Landing Hotel, in case the aircraft were needed at short notice. The first escort was flown on September 12 and anti-submarine operations continued until October 8 when the unit was withdrawn. Guernsey Airways resumed limited inter-island and Guernsey-Shoreham operations on October 24, though Tangmere was used as the terminal for a spell early in 1940.

On April 24 1940 the School of General Reconnaissance arrived from Thorney Island. With 27 Ansons and 95 pupils, the unit rapidly settled down to a full programme, operating three courses simultaneously.

The German breakthrough in France and the entry of Italy into the war changed the situation dramatically. On June 11 instructions were given for the school to move out of Guernsey, and following the refusal of the French to allow Wellingtons to bomb Italy from southern France, the Channel Islands were used as a refuelling base by 36 Whitleys from 4 Group squadrons. Half of them used Guernsey Airport, taking off during the night of June 11 with the Fiat aero engine works in Turin as the primary target. Ten crews claimed to have attacked it, while two others of the force bombed the Ansaldo aircraft factories in Genoa. The other 23 aircraft were

defeated by the severe weather over the Alps and returned early.

Three days later all School of General Reconnaissance training ceased and the air party of 16 officers and 52 men flew out in 26 Ansons on June 16, leaving the unserviceable *K8825* behind (it was destroyed on July 5). The ground echelon left aboard the SS *Brittany* on the 18th, leaving two parties on Guernsey as the nucleus of Nos 32 and 64 Fighter Wing Servicing Units, the former intended for operations on Jersey. 17 Squadron operated a short-lived detachment of Hurricanes, but on the 19th the servicing units left in a train ferry and rejoined the school at Hooton Park.

Between June 19 and 21 both Jersey and Guernsey Airways, based at Exeter, operated evacuation services from the Channel Islands carrying 319 people to the mainland in their DH86s. Then came a lull and anti-climax, for nothing happened until the 28th when three Luftwaffe aircraft reconnoitrered the island, followed by Ju 87s which dive-bombed St Peter Port killing 33, and wounding many more. As directed, white flags were put out on the airfield and in the town square, and on July 1 the advance guard of the Wehrmacht arrived at the airport in Ju 52/3ms.

Within a month the Luftwaffe was using the airport as a forward fighter base. At intervals during the Battle of Britain JG27 and JG53 operated their Bf 109s from the small grass field, but not without problems. On August 9 an aircraft of 1/JG53 made an emergency landing following engine failure and collided with a flak emplacement killing three men and injuring three more. To support bombing attacks on the West Country, such as that by KG55 on Filton during September 25, 4/JG53 flew from Guernsey—but could still only provide cover to the English coast. After the Battle the airfield remained in Luftwaffe use, but only for communications aircraft.

The Germans evacuated Guernsey on May 9 1945 and 160 Staging Post moved in from Ibsley to set up a base for RAF transport aircraft. Distinguished early visitors were their Majesties the King and Queen who landed from Jersey in Dakota *KN386* on June 6. They left 3½ hours later having visited St Peter Port and

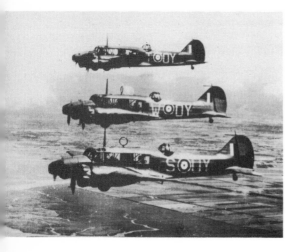

Three Ansons of 48 Squadron in formation—the unit spent just a few weeks in Guernsey.

other parts of the island. Jersey Airways restarted services from Guernsey to London (Croydon) on the 21st, followed by inter-island operations on July 18.

The airport was still grass-surfaced in 1959 but was often waterlogged. As part of a major development programme a 4,750 ft (1,448 m) tarmac runway was laid and opened in time for the 1960 summer season.

The RAF association with the island ceased soon after the war, but ever since the original opening in May 1939 201 Squadron has been known as 'Guernsey's Own' and after the war these links were strengthened by the formation of a unit museum in Castle Cornet, St Peter Port. Opened by the AOC 18 Group on May 20 1975, the museum contains material from the squadron records, and equipment used by the unit throughout its long career, in an attractive display.

Haldon, Devon

SX915765. 2 miles NW of Teignmouth

The increasing use of the Lyme Bay gunnery ranges by the Fighter School at Yeovilton caused the Admiralty to look for a landing ground in the area which could be used for their target-towing aircraft. They chose the small moorland airfield of Haldon, high above Teignmouth on the western side of the bay.

The field had been developed by Mr Parkhouse of the Agra Engineering Company, a Teignmouth motor firm, on rough moorland just north of the golf course at Little Haldon. With a hangar erected and the surface reseeded with grass, the first public flying meeting was held on September 21 1929. Due to the enthusiasm of Mr Parkhouse and a small band of private owners, the aerodrome prospered despite its rather isolated position and poor weather factor.

Air meetings at Haldon became extremely popular during the 1930s, with the Teignmouth Air Race Cup strongly contested by many well-known British pilots. The British Hospitals Air Pageant visited in 1933, the year that the Great Western Railway Company inaugurated a Cardiff-Plymouth (Roborough) service which called at Haldon. Alan Cobham also brought his circus to Haldon annually, and in 1934 Provincial Airways and Railway Air Services started services through Teignmouth Airport.

On January 1 1937 the Straight Corporation took over management of the aerodrome and regular summer services continued on a request stop basis until September 1939 when all civil flying ceased. Later Haldon was requisitioned by the Air Ministry and used in a desultory fashion by communications aircraft from Boscombe Down during armament trials using the Lyme Bay ranges. Transferred to the Admiralty, Haldon was commissioned as *Heron II*, a satellite of Yeovilton, on August 18 1941 for the use of detachments from 794 Squadron flying Skua target tugs, and 761 with Masters.

The Hjordis glider at Haldon on September 26 1937 about to be flown by Philips Wills. The rough terrain is readily apparent.

The airfield was extended by requisitioning land to the north and south, including a small portion of the golf course. Haldon Tea House was used to accommodate the military guard and billets found for other personnel in Teignmouth. The aircraft towed targets for Yeovilton-based units and for naval ships, but operation from the aerodrome proved very difficult. During 1942 land drainage was undertaken, a macadam hard-standing and Sommerfeld steel tracking was laid, and Haldon Camp (SX889849) was taken over from the War Office in April to provide additional accommodation.

With these improvements completed, Defiants, and probably Martinets, were introduced to Haldon but high winds and low cloud often caused cancellation of the programme. In May 1943 the Admiralty reduced the airfield to C&M, having already transferred the name *Heron II* to Charlton Horethorne the previous January. It is believed that the airfield was used as an emergency crash strip for USN Liberators from Dunkeswell. Occasional aircraft visited, a Tiger Moth of 3 EFTS being flown over on take-off in February 1945, and ATC gliders were accommodated in the hangar.

Efforts were made to re-establish civil flying in 1946 but the airfield soon fell into disuse and has now reverted to rough moorland with only a few concrete foundations remaining.

Hamworthy (Poole), Dorset

SZ035900. 1 mile S of Parkstone (Technical base SY986903)

Even today flying to the United States for the first time is an adventure for most people. Consider what it must have been like in the dark days of 1940. Passengers were taken to Poole by Pullman train, on to a windswept quay at the eastern side of the harbour and into a small pottery factory masquerading as passenger reception. After security and censor checks, they went by marine craft out to a flying boat swinging at its mooring in the open harbour. The Short C boats could not cross the Atlantic direct, going via Foynes in Eire, Botwood in Newfoundland and Montreal in Canada before going on to the blazing night lights of unrationed New York. The change from blacked-out Britain must have been traumatic, but it was only for the few priority passengers, the five return flights made between August and November being mainly mail and freight services for the British Government.

There were other services from Poole harbour, however, for under the aegis of the National Air Communications organisation the flying boats of Imperial Airways had moved their operating base from Hythe to Poole in September 1939.

BOAC's Boeing 314A G-AGCB touches down at Poole Marine Terminal (IWM).

Only makeshift shore facilities were set up, all maintenance being carried out either at Hythe or the moorings just off the main channel, around the north side of Brownsea Island. BOAC, officially formed on April 1 1940, took over the aircraft and responsibility for the propaganda Atlantic services flown in 1940 and the important flights to Africa. The latter were suspended when the French capitulated, but were restarted in August, escorted down the Channel and into the Bay of Biscay by Blenheim fighters.

The famous Short S.21 *Maia*, the lower part of the Mayo composite, was destroyed in Poole Harbour during a night raid on May 11 1941, just before the first of three Boeing 314A boats were delivered to BOAC. They were based at Foynes, a connecting service by Short flying boats operating until late in the war. Then the large Boeings started to fly from Poole via Bathurst and Bermuda to the USA.

Pressure on the flying boat stations at Pembroke Dock and Mount Batten caused Coastal Command to look for another site in 1942. After much discussion and argument Poole Harbour was chosen although it was already a heavily congested area. The naval and Army authorities had requisitioned all the best sites and properties, and the opening-up party finally selected a location about 1½ miles west of Poole on the northern side of the Wareham Channel. Work started on a slipway at the end of June 1942, but there was no room for hangars or buildings and a number of houses in the Lake Estate district were used as workshops. For domestic, administrative and operational purposes, properties all over Poole and Parkstone were earmarked.

When the Station Commander and operations staff arrived they were very unhappy about the dispersed nature of the new base and the prospect of having to use the Wareham Channel for operations. Pressure was applied and soon after RAF Hamworthy opened on August 1 they obtained approval to move the operational base to Salterne Pier in the Parkstone/Lilliput area. 461 (RAAF) Squadron arrived with their Sunderlands at the end of August. It was a depressing scene which met them. The harbour was a difficult shape, full of dangerous sandbanks. BOAC already had the best area, and depending on the weather the

RAF trots, as the moorings were called, were anything up to four miles away from Salterne Pier. The navigation channels were narrow and there were no night flying facilities. On shore the slipway was makeshift and there was insufficient room to park the Sunderlands properly. Even such commonplace events as an engine change became a major headache.

Patrols over the Bay of Biscay continued without a break, crews flying to Mount Batten for operational night take-offs. The Luftwaffe was also active over the Bay and during September 1942 three of 461's Sunderlands were intercepted by Ju 88s, and one shot down. However, eight attacks were made on U-boats and a blockade runner was seriously damaged 700 miles west of La Pallice, and forced to return for lengthy repairs. In October the squadron concentrated on transport work flying essential freight and groundcrew to Gibraltar for 210 Squadron in preparation for Operation *Torch*, but it was back in action over the Bay the following month—though with little to show for its efforts.

With the Army moved from Salterne Pier, an operations centre was set up in the Harbour Yacht Club, and accommodation gradually concentrated in the Parkstone, Lilliput and Sandbanks districts. The 'Harbour Heights' Hotel was taken over as an Officers' Mess and 461 Squadron HQ transferred from Hamworthy in January 1943.

When the establishment increased to 12 aircraft it was obvious that the limited facilities would not cope with the added commitment. 461 Squadron thankfully moved to Pembroke Dock in April, on exchange with 210 which were equipped with the smaller Catalina. It is not recorded what 210 thought of this, but perhaps they felt compensated by the better facilities off base!

No 210 Squadron became involved in a phase of the long-running Biscay offensive, known as *Enclose 2*. Strengthened by six crews from 119 Squadron, it helped set up patrol lines across the Bay designed to force U-boats to transit submerged and exhaust their batteries. Tactics on both sides changed, the Germans entering and leaving the Bay at Cape Finisterre and Cape Ortegal and creeping along the coast. *Precussion* patrols were then introduced, Catalinas flying along the north-west coast of Spain by day and night.

Despite improvements, Poole Harbour

A Sunderland of BOAC is serviced at Hamworth (Poole) in September 1943 (via British Airways).

continued to be unsatisfactory for operations, night flying being particularly hazardous. In December 1943 19 Group decided to re-establish Calshot as the main diversion and to vacate Hamworthy. A meeting was held with representatives of Transport Command and the Director General of Civil Aviation, and on January 13 1944 Hamworthy was transferred to 116 Wing, Transport Command for M Flight (BOAC) Sunderland services to Lisbon and India. These services had been running since March and October 1943 respectively, the latter in RAF markings because it passed through military zones in Egypt. On January 29 1944 a Horsa glider ditched on the flare path just before a flying boat commenced take-off and in March more excitement was caused when a Dakota circled the harbour with a parachutist dangling below it. He was finally cut free but was found to be dead when picked out of the water.

During February much of the re-quisitioned accommodation was returned to the owners including the whole of the Hamworthy site, but Salterne Pier together with the 'Harbour Heights' Hotel and Harbour Yacht Club were handed over the DGCA when RAF Hamworthy closed on May 1 1944. Renamed Poole, the base was operated by the DGCA on behalf of BOAC and was

used to pioneer the immediate post-war flying boat routes of the company, Hythe-class *G-AGJM* making a survey flight from Poole to Australia, New Zealand, Hong Kong, China and Japan during February/April 1946.

BOAC finally left Poole on March 31 1948 when they transferred their marine operations to Southampton. It was the end of an uneasy partnership between Poole and the flying boat which always had a very temporary feeling about it. Little did anyone realise how temporary the move to Southampton would also be.

Haresfield (Moreton Valence), Gloucestershire

See Moreton Valence

Harrowbeer, Devon

SX513680. ½ mile W of Yelverton on A386

Built as a 10 Group fighter station, Harrowbeer was one of those rare airfields that was used as intended. Constructed during 1940-41 on a triangular piece of heathland between Yelverton and Crapstone, it opened on August 15 as a satellite for Exeter complete with three tarmac runways.

The first aircraft were involved with an Army exercise at the end of August 1941 and a fortnight later a 500 Squadron detachment moved in to fly Blenheim intruder missions over enemy-occupied airfields—a very dicey activity. The first fighters were Spitfire IIs of 130 Squadron which arrived from Portreath in October to work up on their new aircraft. 276 Squadron formed at Harrowbeer on October 21 as the second of the new Air Sea Rescue units, replacing the rather *ad hoc* organisation used previously. A Flight and the HQ soon moved to Portreath but B Flight with two Walruses and three Lysanders remained to cover the Exeter Sector.

Only after these preliminaries did an operational fighter unit appear at Harrowbeer. This was 302 (Polish) Squadron, a veteran of the Battle of Britain, which flew in from Ibsley early in November and after some convoy patrols started escorting bombers over France. Some of these *Circuses* were mounted from Harrowbeer, but most meant flying east to 11 Group stations for briefing and rendezvous with the bombers. A Bf 109 was claimed during a raid on Cherbourg docks on April 17 1942 followed a week later by a probable Fw 190.

The station was now in the final stages of completion, with the watch office coming into use during April 1942. This coincided with the first bombing of the airfield by the Luftwaffe but there was little damage and no casualties.

No 312 (Czech) Squadron replaced the Poles during May and their Spitfire Vs started sweeps over France. On June 3 they met up with some 30 Fw 190s near Cherbourg and during the ensuing mêlée lost two aircraft—though they claimed one Fw 190 destroyed and four damaged. The Czechs moved up to Redhill for Operation *Jubilee* on August 19, but

were soon back and remained at Harrowbeer until October.

Harrowbeer concentrated on fighter-bomber operations with the arrival of Hurri-bombers of 175 Squadron. Their main work was low-level shipping strikes, including against E-boats which proved very unpleasant adversaries. The scene was enlivened by a visit from 1426 (EAC) Flight on October 24 when captured Luftwaffe aircraft were demonstrated. Two months later 193 Squadron formed as a new Typhoon unit but with no aircraft immediately available the pilots were seconded to 257 and 266 Squadrons until January 1943. Operations began in April with shipping recces and MTB escorts, but they soon took the offensive with a very successful dive-bombing attack on Guipavas airfield and *Anti-Rhubarb* sorties against Bf 109G and Fw 190 fighter-bombers raiding coastal towns.

The Typhoons were joined by Whirlwinds of 263 who spent a month at Harrowbeer early in 1943 for night *Rhubarbs* on airfields in occupied France. The arrival of 183 Squadron 'Tiffies' in June meant that Harrowbeer could operate as a Wing for the first time, and attacks were made on rail communications and airfields in France. Both Typhoon squadrons left for 11 Group stations in August, but 193 was back in September for operations with 266 Squadron. The former unit was adopted by Brazil in October, the squadron being visited by the Ambassador for a formal ceremony. In November the Harrowbeer Wing started to concentrate on the well hidden V-1 sites—these becoming known

Harrowbeer, looking to the west from above Yelverton (via D.C. Teague).

Above *Typhoons of 193 Squadron at Harrowbeer in 1943* (F.H.B. Hulbert). **Below** *A double fighter blast pen at Harrowbeer still visible late in 1980 though showing signs of erosion due to the activities of children.*

as *Noball* operations. A typical day was December 5 when a sweep was made in appalling weather which forced the Typhoons to fly on the deck all the way. A quick refuel and another sweep provided forward cover for a USAAF B-17 formation, and on the return flight they gave close escort to 60 Liberators found north of Lorient.

The months immediately prior to D-Day were ones of change and movement. 193 and 266 Squadrons left Harrowbeer and were replaced by the Typhoons of 263 and various Spitfire squadrons. No 156 (GR) Wing, Coastal Command, arrived on April 20, its operational element being the Swordfish aircraft of 838 Squadron, FAA, from Inskip. They were intended for smoke laying to cover beach landings but started badly, losing three aircraft on

their first practice before they learnt the specialised techniques involved.

During May 1944, 610 Squadron brought its brand-new Griffon-engined Spitfire XIVs to Harrowbeer and 263 converted from bomber to rocket-firing Typhoons to concentrate on ships and radar sites with these devastating weapons. The airfield was also used by 124 Wing (193, 197 and 257 Squadrons) for operations against communications in France just prior to the invasion, and for sweeps by Spitfire IXs. Nos 1 and 126 Squadrons carried out close support to the Army in Normandy after D-Day, and later in June 64 and 611 Squadrons arrived from Deanland to concentrate on shipping strikes in the approaches to the Channel. They had some successes in the air also, the Wing Leader, Wing

Commander Bird Wilson, destroying two Bf 109s on August 1 while escorting Mosquitoes, and on the 14th 126 Squadron swept over an airfield just as a Luftwaffe unit was landing. They shot down six and claimed another probable.

All operational units left during August and Harrowbeer was placed on Care & Maintenance by 10 Group. The station continued to be used by communications aircraft, however, in particular by the US Navy for visits to Fleet Air Wing 7 HQ in Plymouth, and they took over air traffic control.

When Exeter was transferred to Flying Training Command in January 1945, Harrowbeer was reopened as a self-supporting 10 Group station with parenting responsibilities for Bolt Head and the GCI stations at Exminster and Hope Cove. Air traffic control was taken back from the US Navy and 275 (ASR) Squadron arrived from Exeter with their Walrus amphibians. Five days later the Mustangs of 26 Squadron flew in for strike training and 691 Squadron was transferred from Roborough. Their aircraft included Blenheims, Oxfords, Hurricanes, Defiants and even Barracudas for the multitude of tasks which went under the heading of anti-aircraft co-operation. The weather, however, was extremely bad during the winter of 1944-45 and operations were severely restricted by snow for several weeks.

Immediately after the war 329 (French) Squadron flew down from Skeabrae in readiness for a brief trip to France to take part in a triumphal Air Pageant for General de Gaulle. They finally left for Exeter in August together with 691 Squadron, and Harrowbeer reverted to C & M. No 229 MU used some of the storage space for a few months, but Fighter Command closed Harrowbeer down on May 13 1946.

The airfield was transferred to the Ministry of Civil Aviation who planned to use it as Plymouth Airport in preference to Roborough. There was strong local opposition, but it remained open though largely unused, until December 1947 when 19 Group Communications Flight arrived from Roborough with Dominies and Ansons. The Comm Flight stayed until August 1948 by which time the airport project had been dropped. Once again Harrowbeer was under C & M until transferred to 90 Group in October 1949 for use as accommodation by RAF Sharpitor.

With the closure of Sharpitor the airfield was finally relinquished. The site was cleared of buildings the runways broken up, and the ground returned to heathland. It is now common land, grazed by sheep but open to the public, with the perimeter track forming an internal road and the old blast pens alongside the A386 providing a reminder of its wartime activity, and a play area of children. On August 15 1981 the station's first CO, Group Captain the Hon E.F. Ward, unveiled a granite memorial stone at Leg O'Mutton Corner, Yelverton, dedicated to those who served at Harrowbeer.

Henstridge, Dorset

ST752205. 1½ miles E of Henstridge off A30

Travel along the A30 past Henstridge and one could easily miss the airfield, but in 1943 the place was literally swarming with Seafires for it was one of the Navy's main training bases. Some would be practising normal circuits at about 400 ft (122 m), while others flew on to a special runway laid out like a deck. This was complete with arrestor wires and all the other paraphernalia associated with an aircraft carrier.

Preparatory work started in August 1941 on 355 acres of farmland near Henstridge village, contracts being placed for a five-runway layout specially designed for deck landing training. Drem lighting was installed, numerous dispersed hangars and accommodation areas built, but progress was slow and it was not until April 1 1943 that the station was commissioned as HMS *Dipper* and No 2 Naval Air Fighter School moved in from Yeovilton. The school's flying unit was 761 Squadron equipped with Seafire 1Bs, hooked Spitfire Vs and Masters. During 1943 an additional 18 acres were taken over at Gibbs Marsh Farm for the construction of an Aircraft Rectification Hangar and ancillary installations, and as the station grew in size extra accommodation was requisitioned at Fifehead Magdalen.

No 894 Squadron disembarked from *Illustrious* with Seafire IIs on October 18 1943 and settled into the newly opened B Camp (Priors Down). New Seafire IIIs were received and they formed a Wing with 887, the two squadrons moving to Burscough in January 1944. They were replaced in March by No 3 Naval Fighter Wing from Lee flying Spitfire Vs on low-

Left *HMS* Dipper *(Henstridge) in July 1944* (SAA Museum).

Right *Oblique of Henstridge from the west in October 1945. Note the Seafires in front of the Mains hangar near the electrical workshop* (FAA Museum).

level exercises working up for Operation *Neptune*—bombardment spotting during the invasion of Europe. The Wing, consisting of 808, 885, 886 and 897 Squadrons with 42 aircraft and 60 pilots, returned to Lee before the end of March, leaving Henstridge to the Naval Air Fighter School. This was joined by 718 Squadron, formed on June 5 for Army Co-operation training using both Seafires and Spitfires, among the latter the rare PR XIII, passed on to the FAA after their *dicer* days were over.

Henstridge became the only Naval Fighter School operating Seafires in October 1944 and thus responsible for all training on the type, though extra squadron conversion had to be given when Griffon-powered aircraft were introduced into the front line during 1945. The Naval School of Army Co-operation (and 718 Squadron) moved out to Ballyhalbert, NI, in August 1945, leaving 761 Squadron as the sole occupant until the following March when it was disbanded.

Taken over again by Yeovilton as a satellite, Henstridge was little used until August 1949 when 767 Squadron started using the dummy deck for the training of deck landing control officers. By 1951 this unit was flying Firefly 1s and Sea Fury FB

11s, the aircraft remaining at Henstridge while the personnel lived at Yeovilton. On June 18 the whole squadron moved into Henstridge for a week of concentrated ADDLS (aerodrome dummy deck landings) prior to embarking in HMS *Triumph*, the training carrier.

Further training sessions on *Illustrious* and *Triumph* broke up 767's time at Henstridge but at the end of December 1951 they moved in completely while Yeovilton's runways were resurfaced. In March Firefly 4s started to arrive as replacements for the Mk 1, and in September they were fitted with ASH radar ready for Exercise *Mainbrace* which was flown in appalling weather from HMS *Triumph*. The aircraft were flown direct from the ship to 767's new base at Stretton, and with the removal of stores and equipment, Henstridge was reduced to inactive status.

In 1953 Air Whaling Ltd was formed by ex-naval helicopter pilot Alan Bristow, and used Henstridge as a base. He was involved with the operation of a Dragonfly leased to a Norwegian firm by Westland and also experimented with a Hiller 360. In 1954 four Westland S-55s were sold to the South Georgia Co Ltd for whale spotting and until 1957 they received an annual overhaul at Henstridge

before going to the Antarctic each October.

Henstridge reopened as Yeovilton's satellite in 1954 and much to the consternation of local residents was used mainly for night deck landing practice. It finally closed as a naval base in June 1957.

During 1955 a new company, Bristow Helicopters Ltd, was formed with its headquarters at Henstridge. Four Widgeons were lease-purchased for oil exploration work in the Persian Gulf on behalf of Shell but in 1958, when the firm started to prosper, Bristow moved to Redhill. The Admiralty then sold off the hangars and the site nearest the A30 became the Henstridge Trading Estate, occupied largely by agricultural engineers. The airfield itself was later sold to local farmers, one of whom reopened part of it for use by aircraft. The number of residents gradually increased to about 16 light and executive machines. These included the Wessex Strut of the FPA who held an annual fly-in during the 1970s.

In 1980 it was announced that the airfield was to be sold to the BBC for use as a broadcasting relay station, and notice was given to the aircraft owners. A strong local campaign against the BBC was mounted and they were refused planning permission in 1981 so flying continues.

There are still numerous derelict buildings on the site including the large ATC tower and several hangars.

High Post, Wiltshire

SU145372. 4 miles N of Salisbury on A345

A grass airfield at the highest point on the road between Salisbury and Amesbury, High Post was opened by the Wiltshire Light Aeroplane & Country Club in 1931—probably in May. Certainly it was well established by October when the clubhouse was opened, and with a number of private owners giving support the club prospered.

In common with all private flying, the club was grounded in September 1939 and the aircraft, mainly Piper Cubs, were stored in the hangars. The airfield remained deserted until February 1940 when D Flight, Old Sarum, spent some time at High Post collecting equipment.

On June 6 1940 the advance party of 112 (RCAF) Squadron arrived at High Post and with invasion expected at any minute work went on at a frantic rate. A tented site was completed on the 14th, air raid shelters were dug on the 15th, defences set up, and camouflaging of buildings commenced on the 20th. The 'High Post' Hotel was taken over as an

High Post on July 17 1958. The farm track diverted around the 1944 extension can be plainly seen (DoE).

officers' mess, and all was ready for the main party, which crossed the Atlantic on the *Duchess of Atholl.*

The first three Lysanders arrived for 112 (RCAF) on June 23 and flying started early in July with training in artillery observation and live shoots on the Larkhill ranges. Following the shooting down of a Hart Trainer from Netheravon on July 21, all Lysanders were flown fully armed and manned, but there were no incidents. On August 3 two gliders of the Special Defence Flight, Christchurch, were at High Post for towing trials and a Viking crashed after a wing touched the ground while avoiding the other sailplane. A month later one of 112 Squadron's Tiger Moths was destroyed in a crash just to the north-west of the airfield.

With winter approaching 112 Squadron was moved to Halton, seven Lysanders and two Tiger Moths flying out on November 13. A week later the Piper Cubs of the Wiltshire School of Flying were taken out of the hangars and sent to Old Sarum for assembly and delivery to Larkhill for D Flight.

Supermarine's main Spitfire production factory at Woolston was heavily bombed on September 26 1940 and it was obvious that the assembly and flight testing facilities at Eastleigh were equally vulnerable. It was decided to disperse both production and assembly to 35 sites in Hampshire and Wiltshire, among them High Post. Supermarine arranged the manufacturer of small components in Salisbury garages with main assembly in the Wilts and Dorset Bus depot, and following the take-over of the airfield by Vickers Supermarine in 1941 the aircraft were erected and flight tested at High Post.

From November 1940 onwards it was also used for circuit training by Netheravon and Upavon, first with Masters and Battles and later, Oxfords. One of the latter, *EB981,* collided on September 10 1943 in the circuit with Lancaster *JA894,* which was on test from Boscombe Down. The two circuits overlapped and such an accident was always a possibility.

Many of the Spitfire Vs, VIIIs and all the Mk XIIs were manufactured in Salisbury and after test at High Post were collected by 15 Ferry Pilots Pool, Hamble, for distribution to MUs. The airfield also gradually took over from Worthy Down as the home of Supermarine's Experimental Flight Test Department. One early test was on a rear fuselage tank—the aircraft flying to Bramford in Scotland and back, non-stop. In 1944 the *ad hoc* collection of garages and bus depots in Salisbury was replaced by a proper manufacturing plant (now the Sadia Water Heater factory), assembly sheds were built alongside the A345 just south of High Post, and the airfield came into its own.

The east-west grass runway was extended across the Upper Woodford-High Post road, which was closed off very

A line-up of experimental Spitfires believed at High Post in 1943-44.

effectively in April 1944 by a barrier made up of three Hawker Tomtit fuselages. The number and variety of types on test now increased, with up to 30 Spitfire and Seafire variants on the flight line, including the Seafire prototype *TM379* and the hybrid Spitfire/Spiteful *NN660*. The latter made its first flight from High Post on June 30 1944 flown by Jeffrey Quill, but less than 2½ months later it crashed on the airfield killing the pilot, Frank Furlong.

After the war High Post continued as a test centre for Supermarine and the first Attacker, *TS409*, was assembled there before being towed down the road to Boscombe Down for its first flight. Even more surprisingly, it later carried out a few trial flights from High Post before transferring to Chilbolton in 1947.

Meanwhile, the Wiltshire Flying Club reopened at High Post on April 16 1946 and commenced flying with Austers and a Magister. The Royal Artillery Flying Club also re-established itself, but with the expansion of Boscombe Down the airfield was obviously untenable and it closed in June 1947 when both clubs moved to Thruxton.

Subsequently the ex-WD/Supermarine buildings on the western side of the field have been extended and in 1980 were in use by Pains Wessex to manufacture explosives/fireworks. A garage has been built alongside the hotel and the assembly hangars are used for storage. I still find it hard to believe that High Post not only reverberated to the sound of the Griffon, but was also blasted by the Nene of the tail-dragging Attacker! Airfields are full of surprises.

Holmsley South, Hampshire

SZ215988. 5 miles NE of Christchurch on A35

Carved out of the New Forest, Holmsley South was built as a standard three-runway airfield during 1941-42. It was opened in a terrible rush on September 1 1942 to accommodate reinforcements for 19 Group, Coastal Command, during Operation *Torch*.

None of the domestic sites were complete when RAF personnel began to arrive and the first weeks were utter chaos. Fortunately last minute changes delayed the first flying unit until October 21, and then it was only the nucleus of 547 Squadron. Four days later, however, two USAAF officers arrived, and galvanised the station into action by stating that eight Liberators were flying in that afternoon to start operations. These B-24Ds were from the 330th Squadron, 93 Bomb Wing, VIIIth AF, seconded for anti-submarine work with 19 Group. With only two hardstandings completed, the aircraft were parked on the secondary runways and missions started on October 28 with a Bay of Biscay search. More aircraft arrived and the 330th rapidly increased their sortie rate, though like most bomber units they found the anti-submarine role difficult, and while a number of sightings were made, no follow up attacks resulted.

Holmsley South taken by 543 Squadron on May 24 1960 before the Forestry Commission started to reclaim large parts of the eastern area (DoE).

Two aircraft were intercepted by Luftwaffe fighters, one being attacked by five Ju 88s on November 21. The fighters' clumsy approach enabled the American gunners to shoot two down and claim a third damaged before the Liberator reached the safety of cloud.

With *Torch* over the Americans returned to Alconbury and 58 Squadron, RAF, arrived from Stornoway to re-equip with Halifax GR IIs, replacing 547 which left for Chivenor after working up on Wellingtons. In March 1943 502 Squadron flew in from St Eval to complete conversion from Whitleys to Halifaxes, 58 moving out during the following month.

Holmsley South was being used as a conversion base for Halifax squadrons, amongst them a 38 Wing unit, 295 Squadron, which arrived from Netheravon in May. Previously flying Whitleys, they were to tow 36 Horsa gliders over Sicily. Intensive crew conversion and glider towing resulted in three crashes while at Holmsley, but both crews and Halifaxes were ready in time for the operation.

The airfield was now almost complete, a large number of panhandle dispersals having been cut into the woods around the airfield and two Bellman hangars built. During July 1943 Nos 58 and 502 Squadrons returned for intensive anti-submarine operations. They were soon in

action, a pack of three U-boats being caught on the surface by a Sunderland and two of 502's Halifaxes on July 30, while on August 2 Flying Officer Biggar took on a German destroyer and claimed it damaged. This period coincided with increased activity by Ju 88s in the Bay and 58 Squadron lost three Halifaxes during August to these formidable aircraft. Two more were lost in accidents, a total of five in nine days. Things looked even blacker when Halifax *58/B* failed to return on September 27. It was carrying the Station Commander, Group Captain Mead, DFC, on his first operational sortie with the squadron. The crew sighted, attacked and sank *U-221*, but the Halifax was set on fire and the captain forced to ditch the aircraft. Six of the crew managed to scramble aboard their dinghy and after 11 days at sea they were found, by chance, by two destroyers. It was a thinner and wiser CO who subsequently returned to Holmsley. In December both Halifax squadrons left for St Davids, South Wales, and early in 1944 the station was transferred to 10 Group for fighter operations.

Three Canadian squadrons, 441, 442 and 443, moved in from Digby with their Spitfires and worked up as 144 Wing before exchanging places with 121 Wing (174, 175 and 245 Squadrons) which flew Typhoons and arrived from Westhampnett in April as 83 Group lodgers. This Wing had recently converted to rocket work and spent D-Day in direct support of troops on the beachhead. When the Army was established, they turned their attention to communications, harassing motor transport in the immediate rear of the front line.

Meanwhile, 418 (RCAF) Squadron, equipped with Mosquito FB VIs, started intruder operations from Holmsley South. On June 14 one of the crews reported the first V-1 sighted in flight and together with three other Mosquito squadrons they concentrated on night *Anti-Diver* patrols. During the first night operations the squadron accounted for three V-1s and a probable in the five sorties flown.

No 121 Wing moved to the Continent in mid-June and was replaced by Nos 129, 306 and 315 Squadrons from Coolham. They went on armed recce, some of their Mustangs carrying bombs, but also became involved in several dogfights heavily outnumbered by German fighters. They also suffered from flak, losing several aircraft while at Holmsley South, but within days they were transferred to Ford and the airfield handed over to the IXth AF, USAAF, as Station 455.

It was used by the B-26 Marauders of the 394th Bomb Group (584-587 Squadrons) which moved forward from Boreham on July 24 and flew medium-level bombing raids behind the front line in France. Typical were operations on August 7 1944 when the 394th despatched 36 Marauders for a morning attack on the bridge at Nogent-sur-Seine and successfully severed this important communications link despite heavy flak. In the afternoon 34 B-26s were sent to an ammunition dump south of Nantes, leaving it in flames.

After a month at Holmsley the unit moved on to the Continent and the airfield was left empty until 116 Wing, Transport Command, took it over during October. Newly formed on the very troublesome Warwick transport, 167 Squadron began services to the liberated parts of the Continent in December. 246 Squadron arrived from Lyneham during the same month and flew to the Middle and Far East using Liberators and a few Yorks. The squadron absorbed the VVIP Flight of the Metropolitan Communications Squadron, Northolt, in February 1945 and received its first Skymaster in April, giving up its Halifaxes at the same time.

Meanwhile the unhappy 167 Squadron had moved to Blackbushe, and the long-range 246 settled down to operations to India on trooping until it merged with 511 Squadron at Lyneham in October 1946. A Battle of Britain display was held in September 1946 but it was virtually the end, for on October 16 Holmsley South was placed on Care & Maintenance as an inactive site.

Parts of the runways remain on the privately owned western end, but the rest of the airfield has been reclaimed by the Forestry Commission, except for a section used as a public road and a caravan site on one of the old dispersals.

This Whitley towing a Horsa off Holmsley South on June 24 1943 was probably from 295 Squadron (IWM).

Hucclecote (Brockworth), Gloucestershire

See Brockworth

Hullavington, Wiltshire

ST900810. 5 miles N of Chippenham

The 1936 Air Estimates included a vote of £146,000 as the first stage of an expected total cost of £347,500 for the construction of a flying training station with a storage unit attached on flat ground near the Wiltshire village of Hullavington. Work proceeded smoothly and Hullavington was opened on June 14 1937 with permanent domestic and technical accommodation on the main site, much of it in attractive local stone. 9 FTS arrived from Thornaby on July 10 with Hart (T) and Hart Specials, but these biplanes were soon supplemented by the comparatively advanced Anson on which training commenced in March 1938.

Administered by Kemble, 9 MU formed at Hullavington on July 8 1938 and was used initially for the storage of MT vehicles. Probably to prevent confusion with 9 FTS, it was renumbered 10 MU in February 1939, when aircraft were arriving in increasing numbers. Hangarage was already a problem and all-metal aircraft such as Harvards were being picketed out in the open.

Mobilisation brought an influx of personnel and on September 1 1939 ten

Blenheims of 114 Squadron arrived on dispersal from Wyton. Six days later they were joined by seven from 139, but with no sign of the expected assault on East Anglian bomber bases all the Blenheims had left by the 16th. Oxfords replaced Ansons on the FTS during September, but it was on the MU that the greatest turmoil was experienced. Fields near the dispersed sites were acquired and aircraft soon covered them as the number in storage increased rapidly. Security was a continual problem and some malicious damage, or possibly sabotage, was experienced.

The severe winter of 1939/40 caused great difficulties. Some airmen were under canvas and they suffered considerable hardship, while flooding, and then a freeze-up, prevented work on many MU aircraft. The training unit, which became 9 SFTS in November, had to extend courses and the backlog was not cleared until April.

Training Command Operation Order No 1 issued on May 14 1940 required Hullavington to prepare eight Ansons and 12 Audaxes, fitted with bomb racks, for possible deployment to Wattisham as an anti-invasion force. Invasion was indeed a serious threat, and station defences became top priority. Concrete pillboxes were built, trenches dug, and 20 mm Hispanos supplemented the rather ineffective Lewis gun posts. The crews did

Hart Trainer K6476 of 9 SFTS taking off from Hullavington in 1940. The 'C' Type hangars visible are on the main technical site (B.R.W. Hallows).

not have long to wait for, during night flying on June 25, five bombs were dropped just outside the boundary. Night flying was continually interrupted by raid warnings during July, and a RLG at Babdown Farm was brought into operation to try and catch up on training. Meanwhile the airfield was camouflaged and three Hurricanes supplied for 9 SFTS instructors to use on local defence.

Unfortunately, the Hurricanes had just landed from a patrol when 16 bombs were dropped by an He 111 on August 14. Four airmen were killed and ten people wounded. A hangar was badly damaged and a bowser exploded damaging several Harts and two of the defence flight Hurricanes.

No 9 SFTS became an intermediate instruction unit during the autumn and by February 1941 had 56 Masters and 16 Hurricanes on strength, the latter flown by pupils towards the end of the course. A low level daylight attack by an He 111 on February 27 resulted in damage to a Hurricane and a Hampden, but it was engaged by ground defences who claimed three hits. The only other Luftwaffe attack during 1941 was not premeditated— the bomber was being pursued by a night fighter and jettisoned his load, causing slight damage to dispersed aircraft.

Landing Grounds Corporation Ltd started work laying runways during October but progress was slow, and not helped by the decision to further extend the main runway to 4,300 ft (1,311 m) early in 1942. Meanwhile the task of the SFTS had changed again. It started advanced training for pilots arriving from Dominion FTSs and to fit the name to the task became 9 (Pilot) Advanced Flying Unit. More changes took place in March when the Empire Central Flying School was formed at Hullavington, tasked with standardising training procedures throughout the RAF and Dominion air forces. It quickly settled down to a 13-week course during which some 140 students, picked for executive positions at training schools, were put through their paces on Harvards and Oxfords, but also had the opportunity to fly a variety of other types.

To make room for the ECFS, 9(P) AFU was first reduced in size and then moved its aircraft to Castle Combe, leaving just its HQ at Hullavington. Another hit and run attack was made on July 27 1942 when a Do 217 dropped four 500 kg bombs from 300 feet (91 m). They fell between two hangars of the MU causing considerable blast damage.

No 9 (P) AFU was replaced by No 3 Flying Instructors' School at the end of July, but most of the flying on their Oxfords and Magisters was also at Castle Combe to allow the ECFS full reign at Hullavington.

Busy on a wide range of aircraft during 1942, the MU lost its cosmopolitan appearance in May 1943 when its work involved Mosquitoes and Stirlings exclusively as part of a general rationalisation in 41 Group. At the end of the war it became a long-term storage unit and the number of aircraft on charge increased rapidly to over 1,000. Scrapping of obsolete types started, a party from Reid and Sigrist cutting up 68 Defiants in 1945, but the storage task remained until the MU finally closed in December 1959.

The inevitable economies after the war brought changes. In April 1946 the ECFS was renamed Empire Flying School and concentrated on the introduction of all-weather flying in the RAF. It remained at Hullavington until absorbed by the RAF Flying College at Manby in July 1949.

The EFS was replaced by No 1 Air Navigation School which moved in from Topcliffe with Anson T21s and Wellington T10s—later replaced by Valettas, Varsities and Marathon T11s. Accidents happened, one of them during the early hours of May 29 195i when a Wellington crashed and burned about three miles from Hullavington. LAC Jarrett was in charge of the crash crew that night and with complete disregard for his own safety he pulled out one crew member and attempted the rescue of another. His gallantry earned him the George Medal.

The ANS was disbanded in July 1954 when the training of navigators recommenced in Canada as part of a NATO plan. Its replacement at Hullavington was 2 FTS which had already arrived from Cluntoe in May and remained for 3½ years using Provost T1s for elementary training. It also pioneered *ab initio* jet training when a number of experimental courses used a trials batch of Jet Provost T1s and several pilots went solo without any previous piston-engined experience.

Varsities returned in 1957 when the Air Electronics School replaced 2 FTS, but it moved to Topcliffe in 1962 and the station was taken over by 2 ANS until September 1965, when Hullavington ceased to be an

The newly completed runways at Hullavington in April 1942 have already been painted to break up the outline (RAF Museum).

active flying unit. Instead the NATO Codification Computer Centre was established early in 1966, followed by the Balloon Unit from Cardington and the Parachute Support Unit, which arrived from Upper Heyford in 1967. Five years later the Parachute Servicing Flight took up accommodation in a purpose-built unit converted from the hangar used in 1970 for the World Aerobatic Championships, and all balloon and parachute support units were together on one station.

In 1976 there was talk of the airfield being taken over by the Army as a barracks, but it was retained as an RAF unit. Though closed to general flying when balloon training by No 1 Parachute Training School was transferred from Weston-on-the-Green, it has remained in pristine condition and is used by UAS Bulldogs during their summer camps.

Hurn, Hampshire (now Dorset)

SZ115980. 4 miles NE of Bournemouth

What a sight Hurn must have presented in the early days of June 1944. Although an 11 Group station, it was host to two Typhoon fighter-bomber Wings of 83 Group and a Mosquito night fighter squadron from 85 Group, as well as its own night fighter unit. When one remembers that 124 and 143 Wings both had three Typhoon squadrons, and each squadron had 24 aircraft plus another six

in reserve, while the Mosquito units had 18 each, it becomes obvious that even the maze of dispersals on the north side of the airfield would be crowded. The reason for all this activity was the imminent invasion of 'Fortress Europe'. All available airfields in the south of England were swamped with aircraft, but none more so than Hurn.

Construction of the airfield started in 1940 and by the following March it was well advanced with runways and some of the dispersal pens complete. Squadron offices, a watch office and armoury were under construction, and the four domestic sites around Hurn village already had accommodation for about 600 men. Hurn opened as a satellite to Ibsley in July 1941, but was only used occasionally by that station's aircraft prior to the arrival of the Special Duty Flight from Christchurch in November 1941. Its miscellaneous collection were used for radar trials by the Telecommunications Research Establishment at Swanage.

A detachment of Liberators from 1425 Flight, Honeybourne, arrived at the end of the year, but both it and the Telecommunications Flying Unit (SDF renamed) had gone by the end of May 1942 in readiness for Hurn's first major job—as a 38 Wing, AAC base. 297 Squadron brought its Whitleys during June and continued paratroop exercises, two months later being joined by the similarly equipped 296 Squadron. Both units

Hurn on March 13 1956 but still in its wartime state except for the Vickers factory built on the north-westerly dispersals (DoE).

commenced *nickelling* over France before leaving at short notice on October 25 1942. This was for the build-up in North Africa after Operation *Torch* when Hurn, with other airfields in the south, was used as a departure point for units flying out en masse.

No 296 Squadron returned from Andover on December 19 to join 1458 (TT) Flight which had formed at Hurn earlier in the month with Lysanders. Night towing of Horsas commenced in January 1943 and the following month the first Albemarles arrived, the squadron being completely re-equipped by the end of May. The Albemarle, an aircraft rejected for the bomber role, found its niche as a glider tug, proving well able to cope with a loaded Horsa or Hadrian. The first operational flight was on February 9 when an Albemarle dropped leaflets on Lisieux, Normandy, and this was followed, strangely in view of its earlier rejection, by bombing attacks.

In June 1943 the squadron left for Froka, Algeria, in preparation for Operation *Beggar*, the invasion of Sicily. For the same operation 295 Squadron used Halifaxes which had been modified at Hurn for glider towing by a working party from 13 MU, while the Heavy Glider Maintenance Unit prepared the Horsas. 295 Squadron collected the combinations from Hurn at the beginning of June and flew them to Portreath, ready for the long flight to North Africa.

No 296 Squadron returned from the Middle East in October, to be joined by part of 295. The latter converted to Albemarles and built up to squadron strength, while in November 570 Squadron was formed with the same aircraft. All three squadrons then undertook a heavy training programme, and also did supply drops over France, despatching arms and equipment to the Maquis.

For *Overlord* the 38 Group units moved further inland, giving up Hurn to 11 Group on March 15 1944. 125 Squadron moved its Mosquito NF XVIIs down from Valley and immediately found itself involved on Operation *Eric*, supporting decoy bombing raids dropping *window*. On March 18, 143 Wing, consisting of 438, 439 and 440 (RCAF) Squadrons, arrived fresh from fighter training at Ayr. All three squadrons had flown their first sweeps by the end of the month and their Typhoons were soon a regular sight over the Cherbourg peninsula. They went to Funtington for dive bombing training, exchanging places with 124 Wing whose squadrons, 181, 182 and 247, concentrated on rocket firing.

No 143 Wing returned to Hurn later in April, and the six squadrons started full scale operations over France, attacking *Noball* sites and bridges. 438 Squadron became the first Typhoon unit to drop 1,000-lb bombs operationally, and from May 10 an all-out offensive was begun on radar stations along the French coast. Meanwhile 604 Squadron had joined the Hurn-based units on May 3 to strengthen the 85 Group Mosquito night fighter force in readiness for D-Day. During the last major night raid on Britain, on May 15/16 1944, 125 Squadron shot down a Ju 88 near Cherbourg and 604 got a Ju 188. A week later, despite only spasmodic activity by the Luftwaffe, 125 was able to claim another Ju 88 and a '188 in the Southampton area.

All squadrons were on alert for operations on D-Day, the night fighters having started covering Allied forces during the previous night. During June 6/7 604 Squadron shot down five enemy aircraft, and another five on the 8th. This extraordinary success included two He 177s, but it obviously could not be sustained and indeed night activity dropped off considerably as the month progressed. However, standing patrols over the beachhead at the end of June netted 125 Squadron four destroyed and one damaged in three nights, the unit then transferring to *Anti-Diver* patrols and leaving Hurn.

The six weeks prior to D-Day had resulted in heavy losses for the Typhoon squadrons, and the all-out attacks on German armour which followed did not provide any respite. On June 20, 124 Wing moved to the Continent and was replaced at Hurn by 164, 198 and 609 Squadrons (136 Wing). 143 Wing also moved to France to keep the *cab rank* going and by the end of the month all 83 Group Typhoons were on the Continent.

All three 84 Group Typhoon Wings, 123, 136 and 146, now consolidated at Hurn, the squadrons flying daily to landing strips in France to carry out sweeps, attacking railway communications in the German rear areas. During July they gradually moved to France, leaving 183 Squadron to attack the remaining German coastal radar sites.

After a short visit by 418 (RCAF) Squadron with its intruder Mosquito VIs, Hurn was suddenly empty. But not for long, for on August 5 the B-26 Marauders of the 397th Bomb Group arrived from Rivenhall for operations over France. An attack on the rail marshalling yards at Corbiel provided them with their most impressive results when their first bombs hit trucks loaded with explosives, and sympathetic detonations destroyed the whole complex. The units moved to France as soon as an airfield became available, but the USAAF retained Hurn for another month.

Handed back in October, the airfield was taken over by BOAC, who transferred their main landplane base from Whitchurch on November 1 1944. The airfield had already been used for some BOAC flights but these now increased markedly as routes across France became available. The airfield was transferred to the Ministry of Civil Aviation and BOAC was joined by KLM and Sabena, and before long by Pan American and American Overseas Airways who started the first regular

Near the control tower on the eastern side of Hurn airfield is G-AGLV of BOAC about to leave on the first eastbound England-Australia Lancastrian service on May 31 1945 (Qantas).

landplane services from the United States. The airport was very busy during the immediate postwar era but on January 1 1946 London Airport opened and the services were gradually transferred. The BOAC Development Flight and some maintenance work continued at Hurn which was also used for crew training, but by the mid-1950s it was very run-down.

During 1951 Vickers-Armstrong Ltd took over one of the old BOAC hangars on the north side and used the airfield for flight testing the prototype Valiants while a runway was laid at Wisley. Production of the Varsity was then transferred from Weybridge and, with more factory buildings completed, a Viscount line was established. Airwork Services Ltd formed a Fleet Requirements Unit for the Admiralty, unique in having civilian aircrews flying Service aircraft. The unit worked its way through most postwar naval types, starting with the Mosquito and Sea Hornet, and ending with the Hunter and Canberra. On December 1 1972 the Airwork FRU was amalgamated with the Air Direction Training Unit at Yeovilton and consolidated at HMS *Heron* as the Fleet Requirements and Air Direction Unit.

This was a serious loss of revenue to Hurn Airport, which had been purchased by a consortium of the Bournemouth and Dorset Councils in April 1969. Hurn has faced closure several times, but with the continued occupation of the factory area by British Aerospace, some viable services to the Channel Islands, summer tourist flights, and the recent move of Flight Refuelling Ltd from Tarrant Rushton, the future looks reasonably secure.

Ibsley, Hampshire

SU155090. 2 miles N of Ringwood on A338
Built on low ground near the western edge of the New Forest, Ibsley was opened as a satellite of Middle Wallop on February 15 1941, though it was far from ready. 32 Squadron moved its Hurricanes in only two days later for convoy patrols, and the Luftwaffe soon took an interest, damaging one Hurricane during the night of March 13 when they dropped 30 small bombs.

The airfield was virtually completed around 32 Squadron, and things were just getting organised in April when they were replaced by the Spitfires of 118 Squadron. Engaged on defensive patrols over the south coast, they started badly by

shooting down a Whitley on May 4, but were soon on the offensive, escorting Beauforts on dangerous anti-shipping strikes. They also flew some night patrols and during one of these the CO shot down an He 111. When 501 Squadron arrived in August the accommodation built on the north-east corner of the airfield was usable, but much requisitioned property had to be retained as the station's strength steadily increased. Equipped with Spitfire IIs the two squadrons launched into a round of *Rhubarbs, Ramrods* and *Roadsteads* as well as the inevitable convoy patrols.

Numerous squadrons used Ibsley for operations over France, but the most significant event was the arrival of 234 Squadron in November 1941 and the commencement of operations as a Wing under the dynamic leadership of Wing Commander 'Widge' Gleed. The Wing was soon escorting bomb-carrying Hurricanes, 2 Group light bombers and the heavies of Bomber Command. Many of the *Circus* operations were very successful but a long-range sweep of 300 miles (482 km) made on March 16 nearly ended in disaster. Short of fuel in bad weather, 28 Spitfires landed at Exeter, four scraped into Bolt Head and four crash-landed with the loss of one pilot.

Meanwhile, ten months' hard work by a Works Flight had provided double fighter pens around the perimeter together with the only weather protection at Ibsley, nine oversize Blister hangars. On May 15, just after 66 Squadron replaced 234, the whole Wing was involved in a very sticky mission escorting eight Hurri-bombers of 175 Squadron against three minesweepers off Cherbourg. As they left the area one ship blew up, another burst into flames and the third was listing badly, but despite heavy flak only two Spitfires were damaged, and all the Hurricanes got back to base.

Operations continued at a slightly reduced rate throughout June, but then Gleed was posted and the Wing dispersed, Ibsley being handed over to the USAAF. A few days later the American advance party arrived and on August 27 the 1st FG (71 and 94 Squadrons) flew their P-38F Lightnings in from Goxhill. On the 29th came the Group's first operation, the 94th scrambling two aircraft to intercept a Luftwaffe bomber, but they did not make contact. By the time the 1st FG left for Tafaraoui, Algeria, on November 14 they had flown 273 sorties and claimed one victory.

Ibsley transferred to 10 Group on December 12 when 66 and 118 Squadrons returned from Zeals, to be joined later in the month by 504 Squadron. Only 504 stayed very long and with 129 and 616 Squadrons it was soon heavily engaged in sweeps, *Circuses, Ramrods* and *Rhubarbs*, including top cover to the murderous B-17 daylight raids over France. The winter revealed one of Ibsley's main problems—flooding. Work was started on widening and straightening drainage culverts but proved of little value during severe gales in January when the southern half of the airfield was soon under water.

The Wing took part in the large-scale Army Co-operation exercise *Spartan* in March 1943, while 616 Squadron provided close escort to the Prime Minister's Liberator on his return from Casablanca, and later for HM the King homebound from North Africa. 310, 312 and 313 Squadrons were then gathered in from Scotland, Wales and south-east England and established at Ibsley in September as the Czech Wing. Still flying Spitfire Vs, the Wing concentrated on bomber escorts over France but saw little action apart from an early skirmish with Bf 110s on September 21. 263 Squadron arrived in December to convert to Typhoons but all RAF units left early in 1944 when the Americans returned.

The HQ of the 100th FW, IXth AF, moved in on January 13 and the aircraft dispersals and airfield defences were strengthened. The 48th FG (492, 493 and 494 Squadrons) arrived from the USA on March 29 and flew their first P-47 mission over France three weeks later. They were joined briefly by the 371st FG in April due to the condition of their base at Bisterne, but they left early in May. Intensive training using the bombing range just to the east of the airfield quickly brought the 48th up to operational standard and they carried out numerous sweeps before D-Day, attacking marshalling yards, airfields, bridges, coastal batteries and radar stations. D-Day itself was something of an anti-climax for they were confined to convoy and beach cover, but afterwards they reverted to their destructive sweeps. During June the 48th flew 68 missions involved 1956 individual sorties.

As soon as ALGs on the Continent became available the squadrons moved in, the last leaving Ibsley on July 4. A liaison squadron was then based for about a week before being replaced early in July by the 367th FG from Stoney Cross. Flying P-38 Lightnings, their stay was also short and they left for Beuzeville, France on July 22.

With the end of the American occupation in October, Ibsley was used temporarily by Oxfords of 7 FIS, Upavon,

Photographed by 82 Squadron on July 26 1956, Ibsley was still in its wartime state before gravel pits despoiled it (DoE).

During the war the tower at Ibsley was almost buried in the trees—but by the early 1970s its derelict state was painfully obvious (D.J. Smith).

and on March 9 1945 the airfield was transferred from 11 to 46 Group, Transport Command. No operational units were based here, it being used as a satellite by Stoney Cross and Holmsley South, and for the Glider Pick-up Training Flight, which arrived from Zeals with Dakotas and Hadrians. A variety of small ground units also appeared, including 160 Staging Post awaiting a move to Guernsey, and 200 and 201 Signals Unit which assembled at Ibsley in readiness for Tiger Force.

The Glider Pick-up Training Flight moved to Ramsbury in October and the station joined 47 Group, though the last flying unit had already gone and Ibsley had started to run down. Amazingly, work started on a new Station HQ in January 1946, but by March the grass between the runways was being ploughed up and Nissen huts were being sold off to local purchasers. Some of the Blister hangars were used by a detachment of 49 MU for storage but Ibsley became an inactive site in 1947 and was soon de-requisitioned. The minor road between Ellingham and Rockford Common, which cuts across the old north/south runway, was reopened and in the early 1970s the airfield itself became an Amey Roadstone gravel pit and is now fast disappearing. A few air-raid shelters, a number of derelict huts and the large ATC tower remain as reminders of a short-lived but important airfield.

Isle Abbots (Merryfield), Somerset

See Merryfield

Jersey, Channel Islands

4 miles WNW of St Helier

Jersey's first air services were provided by flying boats, replaced in 1933 by DH Dragons flying from the beach at St Aubins Bay. During 1936-37 a land airfield was developed at St Peters and when opened on March 10 1937, Jersey A/W transferred its operations immediately and extended their services, adding Shoreham and Portsmouth to the destinations offered.

The following year Air France commenced operating into Jersey Airport, the service being pooled with Jersey A/W in September 1938. The local airline rapidly gained strength, putting the DH Flamingo on its prestige routes in July 1939. With the outbreak of war all civil schedules were suspended but on October 24 Jersey A/W resumed limited flying using DH86 aircraft on inter-island and Shoreham services, the latter transferred to Heston Airport on June 2.

Meanwhile, the Admiralty had commissioned the airport as a RNAS base in May 1940. The Albacores of 828 Squadron flew in on the 21st, not for operations, but for a week of night flying, formation flying and dive bombing training.

Following the refusal of the French to allow Wellingtons of 99 Squadron attack Italian targets from southern France, it was decided to mount a raid on the Fiat aero-engine works at Turin from the

Channel Islands. Thirty-six Whitleys from 4 Group were despatched to Guernsey and Jersey Airports during the afternoon of June 11 for refuelling. Taking off later that night, they flew across France into severe weather over the Alps. Badly iced up, most were forced to turn back, but two of those from Jersey reached the northern Italian plains and one claimed to have bombed the primary target, the other going on to Genoa and the Ansaldo works.

As the Germans advanced through France 17 Squadron was forced to withdraw from Le Mans and Dinard and moved their Hurricanes into Jersey. 501 Squadron joined them from Dinard on June 18 and both units attempted to cover the evacuation from Cherbourg before being recalled to the mainland the following day.

With the collapse of Allied forces in France all passenger services from Jersey were again suspended until, with the declaration that the Channel Islands could not be defended, evacuation started. Most went by sea but between June 19 and 21 Jersey and Guernsey A/Ws carried 319 people from the islands in their DH86s and an AW Ensign, having found Nantes deserted and on fire, flew to Jersey and picked up a load of evacuees.

The town of St Helier was bombed by Ju 87s on June 28 and 11 people were killed. The Germans ordered white flags to be put out at the airport and in the town square and on July 1 1940 the advance elements of the occupation forces landed by Ju 53/3m transports on the airport.

Bf 110Cs of ZG76 used the field during the Battle of Britain, one aircraft being damaged in a taxying accident on August 22. But Jersey had no real advantage over French mainland bases and rapidly became congested, so it was little used operationally. During the occupation the Germans extended the airfield to the south of the terminal building by adding a large field to the original area which allowed a 3,000-ft (930-m) NW/SE landing run. It was used for communications between the garrison and HQ in France.

The Channel Islands were freed on May 9 1945 and on the same day the RAF showed the flag by flying Mosquitoes of 151 and 456 Squadrons low over the islands. An RAF Staging Post was established at the airport and the first Jersey A/Ws arrival was a DH Rapide which landed on May 26 carrying executives of the company. Regular services were not started until June 21, by which time Their Majesties the King and Queen had paid a visit—on June 6, when they spent 3½ hours on the island.

The RAF operated the airport until October 1945 when it was handed back to States of Jersey control. The scheduled services were gradually extended and in 1953 a 4,750 ft (1,448 m) tarmac east/west runway was constructed. Two further extensions have brought it up to its current 5,600 ft (1,707 m) length which is sufficient for all the twin turboprops and turbojets likely to be required for the foreseeable future.

Keevil, Wiltshire

ST922571. 5 miles E of Trowbridge

All personnel had been confined to camp and the mail censored for several days. With glider training complete at the end of May 1944 the squadrons were ready and tension rose as the crews of 196 and 299 Squadrons were called for briefing during the afternoon of June 5—Operation *Tonga* was on for that night and the news quickly spread around the camp. The Keevil Stirlings were to drop troops of the 6th Airborne Division on the eastern bank of the river Orne near Ouistreham. The capture of bridges over the Orne and the Caen canal was their objective—the invasion of Europe was underway.

The 46 Stirling C IVs, each carrying 20 troops and their equipment, were carefully lined up on the bar and rod tracking which flanked the threshold of the main runway. It was essential that they took off at short intervals, and even at night this was achieved, the first aircraft rolling at 23:19 hours, followed at ½-minute intervals by the rest. They encountered light flak and one aircraft was lost, but the others delivered their troops and were soon back at base. During the daylight hours of June 6 the crews attempted to sleep in readiness for Operation *Mallard*. Meanwhile, the complicated task of marshalling gliders and tugs into position took place and all was ready when troops of the 6th Airborne filed aboard their 36 Horsa gliders shortly after 18:00 hours. Again it went well, though many of the gliders were badly damaged by obstructions on the DZ—Keevil had come through its big test.

Planned as a fighter OTU, Keevil was actually built as a bomber OTU, and opened on July 15 1942 as a typical three-runway airfield with numerous panhandle dispersals—but in Army Co-operation Command. Delays in the build-up of airborne forces meant that there was no immediate operational use for the airfield, but it was perfect for the testing of Spitfires being manufactured under the dispersal scheme at Trowbridge. A large assembly shed was built near Steeple Ashton village together with offices, dispersals and a taxiway to the airfield, and testing was soon in full swing. Meanwhile, the construction of domestic sites and other facilities on the station continued, resulting in Keevil having three Teeside and seven Blister hangars when completed.

In September 1942 the XIIth AF, USAAF, took over Keevil as Station 471. Ground echelons arrived on the 7th followed by Douglas C-47s and C-53s of the 62nd TCG (4, 7, 8 and 51 Squadrons) direct from the States via the North Atlantic ferry route. They flew paratroopers to North Africa between November 11 and 18 for Operation *Torch*, and a week later left Keevil in the hands of a 70 Group Care & Maintenance party. Again the airfield was surplus to requirements, but was earmarked for the expected build-up of USAAF units during 1943. After a delay of several months the VIIIth AF took over in August and used it as a supply base for their Air Support Command. They were joined by the 363rd FG, 70 FW, IX Fighter Command in December. They received Mustangs in January 1944 but left the following month after work-up to operational standard.

Keevil now joined 38 Group and with the arrival of 196 and 299 Squadrons in March, together with 1 and 2 (Horsa) Glider Servicing Echelons, the airfield realised its full potential for the first time. 196 Squadron used their Stirlings for SOE

Above *The dispersals near Steeple Ashton were used by the MAP for Spitfire production at Keevil and are seen in this October 1943 photograph (USAF).*

Right *Two USAAF Spitfires on a panhandle dispersal at Keevil in October 1943 (USAF).*

Spitfire LF XVIe of 61 OTU at Keevil in June 1947 (via M.A. Garbett).

supply drops over France, and 299 underwent training before beginning operations on April 5. Their main task, however, was glider towing in preparation for the invasion. After *Overlord* they carried out re-supply, SOE and a number of top secret operations, in addition to more glider training. The small losses experienced during the invasion resulted in the strength of the squadrons handsomely exceeding their establishment of 22 Stirlings, and Keevil became very crowded. The number of assembled gliders also increased steadily, reaching 130 by early September.

Operation *Market*, the next major airborne assault, was now in the final planning stages, and again personnel were confined to camp for several days. Both squadrons towed Horsas carrying the 1st Airborne Division to Arnhem on September 17 and 18. Fog delayed departure and with flak trucks in position on the approach tracks to the DZ, it was no picnic—and many Stirlings were damaged, though losses were light at first. On the 19th plans to drop more troops were abandoned and re-supply drops were against increasing opposition which resulted in the loss of ten Stirlings, one from 299 Squadron. A major effort of the 20th involved 33 Stirlings from Keevil and again they had to brave heavy flak and fighters. 196 Squadron were attacked by five Fw 190s after dropping their loads and three were quickly shot down despite flying at low level, while 299 lost one to flak. The attempted re-supply continued for three more days, though the weather

was so bad on the 22nd that no flying was possible. The next day they were supported by fighters but flak was still heavy and 299 had three badly damaged, and one forced down. 196 Squadron sent 13, four of which were badly damaged. Keevil spent some time licking its wounds after that.

With airfields in East Anglia available, the Keevil Wing went *en bloc* to Wethersfield on October 9 1944 to reduce towing distances to likely dropping zones. Keevil was transferred to 23 Group and on October 15 No 22 Heavy Glider Conversion Unit/Operational Refresher Training Unit was formed with Fairford as a satellite. The establishment was 58 Albemarles and 46 Horsa/Hadrian gliders, and the area was soon swarming with aircraft as replacement crews were trained for the front-line squadrons.

No 22 HGCU and Keevil were transferred to 38 Group in March 1945, but in June the unit moved to Blakehill Farm. With hardly a break 61 OTU moved in from Rednal. It flew Spitfire Vs and Mustangs, later replaced by Spitfire LF XVIs, and was responsible for some spectacular accidents, on and off the airfield. Renamed 203 AFS in July 1947, the unit left for Chivenor a couple of months later. It proved to be the last flying unit at Keevil.

At the end of July the outlying domestic sites were released, some to the Ministry of Health, others to the Ministry of Works. In October 1948 the boundaries of the airfield were revised, but it was retained by the Air Ministry, and in

December 1955 was transferred to the USAF as a stand-by base for the 3rd Air Force. They kept it as a non-operational site for nearly ten years, the airfield being used for paratroop training by Transport Command. Latterly Hercules of 38 Group have continued such training, while aircraft and helicopters have been deployed at Keevil during large scale tactical exercises such as *Avon Express*.

Keevil is still owned by the Ministry of Defence but they allow the Bath & Wiltshire Gliding Club to use the airfield. The large ex-MAP hangar is in very good condition and some of the other buildings on Keevil are still in use, including two of the 'T2' hangars. To the south some Maycrete huts on a dispersed site have been converted into animal breeding units and there are many others derelict in the area. Access to the airfield (to visit the Gliding Club) is from a minor road south of Steeple Ashton.

Kemble, Gloucestershire

ST960965. 4 miles SW of Cirencester on A429

There can be few RAF airfields whose main task has remained unchanged for over 45 years—one of them is Kemble, yet it would be unknown to the general public but for its association with the famous 'Red Arrows' aerobatic team.

No 5 Maintenance Unit formed at Kemble on June 22 1938 as an aircraft storage unit. The brand-new airfield astride the Fosse Way had three large hangars on the main technical site when it opened, but plans were already being made for expansion. The MU absorbed

the personnel and equipment of H MU, Waddington, in February 1939 and was placed on a war footing in August when Army guards arrived. Early in September barriers were placed across the Fosse Way and on the 6th 14 Wellingtons of 37 Squadron suddenly appeared—to go just as quickly two days later when the expected attack on East Anglian airfields failed to materialise.

In October land for an additional four hangars was acquired and by December 500 aircraft were in storage, some of them dispersed beneath trees around the airfield because of the risk of air attack. This dispersal caused several problems during the first winter of the war, among them the difficulty of guarding aircraft, waterlogged access tracks and damage in high winds and frost.

Aircraft delivery problems also grew as the output increased and in May 1940 it was decided to form a Ferry Pool at Kemble. Tented accommodation was prepared for 300 personnel and No 4 Ferry Pilots' Pool arrived from Cardiff on June 1 as C Site was prepared for them.

On July 3 the 1,000th aircraft since the declaration of war was despatched but any feeling of celebration was tempered by the need to strengthen the defences of the station following the fall of France. A defence flight of Hurricanes was formed by the MU and quickly brought results for a Ju 88 was intercepted and shot down on July 25. Jubilation was shortlived for the Hurricane went into a spin and hit the ground, the pilot being killed. On August 14 the Luftwaffe made a long-awaited first visit when two bombers dropped 18 HE and four large oil incendary bombs. No casualties resulted but nine Whitleys

Kemble in September 1942 soon after completion of the two runways. The main technical and domestic site is in the foreground (RAF Museum).

were damaged. Members of the Pioneer Corps arrived for airfield repair and in September, with invasion fever at its height, all Whitleys and Hinds on strength were fitted with bomb racks.

No 4 FPP left for Hawarden in October 1940 and was replaced by an Overseas Air Delivery Flight which became operational in January 1941. Meanwhile, the station had been attacked again during October and November but with only minor damage to hangars on a dispersed site. Dispersal continued to be a problem and some aircraft were sent to other airfields, such as Stoke Orchard and Watchfield. They soon became overloaded and specially camouflaged landing grounds were developed instead, Kemble using Bush Barn (44 SLG), Berrow (5 SLG) and Beechwood (12 SLG) with varying success.

In September work started on the construction of two runways which were officially opened in April 1942. Glider assembly started in July and another task involved the conversion of Hurricanes to fighter-bomber standard. At the end of the year the output consisted of Hurricanes, Typhoons, Albemarles, Beauforts and Lancasters. 44 Group decided that the OAPUs should have numbers and the unit at Kemble became No 1 in December, when the unit was mainly concerned with Wellingtons, over 500 being modified and delivered to the Middle East. During 1943 work started on an extension to the main runway and taxiways were built connecting the maze of dispersal fields to the west of the main

The inside of a Kemble storage hangar revealing the construction and a Meteor TT 20 destined for France.

airfield, some of which nearly reached the village of Culkerton, 1½ miles away. This work severely restricted output of the MU but the airfield was fully operational by January 1944 as work built up on Typhoons in readiness for D-Day. Because of the high turnover of these aircraft this work continued until late summer when the major task changed to the re-engining of Lancasters with the much improved Merlin 24.

In January 1945 Kemble became part of 47 Group, Transport Command, and continued to operate the service Ferry Pool HQ, with 5 MU as a lodger unit. At the end of the war a Transport Aircraft Modification Section was formed to undertake a number of special installations on aircraft for overseas tours.

The number of aircraft held by the MU rapidly increased, reaching a peak of 1,030 in December 1945. The first sales of impressed civil aircraft were held at this time and the number on strength gradually reduced as airframes were either sold or scrapped.

Transport Command relinquished Kemble during 1946 when it returned to Maintenance Command and became one of the premier MUs in the country. Operation *Beechers Brook*, the transatlantic ferrying of over 550 Sabres from Canada in 1952, resulted in batches of up to 30 aircraft arriving at Kemble for

117

modification and painting in camouflage colours. The paint shop, given the name Surface Finish Section in 1955, became justly famous for its high standard and has been responsible for most of the special schemes seen in recent years of RAF and MoD (PE) aircraft.

From 1954, until threatened with closure, 5 MU has been concerned with Hunter modernisation programmes which have kept this fine aircraft fit for many tasks. The Hunter has also seen service with the Central Flying School at Kemble following its introduction on their Types Flight in 1955. Little Rissington was also found unsuitable for the Gnat when it entered service with CFS and they were transferred to Kemble from where flying was carried out by student instructor courses.

Following the demise of the 'Red Pelicans' as the official team, the CFS element at Kemble formed the 'Red Arrows' using bright red Gnats. After four years of *ad hoc* operation they were established as a full-time display team in 1969. When 4 Squadron (CFS) moved to Valley in April 1976 the 'Red Arrows' remained at Kemble and changed to the more powerful Hawk for the 1980 season.

Now established as part of the Kemble scene, the 'Red Arrows' can be watched, together with aircraft on test or delivery, from an official spectators' area located near Kemble Wood at the end of the 27 runway. The Fosse Way would given an even closer view of activities, but it bisects the main runway so is understandably still closed under the Defence of the Realm Act. It has recently been announced that RAF Kemble will close on March 31 1983 when its aircraft overhaul and storage facilities will be re-allocated to Abingdon, Shawbury and St Athan and the 'Red Arrows' will move—somewhere.

Land's End (St Just), Cornwall
See St Just

Larkhill, Wiltshire
SU120455. 4 miles NW of Amesbury

Larkhill—one of the oldest and most revered names in British aviation—and also one of the most difficult airfields to locate. Several sites in the Salisbury Plain area have carried the name, and this has caused much confusion.

The first Larkhill was on Durrington Down, a stretch of rough land south of the Packway, known locally as the Hill of the Larks. Horatio Barber obtained permission from the War Office to use this ground for aeronautical experiments and erected a shed in 1909. He was joined by G.B. Cockburn and Captain J.D.B. Fulton of the Royal Artillery, Bulford Barracks, the following year when the War Office offered free use of the area for flying and encouraged the development of the Bristol School of Aviation on the site.

The first Army experiments in aerial reconnaissance followed when Captain Bertram Dickson of the Air Battalion, Royal Engineers, used a Bristol Boxkite at Larkhill to observe a mock battle. In the spring of 1911 No 2 (Aeroplane) Company was formed and housed their amazing selection of aeroplanes in sheds on the Down while the personnel lived at Bulford Camp.They became 3 Squadron when the Royal Flying Corps was formed in April 1912, and while a new aerodrome was being prepared for them at Netheravon, tents were provided on the site of the present Packway Church for the men, while the officers used the 'Bustard Inn' as their mess.

Auster AOP 1, LB319, believed at Larkhill in 1941 (Museum of Army Flying collection).

In August 1912 Larkhill was the venue for the first Military Aircraft Trials, but with the development of Upavon and Netheravon War Office interest in the original aerodrome waned. The Bristol School was finally closed in June 1914 after training 129 pupils at Larkhill, and with the outbreak of war the airfield site was soon covered with hundreds of corrugated iron huts as the barracks expanded.

Aircraft taking part in the annual Army exercises on the Plain between the wars usually operated from Old Sarum, but in the late 1920s some of them were detached for field training to convenient stretches of Knighton Down, all referred to as Larkhill. Nos 2, 4, 13 and 16 (Army Co-op) Squadrons all used the downs, the main site becoming known as RAF Larkhill from January 1936. In view of the rough ground and lack of facilities there were surprisingly few problems with this flying, though an Audax of 16 Squadron crashed on landing at Knighton Down in June 1937.

This rather vague situation continued during the first year of war but on August 5 1940 Larkhill (Knighton Down) received its first permanent unit. Known as D Flight, the unit had recently returned from France, where it had started AOP field trials using Taylorcraft light aircraft. Accommodated in huts at the School of Artillery, they started training pilots for the first AOP squadron, 651. In September 1941 the unit became 1424 Flight, and a month later was involved in a big demonstration of firepower on Salisbury Plain. The AOP courses concentrated on precautionary landings, quick take-offs and low-level flying to convert Army officers to operational flying after their *ab initio* flying at EFTSs. By the end of the year a hangar had been provided and during 1942 Tiger Moths and Auster AOP 1s appeared at Larkhill.

No 1424 Flight was upgraded in October, becoming 43 OTU and moving to Old Sarum the following month with 32 light aircraft on strength. The airfield on Knighton Down was then relinquished by the RAF and returned to the War Office, but was little used for Austers could land on any cleared stretch of Salisbury Plain. When helicopters took over after the war this state of affairs continued, though various Royal Artillery units, such as 6 and 25 Field Regiments, kept their Sioux at OS Ref SU140450 while acting as

support unit for the School of Artillery during the 1960s.

There is now no designated airfield at Larkhill, but a general helicopter operating area for use when visiting or exercising with the School of Artillery. The position of the pre-1914 aerodrome is marked by a small concrete plinth on which a brass plate states that this was the site of the first military airfield in Britain—it is a simple but strangely moving memorial.

Lavington (New Zealand Farm), Wiltshire

See New Zealand Farm

Long Newnton, Gloucestershire

ST929920. 1 mile E of Long Newnton village on Fosse Way

Many wartime airfields were developed from practice landing fields, but only a few from dummies. Long Newnton was one of the latter, having been selected in July 1940 as the Q Site for Kemble. Occupying a roughly similar position alongside the Fosse Way, some 3½ miles to the south-west, it was perfect for the purpose. But it also attracted the attention of 15 SFTS, Kidlington, who started to use it during November as a night flying RLG for their Harvards.

During February 1941 it was taken over by 3 SFTS, South Cerney, followed by 14 SFTS, Lyneham later in the year when it was developed as a satellite airfield. A perimeter track was laid connecting two Sommerfeld Track runways, and a technical area consisting of four Blister hangars built alongside the Fosse Way. It was reopened during February 1942 but no units were based here until it became a satellite of 3 (P) AFU South Cerney in June 1942.

The airfield had been camouflaged by then and the dispersed accommodation sites to the west of the Fosse were well advanced. From the summer of 1942 3 (P) AFU dispersed aircraft to Long Newnton and as the number of Oxfords increased more Blister hangars were built around the airfield. On the technical site a 'T1' hangar was erected.

An inspection of the airfield was made by 15 (P) AFU Ramsbury in August 1943 and during the following month they took over from 3 (P) AFU, moving in their detached Flights previously at Greenham Common. Heavy rain in October made conditions very difficult and it was not

The painted hedges and small copse would be almost perfect camouflage for Long Newnton in June 1942 if it wasn't for the perimeter track and newly constructed technical site alongside the Fosse Way (RAF Museum).

until the spring that things got better. The same problems attended the winter of 1944/45 and the airfield was hardly back in full operation when 15 (P) AFU left at the end of April prior to disbandment.

Long Newnton was reduced to Care & Maintenance on May 15 1945, becoming a storage sub-unit of 11 MU Chilmark at the end of July. It was still listed as such at the end of 1949, though inactive.

The airfield has now reverted to farmland but the large ATC tower and its attendant fire tender and ambulance buildings are still largely intact. There are also many Maycrete huts and the 'T1' hangar still in use alongside the old Fosse Way. The Roman road is closed through the airfield area and is private property. Visitors are not encouraged.

Lulsgate Bottom (Broadfield Down), Somerset

ST504651. 6 miles SW of Bristol alongside A38

The aerodrome at Lulsgate Bottom was opened in August 1940 as a RLG for the Tiger Moths of 10 EFTS Weston-super-Mare. Its small size and lack of facilities limited its use but any passer-by on the A38 trunk road had a good view of the Tigers on circuits and bumps. A heavy Luftwaffe attack on the adjacent *Starfish* decoy during the night of April 5 1941 caused some disruption when two unexploded bombs were discovered on the edge of the landing ground. But it had already been decided to develop the RLG as a 10 Group fighter station and with

work commencing on the runways 10 EFTS stopped using Lulsgate on June 10 1941.

While under reconstruction the site was known officially as RAF Broadfield Down and it was at this airfield that a Ju 88A-4, lost and short of fuel, landed on a half-built runway at 06:20 hours on July 24. Whether it was the Germans or the British who were most surprised is uncertain, but the aircraft and crew were captured intact. The aircraft was flown to the RAE Farnborough on August 1 for a close examination before joining 1426 (Enemy Aircraft) Flight a year later.

With the original name of Lulsgate Bottom restored, the station was reopened in 10 Group in January 1942. It was not graced with any operational fighters, however, its first occupants being 286 (AA Co-op) Squadron flying Lysanders and Hurricanes and a detachment of 116 (Calibration) Squadron with Blenheims. The latter did little flying and soon departed but 286 Squadron remained until the airfield was transferred to 23 Group on June 1 1942.

This was the start of a long period of steady and productive effort at Lulsgate. Operating as a satellite of 3 (P) AFU South Cerney, two Flights of Oxfords moved in and the surrounding countryside soon became very familiar with the sound of Cheetah engines. The airfield was ideal for Oxfords but the pilots of bigger aircraft found it difficult, as demonstrated by a B-17 which crashed on January 23 1943 after two attempts to land. In April No 1540 (BAT) Flight was

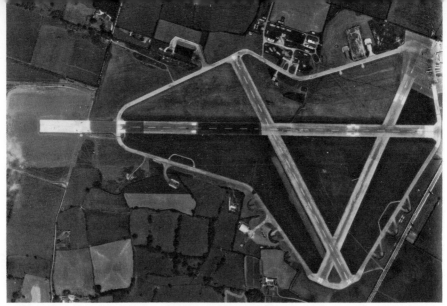

Lulsgate Bottom photographed on July 26 1963. Apart from the runway extension to the west and airport apron it is essentially unchanged from wartime days (DoE).

formed for 3 (P) AFU training and this unit survived a change of major unit when Lulsgate was transferred to 3 FIS at the end of September 1943. On October 1 more aircraft flew in from Castle Combe and as new buildings were completed the station gradually assumed the status of a fully independent, self-accounting unit.

Although not renowned for good weather, Lulsgate received its fair share of diversions. Three Liberators landed on December 31 1943 and during April 1944 no less than 13 BOAC aircraft used the airfield instead of Whitchurch. At this time both Masters and Oxfords were in use with 3 FIS and on a good day the place was like a hornets' nest. In February 1945 F Flight was formed, but it was not to be long before the rundown commenced. As soon as the Germans surrendered the requirement for instructors was cut back and on July 18 No 3 FIS disbanded and Lulsgate Bottom became a satellite for 7 FIS Upavon. The task remained much the same but the level of activity was greatly reduced.

During January 1946 it was decided to move the Upavon satellite to Ramsbury but before this occurred the destination was changed to Little Rissington where 7 FIS was to re-form as the reborn Central Flying School. Late in April the 7 FIS detachment discovered it was to go to South Cerney instead, and they had left by May 7. Lulsgate Bottom was put on Care & Maintenance until it was de-requisitioned in 1947 when the Ministry of

Civil Aviation took it over as the future Bristol Airport.

Conversion was slow, however, and its first regular users were the Bristol Gliding Club who were in occupation by September 1947 when they held an At Home and showed off their new Kirby Cadet and Kirby Tutor provided by the Kemsley Fund. The 300-acre site was purchased by Bristol Corporation in 1955 and development commenced. A terminal building, built alongside the A38 trunk road, was opened by the Duchess of Kent on May 1 1957 when civil operations were finally transferred from Whitchurch. Cambrian Airways had made the first passenger transport landing a fortnight earlier, but after a disastrous year they were forced to suspend operations through Lulsgate during the winter of 1958 leaving the new airport with only one scheduled weekday flight—an Aer Lingus service to Dublin.

During the early 1960s the main 3,930 ft (1,209 m) runway was extended to 6,600 ft (2,030 m) which allowed the operation of medium-sized four-engined transports and increased the number of operators. Slowly the annual number of passengers increased from 30,516 in 1959 to 328,408 in 1972. The rapid build-up in the foreign holiday trade and the steady expansion of internal scheduled services during recent years has meant that Lulsgate has been operating to capacity in the summer months and further building seems inevitable. Evidence of its wartime past still lingers, especially on the north side where a Bellman hangar and a number of Maycrete buildings remain in use and good condition.

Lymington, Hampshire

SZ342960. 1 mile E of Lymington

Built specially for the invasion of Europe, the Advanced Landing Ground of Lymington had minimal facilities. Two temporary runways were produced by laying steel wire mesh reinforcements on low-lying ground on Snooks Farm near Lisle Court, and close to the Solent. A number of Blister hangars were erected but personnel were accommodated in tents.

The 50th FG (10, 81 & 313 Squadrons), IXth Tactical Air Command, USAAF, moved in during March 1944 and started intensive training on their P-47 Thunderbolts. Under the command of Colonel William D. Greenfield they flew their first operational mission on May 1 and soon all three squadrons were hard at work softening up communications on the Continent.

With landing strips available in France, the Group moved over the Channel on June 25 and Lymington was not used again, rapidly reverting to agriculture. A Blister hangar has been used as a farm building for many years and the position of another at SZ344960 can be deduced. Some bar and rod tracking is in use for fencing, but little other evidence of an airfield now exists.

All that now remains at Lymington is this well preserved Blister hangar used to store farm machinery (D.J. Smith).

Manningford, Wiltshire

SU130590. 2 miles WSW of Pewsey

With the outbreak of war in 1939 came a heavy demand for flying instructors and the Central Flying School at Upavon, already using Alton Barnes as a relief landing ground, was soon searching for others in the area.

One of those selected was a large pasture, shown on the map as Manningford Bohune Common, and by the end of September Avro Tutors were busy in the circuit. Inevitably there were accidents as wartime pressures increased, but the LG was retained and handed over to 29 EFTS Clyffe Pypard on November 21 1942 when Upavon became concerned with advanced training and found Manningford unsuitable for its aircraft.

The Tiger Moths and Magisters of 29 EFTS do not appear to have made much use of Manningford but it was still in operation in 1946 and was transferred to Yatesbury as a satellite in May. It was then used by 2 EFTS as a RLG for their Tiger Moths until April 1947 when it closed down.

Throughout its eight years of existence Manningford remained just a large field with a windsock. There is now no sign of occupation by the RAF.

Merryfield (Isle Abbots), Somerset

ST342186. 4 miles NW of Ilminster

In flat country near the ancient town of Ilminster a site for a bomber station was selected during 1942, and the land purchased from the trustees of the Baptist Church at the end of the year. Work started immediately on a typical three-runway layout with extensive dispersals

and accommodation sites. The majority of the living sites lay between Midges' Farm and the small village of Ilton.

Good progress was made on the airfield despite problems caused by an old canal which crossed the site, and named Isle Abbots it was transferred to 70 Group control in April 1943 for administration and development as a USAAF base. The name was changed to Merryfield on September 14 1943 when the airfield was approaching completion.

Merryfield was opened on February 9 1944 and Americans started to arrive in large numbers. During April the four squadrons of the 441st TCG, 50th TCW, IXth Troop Carrier Command moved in from Langar, Notts, with Douglas C-47s and Hadrian gliders. Training for D-Day commenced immediately and by the end of May the 441st was proficient in marshalling its gliders and tugs on the runway so that rapid hook-ups could be achieved and thus produce a concentrated flow of combinations. Together with the other 13 TCGs of IXth Troop Carrier Command, the 441st delivered the 82nd and 101st US Airborne Divisions close to St Mere Eglise on D-Day to seize road/rail bridges and other key points. They followed up with resupply for the next few days and in July the 61st Field Hospital was established at Merryfield. A large tented hospital area and ambulance park was constructed close to the technical site in the south-east corner of the airfield. 813 Air Evacuation Transport Squadron started flying in American casualties from

the Continent, and although the airfield was transferred to 10 Group, Fighter Command, in August the Americans remained until November 1944.

The airfield was taken over by 47 Group, Transport Command on November 30, the nucleus of a new transport squadron, 238, having arrived a week earlier. Intended for Albemarles, it was actually equipped with Dakotas for work in Australia. A change of plan resulted in 238 going to India instead, and 1315 Flight was joined at Merryfield by a detachment of 243 Squadron to form 300 Wing and take over the Australian commitment.

More confusion followed when 187 Squadron formed on February 1 1945, for though intended to operate a special freight version of the Halifax III, none were delivered. Instead, a Halifax Development Flight which started life at Lyneham as part of 246 Squadron moved to Merryfield via Holmsley South and was attached to 187 for servicing. The squadron itself received Dakotas and after operating several freight runs to the Middle East the Development Flight was disbanded on April 3.

When 187 Squadron had settled down with Dakotas they started a trooping service to India in preparation for an assault on the Japanese in Burma. In September 187 moved to Membury to join 525 Squadron and was replaced by 53, an ex-Coastal Liberator squadron from St Davids. After three months trooping from the Far East, 53 Squadron moved to

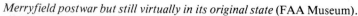

Merryfield postwar but still virtually in its original state (FAA Museum).

208 AFS Vampire photographs are rare. This FB 9 was taken at St Eval in 1953, but hailed from Merryfield.

Gransden Lodge and the Stirlings of 242 Squadron arrived. It converted to the Avro York and then moved to Oakington in May 1946. The station then ran down rapidly, the four Oxfords of 1552 (RAT) Flight leaving just before Merryfield closed on October 15 1946.

Retained as a reserve airfield, it was re-activated by Flying Training Command in November 1951. 208 AFS was formed on the 19th and equipped with Vampire FB 5 and Meteor T7 aircraft. On June 1 1954 the unit was renamed 10 FTS, this designation lasting just a month before it was changed to 9 FTS. Presumably this was to confuse the enemy; it certainly confounded everyone on our side! With the Korean War over and a general retrenchment, 9 FTS disbanded in February 1955.

Two months later the station transferred to 1 Group, Bomber Command, and to relieve the pressure on Bassingbourn the photo-reconnaissance element of 231 OCU moved to Merryfield. They experienced problems operating in poor weather with the low standard of airfield aids and in November 1956 the nomadic PR Canberras moved to Wyton.

Meanwhile, Westland Aircraft Co Ltd had started using Merryfield for Wyvern testing early in 1949 and also carried out air tests on Sabres and Meteors rebuilt at their repair unit at Yeovilton. This work continued through the 1950s, and with extensive reconstruction at Yeovilton 766 Squadron moved their Sea Venoms over on November 24 1956. They were followed by operational Sea Venom squadrons while shore-based during 1957.

No 766 Squadron returned to Yeovilton

on January 20 1958 and Merryfield reverted to Care & Maintenance at the end of the month. For a period in 1960, 700 Squadron used the accommodation but Merryfield was then virtually abandoned, the two 'T2' hangars sold, and the airfield taken over by farmers and a large gypsy camp. The gypsies virtually stripped the place of every movable item, reducing the buildings to shells and spreading their accumulated waste over the runways.

Merryfield remained in this state for over ten years before the Admiralty reopened it as a satellite for Yeovilton. Working parties from Yeovilton, helped by an Army detachment, cleared the site and the gypsies were moved into a compound on the eastern boundary. The original airfield was now bisected by the minor road built across the airfield while it was closed, using one of the runways.

The airfield was named HMS *Heron*, RNAS Merryfield on May 22 1972 and the control tower rebuilt with a greenhouse top. The runways were in poor condition and not used, the western half of the airfield becoming a training area for Commando helicopter squadrons.

Middle Wallop, Hampshire

SU305393. 6 miles SW of Andover on A343

It was a Royal Command performance. After HM King George VI had visited 604 Squadron at Middle Wallop on May 6 1941 he motored to Sopley GCI station near Bournemouth to be shown the operation of that radar unit. Meanwhile, the crews at Middle Wallop got ready for the night's work, Squadron Leader John Cunningham with his radar operator,

Sergeant C.F. Rawnsley, being scheduled for the first patrol. Taking off in their favourite Beaufighter they were soon calling *Starlight*, the codename for Sopley. Almost on cue a bogey appeared and Cunningham was vectored on. Slowly the blip on the GCI screen came closer and at two miles Rawnsley got contact on his AI—the target was ahead and below. Cunningham eased the Beaufighter down and sighted an He 111 against the moonlit sea. He crept up behind the bomber and fired a short burst; it caught fire and plunged to earth. At Sopley the King watched the interception and was then invited to step outside to see the German bomber falling from the sky—a perfect demonstration.

Middle Wallop was planned as a standard bomber station with facilities for two squadrons. It was a grass airfield with a concrete perimeter track and hardstand-ings, the maximum run being 4,200 ft (1,280 m) into the prevailing south-westerly. While still being built the airfield came under 11 Group, Fighter Command, but its first occupant was 15 FTS whose base at Lossiemouth was required for other tasks. The HQ and half the Initial Training Squadron arrived at Middle Wallop on April 18 1940 and took over the partially completed station. The only usable buildings were one 'C' Type hangar, the stores, guardroom, Station HQ and three of the six 'H'-Type barrack blocks, the rest being a mass of open trenches and contractors' debris. Those airmen not accommodated in the barracks moved into tents near the hangars, while the officers were billeted in Andover.

With their Oxfords picketed out and few maintenance facilities, the FTS had trouble completing a training programme but by the end of May was settling down. Events were moving quickly, however, for on May 21 the station received instructions to be prepared to operate fighters—and 601 Squadron Hurricanes arrived shortly afterwards from Tangmere. Mainly employed on Blenheim escort, they also attacked Luftwaffe airfields in France on June 7, in company with 43 Squadron—airfields they had so recently occupied themselves.

No 15 SFTS Moved to Brize Norton on June 11 and Middle Wallop reverted to 11 Group control. While work went ahead on the station a number of squadrons were based here briefly during June/July, including 1 (RCAF) which assembled at

Middle Wallop on June 20 after its sea voyage from Canada. 238 replaced 601 Squadron during June and was quickly declared operational, recording its first victory on July 11 when a Bf 110 was shot down off Portland Bill. Their Hurricanes were joined by Spitfires of 609 and Blenheims of 604 during July, and with a Sector Operations Room, the station could truly be called operational day and night. 238 swopped places with 234 Squadron during August and 609 started spending one day in three at the forward operating base of Warmwell.

The newly formed 10 Group took over the station just in time for the first major assault by the Luftwaffe on southern Britain. On August 13 a strong force of Ju 87s supported by Bf 109s made for Middle Wallop. Short of fuel, the Bf 109s turned back at the coast and Middle Wallop was saved when 609, operating from Warmwell, fell upon a Staffeln of II/StG2 and shot down six of the nine Stukas. The rest scattered and only one of a group of Ju 88s from LG1 found the airfield, the rest bombing Andover by mistake. The next day the Luftwaffe tried sending smaller but more numerous formations to dilute the defence, and this worked, the Germans getting through to Middle Wallop and dropping bombs which hit 609's hangar and offices. Three airmen attempted to shut the heavy hangar doors during the raid, but were killed when it was hit. Three civilians also lost their lives and three Blenheims and a number of Spitfires were destroyed. Two aircraft of 609 managed to take off during the raid and catching up with a formation of three He 111s, shot down the leader.

Yet another attack followed on the 15th when 30 Ju 88s of LG1 forced their way through and 12 made for the airfield. The 12 1,000-kg bombs dropped missed the main camp though one aircraft was destroyed and another five damaged, together with two hangars. Spitfires of 609 and 234 Squadrons took off, the former chasing the Ju 88s and their escorting Bf 110s all the way to the coast, claiming an '88 and four '110s—and a Blenheim of 604 Squadron which got mixed up with the general mêlée! 234 Squadron went for Bf 109s escorting Ju 87s attacking Portland and as attacks on the south coast continued at almost saturation level even the Blenheims of 604 were dragged in for day patrols. On September 2 they collected their first Beaufighter and on November 20

The classical Expansion scheme layout of Middle Wallop technical and domestic site. Though a postwar photo, the bomb-damaged 'C' Type hangar remains derelict (Museum of Army Flying collection).

Cunningham, later to be given a nickname he much disliked, 'Cats-Eyes', by the Press, shot down a Ju 88, the first AI success with a Beaufighter.

Meanwhile other methods of downing night bombers were being tried. 420 Flight was formed at Middle Wallop in September to test a system of laying an aerial minefield rejoicing in the name of *Mutton*. Lumbering Harrows were used to sow the mines. The first operational flight was made on October 26, but it proved very difficult to position the parachute mines accurately in front of the approaching enemy. In December the unit became 93 Squadron and a possible success was gained on the 22nd but *Mutton* was about to be dropped when, during a Luftwaffe attack on March 13 1941, a bomber was definitely destroyed. Though it was not the intended victim, the system received a new lease of life. Havocs were used for some of the later sorties, and the unit also used Wellingtons to test the Mobile High Altitude Barrage in which five 100 lb (45 kg) bombs were towed across the bombers' path. It was even less successful and only one operational patrol was attempted with this weapon.

Deliveries of the Beaufighter to 604 were painfully slow. They only had seven by the end of 1940, but during the winter night offensive by the Luftwaffe the squadron slowly gained the initiative, becoming the top scoring night fighter

unit by destroying 30 aircraft in a two-month period.

Middle Wallop was now developing into a pleasant station. The bombed hangar remained a ruin but the other four were complete, together with much of the planned permanent accommodation. In addition a large hutted camp had appeared on the other side of the A343 and the grass runways had been extended to a maximum of 5,700 ft (1,737 m). Following several minor raids on the airfield during the autumn of 1940 there was a lull until July 7 1941 when it was bombed by moonlight, the Luftwaffe losing four aircraft to 604 Squadron crews. The Beaufighter squadron left Middle Wallop in December 1942 after a very successful 2¾ years—a long time on one station for a wartime fighter squadron.

The usual succession of single-engined fighter units passed through during 1942, mainly involved in bomber escort work. The Turbinlite was given up in January 1943 when 537 Squadron disbanded and the first Mustangs had appeared at the end of 1942 when 400 (RCAF) Squadron carried out *Rhubarbs*. 406 Squadron replaced 604, but with little Luftwaffe activity over the country they concentrated on night intruding over France, attacking MT and rail targets, as did 456 who brought the first Mosquito IIs to Middle Wallop when they swapped places with 406 in March 1943. That same

An Auster AOP V of 227 OCU flying from Middle Wallop in 1947.

month the airfield was used for *Spartan*, a very large-scale exercise involving many squadrons living under canvas, and was then invaded by tactical recce Mustangs, 16, 414 and 169 Squadrons being based at various times.

At the end of August a major change took place when IXth Fighter Command, USAAF, moved its HQ to Middle Wallop. The RAF units left and four squadrons (12, 15, 107 and 109) of the 67th TRG arrived from Membury with Spitfires and F-6 Mustangs. XIXth Air Support Command was formed on January 4 1944 at Middle Wallop with the same commanding officer as IXth Fighter Command, and six days later the station was formally transferred to the USAAF. The strange set-up whereby two different Command HQs had the same CO was further confused by a series of unit changes which was not resolved until March. The IXth Fighter Command at Middle Wallop was in control of all operational and training elements of the Air Support Commands, while IXth ASC carried out administrative work for the combined headquarters.

The 12th and 107th Squadrons became operational in January. Between February 23 and March 20 they carried out oblique photography of 160 miles (257 km) of the French coastline in readiness for D-Day. The 15th and 109th joined them in April and vertical photography was added in June following an exchange of squadrons with the 10th Photo Recce Group. The 67th TRG moved to the Continent on July 2 and Middle Wallop reverted to 10 Group control, two Mosquito night fighter squadrons moving in. They were immediately involved in *Anti-Diver*

patrols, 418 Squadron being particularly successful with an average of one V-1 shot down each night during the first three weeks of August. 402 sorties, resulting in 14 per cent of the total night kills of V-1s, had been flown before the squadron was withdrawn on the 21st.

During September No 3501 Servicing Unit & Pilot Replacement Pool arrived from Cranfield with some 60 aircraft on strength. They carried out servicing on hundreds of Spitfires, Typhoons, Tempests, Mustangs and Mosquitoes flown back from the Continent for base inspections.

The Royal Navy then took over Middle Wallop, it becoming HMS *Flycatcher* on February 16 1945. Its task was the formation and exercise of Mobile Air Operations Bases in preparation for action in the Far East. In addition Mosquito B XXVs were taken on charge by the Navy at Middle Wallop and 700 Squadron carried out maintenance test pilot training from May 1945 until *Flycatcher* was paid off on April 10 1946.

Middle Wallop now returned to the RAF and Fighter Command, 164 Squadron moving in. After conversion to Spitfire XVIs it was re-numbered 63 Squadron and remained on the station until December 1947. Meanwhile the HQ of 62 Group arrived as a lodger and supervised Gliding Schools within Reserve Command.

Though still an RAF station, Middle Wallop then became involved with the Army as the home of the Air Observation Post training organisation in January 1948. Initially 227 OCU, the unit was renamed the AOP School in May 1950, and the flying element became known as the Light Aircraft School during April 1952. As courses completed training, Independent Flights were formed and despatched elsewhere.

A Control and Reporting School was also established for fighter controller training. Initially flying Spitfire LF XVIs and Oxfords, it was just changing to Balliols when the unit became 288 Squadron in May 1953, continuing to fly these aircraft until disbanded four years later. Meanwhile the first tentative steps had been taken with helicopters, resulting in the formation of the Development Flight (CFS) in March 1954 and the Joint Experimental Helicopter Unit a year later. The latter distinguished itself at Suez in 1956 but was back at Middle Wallop when the Army Air Corps was formed on September 1 1957.

Middle Wallop became the Army Air Corps Centre and was formally transferred to the Army on October 1 1958. Pilots were obtained largely from the Glider Pilot Regiment at first, supplemented by officers and NCOs seconded from Regiments while Army technical staff drawn from REME gradually replaced RAF personnel. The Chipmunks and Austers were grouped together as the Elementary Training Flight, later becoming the Basic Fixed Wing Flight when helicopter training commenced. In recent years the basic Chipmunk and Bell 47G phases of the course have been contracted to Bristow while the military conversion and operational flying remains in Army hands.

Early in 1970 the Directorate of Army Aviation moved from the Ministry of Defence, London, to Middle Wallop, the old officers' mess on the west side of the A343 becoming the headquarters. With the Army firmly established a new building programme was started. The blitzed No 5 hangar was rebuilt and much new accommodation completed, including many more married quarters. In recent years the Museum of Army Flying has been established at Middle Wallop on a part-time basis and is open to the public three afternoons a week. It is well worth a visit, as is the station during an Open day. Although it has been occupied by all three British services and the Americans, Middle Wallop still remains the almost perfect example of an Expansion Scheme aerodrome.

Moreton Valence (Haresfield), Gloucestershire

SO796104. 1 mile west of Haresfield village
First opened as Haresfield in November 1939 this landing ground was used by aircraft of 6 AONS Staverton for staff pilot training on Ansons. During 1941 the airfield was rebuilt and on September 9 was renamed Moreton Valence. With three runways completed and a couple of Blister hangars erected, B and C Flights of 6 AONS moved into Moreton Valence on permanent detachment, though their Ansons continued to be serviced at Staverton. Seven days later, on January 17 1942, the unit was renamed 6 Air Observers School but the task of training navigators to OTU standard remained the same.

The Pilot Refresher Training Unit formed during the spring of 1942 and

Looking east across Moreton Valence on July 22 1942. The Gloster factory was later built at the northern end of the airfield which is now split by the M5 motorway (RAF Museum).

Top *The ATC tower on the western side of Moreton Valence is the one obvious airfield structure still standing* (D.J. Smith). **Above** *Glosters in their post-war heyday. Meteors for the RAF, Denmark and Egypt lined up outside the assembly sheds at Moreton Valence in January 1950.*

shared the accommodation at Moreton Valence for a few weeks before moving to Kirknewton in Scotland, leaving the airfield to the navigation school which became 6 (Observer) Advanced Flying Unit in June 1943.

A Ministry of Aircraft Production proposal to build a flight test facility for Gloster at Moreton Valence was accepted and contracts were placed for aircraft assembly sheds to be erected in the northeast corner alongside the B4008 road. An extension to the main runway was commenced and the firm moved in during October 1943. All Gloster F9/40 and Meteor test flying was then concentrated at Moreton Valence, joining a prototype Bell YP-59A which had been shipped to

Britain for evaluation alongside the Meteor. Assembled by Gloster, the YP-59A was first flown on September 28 1943 and remained on test until transferred to the RAE in November.

The (O) AFU closed down in December 1944 but Moreton Valence was immediately taken over by 3 (P) AFU South Cerney as a satellite in place of Southrop. The familiar Anson navigation trainer was then replaced by the equally well-known Oxford pilot trainer, but with the first contractions after VE-Day the AFU closed down and the station was transferred to 6 (P) AFU Little Rissington in July. It remained in operation until December 1945.

Moreton Valence continued to be

parented by Little Rissington but 83 Gliding School was the sole RAF unit and when this moved to Aston Down on October 13 1946 the airfield was left in the hands of the Gloster Aircraft Company. The immediate postwar period was the high point of the Meteors' career and several exceptional flights were made from Moreton Valence. In August 1946 a Meteor IV piloted by Philip Stanbury climbed to 46,500 ft (14,308 m) and during January 1948 a similar aircraft was used to attempt a 100 km closed circuit record, Squadron Leader W.A. Waterton achieving a speed of 660 mph (1,062 km/h) in a trial run over the airfield.

With the decision to concentrate all test work, and much of the final assembly, at Moreton Valence the factory area gradually increased and a single, lengthened runway was made ready as work on the hefty Javelin built up during the early 1950s. The prototype, *WD804*, first flew from Moreton on November 26 1951, and was followed by the first deliveries to the RAF in December 1955. The last production Javelin flew in from Brockworth on April 8 1960 but modification and refurbishing of the Mk 7 to Mk 9 standard continued, and in 1961 a batch of 18 Meteor NF 11s were converted to TT 20 standard.

The last Gloster flight movement from Moreton Valence was a Javelin on July 25 1962 and within days the airfield was inactive. After closure the assembly hangars became a trading estate while the other buildings and runway rapidly deteriorated. The M5 motorway now crosses the centre of the airfield and only

the derelict ATC tower and a piece of perimeter track to the west of the elevated road indicates that it was once the scene of a busy RAF training unit and an aircraft factory.

Mount Batten (Cattewater), Devon

SX483533. 1 mile S of Plymouth, across the Sound

Follow the public footpath around Dunstone Point and RAF Mount Batten is laid out below you. These days you are unlikely to see anything more than a few marine craft alongside the quay, but it is easy to visualise a majestic Sunderland riding at anchor, pulled up on the slipways, or creaming across the Cattewater. Although there were other flying boats at Mount Batten during the war it is with the Sunderland that the base is always associated.

The Cattewater was recognised as a natural seaplane base early in the 1914-18 war and the Mount Batten peninsula was requisitioned as RNAS Cattewater in February 1917. Starting with canvas hangars and a miscellaneous collection of seaplanes, the station slowly built up, two sheds and associated technical buildings being constructed around the old castle at the tip of the peninsula, while the breakwater was used as a pier. After the RAF was formed in April 1918, two large

Mount Batten prewar, but it had hardly changed in appearance by 1939. Across the Cattewater is the famous Plymouth Hoe (via Chaz Bowyer).

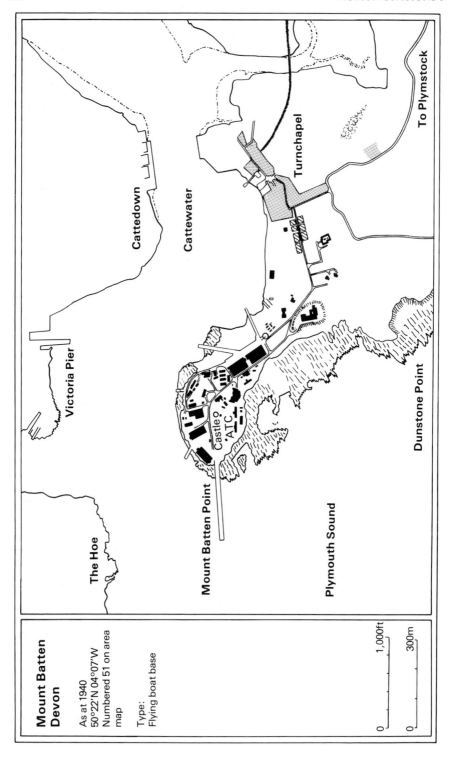

Mount Batten
Devon

As at 1940
50°22'N 04°07'W
Numbered 51 on area
map

Type:
Flying boat base

The Hoe

Victoria Pier

Cattedown

Cattewater

Turnchapel

To Plymstock

Mount Batten Point

Castle
ATC

Plymouth Sound

Dunstone Point

1,000ft

300m

hangars and slipways were built alongside the Cattewater, and during August 237 and 238 Squadrons formed to fly Short 184 floatplanes and F 2A flying boats.

Most of the building work was completed just as the war ended and patrol work in the Channel continued until the end of 1918. 237 Squadron disbanded in May 1919 but 238 remained in cadre form as a storage unit for spare flying boats and seaplanes until closed down in March 1922. RAF Cattewater was put on reserve until 1925 when a special Bill was passed in Parliament to secure the Crown's claim on the site and allow the land to be purchased as a permanent base. Despite this sudden surge of interest the Station remained largely dormant until 482 Flight formed with Supermarine Southamptons in September 1928. Becoming 203 Squadron on January 1 1929, the unit left for the Middle East two months later. However, 204 Squadron had already re-formed at Cattewater and, apart from detachments, remained until 1940.

The base was renamed Mount Batten on October 1 1929 and gradually increased in importance, 209 Squadron forming in 1930 with Blackburn Iris flying boats. 204's first Sunderland arrived in June 1939 and at the beginning of the war the squadron shared the station with Shark floatplanes of 2 AACU which provided training for the Gunnery School at Devonport. With six operational boats, 204 Squadron made its first anti-submarine patrol in the western approaches at dawn on September 4. Fourteen days later it was in the news when, together with a sister boat from Pembroke Dock, a squadron Sunderland alighted in the open sea 70 miles (113 km) west of the Scillies and rescued 33 survivors from the torpedoed SS *Kensington Court*—a spectacular achievement.

On April 1 1940, 10 (RAAF) Squadron brought their Sunderlands from Pembroke Dock. 204 Squadron moved out, going to cold and dreary Sullom Voe, and it was not long before the Australians took over Mount Batten and made it their very own. They were soon very busy, and with the fall of France on June 23 found themselves also acting as long-range transports. One of their first transport flights was to take Lord Gort and Mr Duff Cooper to Rabat, Morocco, to try and secure the continued co-operation of the French in North Africa.

With the Germans in Brittany, Plymouth was in easy reach of the Luftwaffe. The first raid on Mount Batten soon followed, two Ju 88s dropping bombs on July 15, but with little damage. 10 Squadron responded by scoring the first confirmed U-boat kill by a Sunderland two days later. A much heavier raid on Plymouth occurred during the evening of November 27 and a heavy incendiary hit one of the two hangars used by 10 Squadron. A Sunderland in the hangar was destroyed and another, water-borne, was subsequently sunk by four HE bombs, which damaged two other boats. Some 140 incendiaries showered Mount Batten during January 13 1941, slightly damaging three Sunderlands, and another attack on the night of April 20/21 damaged two more in addition to cutting the breakwater and destroying the operations room.

The increasing congestion in the Sound and the encroaching Plymouth balloon barrage forced the decision to move 10 (RAAF) Squadron to Pembroke Dock in May, leaving Mount Batten as a forward operating base for a number of units including 95 and 210 Squadrons. The three Short G boats which had just joined 10 Squadron for special flights to Gibraltar and the Middle East remained and commenced regular flights carrying ammunition and spares for Beaufighters. But on the 20th the *Golden Fleece* suffered double engine failure off Cape Finisterre and was forced to alight in a heavy swell. The hull caved in and nine were drowned, the other five on board being rescued by a U-boat. The other two G boats were withdrawn shortly afterwards.

No 10 (RAAF) Squadron returned on January 5 1942 and a few days later the impressive Boeing 314A *G-AGCA* arrived direct from Bermuda carrying Mr Churchill and the Chiefs of Staff on return from a conference with President Roosevelt and American officials.

Another Australian Sunderland squadron, 461, was formed at Mount Batten on April 25 1942 and worked up with the help of the established unit. The CO, Wing Commander Halliday, made the first operational patrol on July 1 and before the squadron left for Hamworthy at the end of August it had already made a name for itself. When the *Wild Swan* was sunk it was a 461 Squadron Sunderland which rescued the survivors, but while attempting a similar open sea alighting on

A much used Sunderland III, Zebra of 461 Squadron, being winched up the slipway at Mount Batten on a beaching trolley (IWM).

August 13 the CO and crew were lost. This tragedy resulted in such attempts being banned but that did not entirely stop the Aussies, who tended to be a law unto themselves.

The strength of German long-range fighter forces over the Bay continued to increase and took its toll of all anti-submarine aircraft, including the Sunderland, though it proved a difficult adversary. Submarines were also fighting back and a steady run up to the depth charge drop was a daunting prospect. This stimulated efforts to improve the defences of the Sunderland and it was a heavily armed aircraft that Flight Lieutenant Fry took into an attack on *U-454* on August 1. The U-boat stayed on the surface and though the depth charges were dropped accurately and the submarine went to the bottom the Sunderland was also mortally hit and ditched a few minutes later.

Two days later Flying Officer Williams was intercepted by seven Ju 88s over the Bay. While six of the fighters prevented the Sunderland manoeuvring, the seventh attacked head-on. Despite operation of the pilot's battery of four fixed .303-in Brownings in addition to the front turret, the Ju 88 closed to 100 yards, badly damaged the flying boat, and killed the front gunner. The '88s then commenced co-ordinated attacks causing more damage and wounding four of the crew. All the time Williams edged towards cloud and, after severely mauling two of the fighters, was able to circle within it until they gave up.

Although usable in the air, the extra nose guns had been fitted for use against submarines. They proved their worth on January 8 1944 when Flying Officer Roberts attacked *U-426* and prevented any return fire during his run-in to drop six depth charges. 10 Squadron was also responsible for suggesting the installation of Twin Wasps in the Sunderland. After some discussion with Short Bros it was decided to carry out a conversion on the production line and another at Mount Batten. Four Twin Wasp nacelles were delivered and *ML839* was converted and ready for flight in May 1944—the Mk V was born, and for the first time a fully-loaded Sunderland could maintain height with two engines inoperative on one side.

During January 1944 six Sunderlands were prepared by 10 Squadron for despatch to the RAAF and were flown out to Australia by tour-expired personnel from 10 and 461 Squadrons. By this time a beam system had been installed at Mount Batten but operations were still hazardous, especially when approaching over Plymouth to land between the Hoe and the breakwater. Some of the ships in the harbour flew balloons and one aircraft was nearly brought down after hitting one. Other Sunderlands were lost while alighting, hit buoys or, as in the case of *DD852/J* of 10 Squadron on September 2 1944, were hit by vessels dragging their anchors in a gale. Three of the Sunderland's crew were aboard, a standard practice in bad weather, and they signalled for assistance when the boat was driven on to rocks in Jennycliffe Bay. The pilot was washed overboard but

A view of Mount Batten in March 1977. Modern buildings replace many of the earlier huts but the hangars remain, and in the foreground is the combined Southern Maritime Region HQ and Officers' Mess.

managed to swim ashore but meanwhile the Station Commander, the Squadron CO and squadron engineer took a pinnace and made the hazardous journey out to the stricken Sunderland. The two crew members tried to swim to the pinnace but got into difficulties and the Group Captain dived in and supported them until they could all be dragged aboard. Group Captain Alexander received the Royal Humane Society Silver Medal for his bravery.

The period around D-Day was particularly busy, a maximum effort being made to prevent German forces operating in the English Channel. 10 Squadron then returned to its long and generally fruitless patrols over the Bay and Western Approaches. By the end of the war they had lost 25 Sunderlands, 19 from enemy action and six in flying accidents, but had destroyed seven U-boats and damaged eight more, sunk a ship and damaged eight others.

The summer of 1945 was a period of indecision and turmoil but after several changes of plan 10 (RAAF) Squadron left for Australia on October 31 and five days later Mount Batten was placed on Care & Maintenance. 238 MU then moved in as a marine storage unit, the station transferring to Maintenance Command on January 1 1946. 19 Group HQ remained and so did the flying boat moorings, Sunderlands from Calshot and Pembroke Dock visiting occasionally. 84 (Marine Craft Repair Unit) MU was also at Mount Batten from May 1946 until

January 1948 when it amalgamated with 238 MU, which went to Calshot during 1953 in exchange for the Marine Craft Training School.

RAF Sunderlands continued to visit until the last boat squadron in the United Kingdom was disbanded in 1957, but the final appearance of this graceful craft was in 1958 when an Aeronavale machine alighted on the Sound.

Calshot closed in 1961 and the marine craft servicing unit moved back to Mount Batten, amalgamated with the training school, and took the ponderous title of Marine Craft Training and Support Unit. This did not last long for it soon became known simply as RAF Mount Batten. The unit also administered the Maritime HQ and the School of Combat Survival & Rescue which ran courses for all RAF aircrew, using the marine craft facilities for the practical sea work and Dartmoor for land survival training.

The appearance of Mount Batten has changed little over the years. The original wooden huts have largely been replaced by permanent brick but the character of the place, and its tortuous approach from the landward side have been retained. It is truly a maritime base.

Needs Oar Point, Hampshire

SZ402978. 1½ miles S of Butlers Hard

One of the series of Advanced Landing Grounds built along the Sussex and Hampshire coasts, Needs Oar Point could have been scarcely further forward. It was

on low-lying ground near the entrance to
the Beaulieu River, south-west of Fawley.
With clear approaches from the sea, it was
screened by trees on the northern side,
these providing some camouflage for
aircraft.

The site was selected during the summer
of 1942, work commencing in the spring
of 1943. Steel wire mesh was laid as
reinforcement on the grass but other
facilities were minimal, the ALG being
intended for occupation only during the
build-up to the invasion of Europe. All
accommodation would be tented and only
first-line servicing would be undertaken.
Additional work was done on the site by
4842 Works Flight from December 1943
onward in readiness for the HQ of 146
Airfield, 84 Group and 197 Squadron
when they moved in from Tangmere on
April 10 1944. They were joined by
another Typhoon squadron the following
day when 193 returned from an
Armament Practice Camp, and the unit
reached full strength when joined by 257
and 266 Squadrons. Like the other units
of 83 and 84 Groups, it was fully mobile
with some 200 lorries on strength. Each
squadron had 30 aircraft, a total of 120 on
this small landing strip, with 96 in use at
any one time.

During the run up to D-Day the
'Tiffies' concentrated on attacking radar
stations and communications. 193 and 257
Squadrons bombed a rail tunnel on May
19, succeeding in blocking it at both ends,
while the latter squadron fired 9,615
rounds of 20 mm ammunition and
dropped 62 500 lb bombs on just one day.
A few days before the invasion the unit
was renamed 146 Wing.

A maximum effort was made on D-Day
itself when 146 Wing was on *cab rank*
duty, on call to attack any strongpoint
or target designated by the Army. Later
they returned to harrassing enemy
communications. East of Caen they found
a train entering a tunnel, this time
trapping the unfortunate occupants inside
by repeating their earlier blocking tactic.
Their major coup was on June 27 when
the Wing Leader led an attack on a
farmhouse used as the HQ of
Generalleutnant Dohlmann, commander
of the German infantry division facing the
Americans at St Lô. While Mitchells
carried out medium-level bombing the
Wing went in low with rockets, bombs
and cannon. The farmhouse was
completely destroyed and Dohlmann
killed.

This was virtually the end for Need Oar
Point. 257 Squadron left for France on
July 2 followed by 193 and 197 the next
day. 266 Squadron had already gone to
Eastchurch for a rocket-firing APC and
suddenly the ALG was deserted. Within
weeks it was abandoned.

The site was de-requisitioned in
November 1944 and parts of it
immediately reverted to farming, though
it was used for storage by the Royal Navy
as late as 1946. Very little evidence of the
airfield now remains. A thorough search
might produce scraps of wire mesh
reinforcement, but there was never
anything more permanent on the site.

Netheravon, Wiltshire

*SU165493. 6 miles N of Amesbury off
A345*

The sparse population of Salisbury Plain
was nearly as accustomed to the sight of
gliders and parachutists as of soldiers,
tanks and armoured cars by 1944. But any
onlooker could have been excused for
gazing skywards open-mouthed at the
scene presented on May 19 1944. Before
Their Majesties' King George VI and
Queen Elizabeth and many high ranking
officers, Exercise *Exeter*, a demonstration
of the aircraft and equipment soon to be
used in the invasion of Europe, was being
staged on Netheravon airfield. It involved
all the operational squadrons of 38
Group, plus some units of 46 Group.
Dakotas dropped 300 troops of the
Canadian Parachute Training Company,
while Halifaxes cast off tank-carrying
Hamilcars and a hundred Horsas followed
in a tactical landing on the airfield. By any
standards it was an impressive sight.

While ideally suited for such
demonstrations, Netheravon remained a
training base, quite unsuitable for
operations. In 1944 it consisted of two
large undulating fields divided by a single
line of First World War hangars and as
aircraft got larger it became steadily less
suitable—yet 38 years later it is unchanged
in appearance and is still used for flying!

At the end of 1912 the newly formed
Air Battalion of the Army took over some
unused Cavalry School buildings near the
village of Netheravon and work started on
the construction of aircraft sheds, the
rides being considered a good landing area
for aeroplanes. On June 16 1913 No 3
Squadron, RFC, moved in from Larkhill
followed two days later by 4 Squadron
from Farnborough. A year later a

concentration camp for the whole Military Wing of the RFC assembled at Netheravon to test the use of aircraft in war. Soon after the camp dispersed, the original squadrons left for France to join the British Expeditionary Force and were replaced by 1 Squadron in November, this unit acting as a training school until March 1915. Netheravon then continued in this role, concentrating on the build-up of new squadrons. When it was realised that a proper training scheme was necessary, Netheravon became one of the major school airfields, operating a series of Reserve (later known as Training) Squadrons and becoming 4 Reserve Wing in 1917. During 1918 the airfield was operating both 8 and 12 Training Depot Stations flying types as diverse as the Avro 504K and HP 0/400.

With the Armistice came a drastic cut in training requirements and Netheravon became responsible for the disbandment of operational units, among them 35, 42, 52 and 208 Squadrons. 12 TDS staggered on until disbanded in April 1919, but was replaced by the Netheravon Flying Training School in July. Renamed 1 FTS in December it managed to survive, and in 1924 a gradual expansion started, built on a commitment to train Fleet Air Arm pilots.

A number of operational RAF squadrons were also at Netheravon until the station was taken over by 23 Group on April 1 1935 and 6 FTS re-formed, equipped with Tutors and Hart/Audax variants. It also received Ansons before moving to Little Rissington in August 1936. It was immediately replaced by 1 FTS, Netheravon now operating as an advanced flying school, again concerned with Fleet Air Arm trainees. During the spring of 1939 Harvard monoplanes appeared and it was with these extremely noisy but very effective aircraft, and a mixed collection of Hawker biplanes, that 1 FTS entered the war. The station, still with its 1914-18 style accommodation, was full to bursting as the naval courses increased in size, and a number of landing grounds in the area were brought into use.

At the end of 1941 the widely dispersed activities of the airborne forces were gathered together on Salisbury Plain and advance parties of the Glider Exercise Squadron and the Parachute Exercise

Netheravon in April 1944. Close inspection reveals many Horsas on the airfield (Museum of Army Flying collection).

Squadron moved into Netheravon from Ringway. They became 296 (Glider) and 297 (Parachute) Squadron respectively on January 23 1942 and joined 38 Wing, RAF, which was formed at Netheravon to control the embryo squadrons, and provide the link with the 1st Parachute Brigade at Bulford Camp. Meanwhile the Fleet Air Arm had arranged for most of its pilot training to be completed in the United States and 1 SFTS was disbanded in March 1942.

No 296 Squadron used Hector and Hart biplanes to tow Hotspur training gliders while 297 had Whitley Vs, from which ten paratrooopers would be dropped through a hole cut in the floor of the fuselage. In May 1942 296 also received Whitleys and on the 21st the King and Queen paid their first visit to Netheravon for a demonstration by the two squadrons and detachments of the Parachute Regiment. Immediately after the visit six Whitleys were hurriedly converted back to bomber standard and were despatched as reserves for the first Thousand-Bomber raid, made on Cologne. Like many other second-line aircraft, they were found unacceptable

and the crews returned dejectedly on the 30th, feeling very let down.

As the squadrons worked up to operational standard they left Netheravon for better airfields, 297 going to Hurn on June 5, followed in July by 296 which left its B Flight Hectors behind for glider pilot continuation training.

On July 27 the airfield was attacked by a single enemy aircraft whch fired several bursts of machine-gun fire into the WAAF and officers' quarters before hurriedly departing. There was minor damage but no casualties from this, the only raid on Netheravon during the war. Whitleys returned to Netheravon when 295 Squadron formed on August 3 to train ex-bomber crews to tow Horsa gliders, and a week later B Flight of 296 Squadron re-formed as the Glider Pilot Exercise Unit. On November 17 1942 one of the worst accidents occurred when a Whitley of 295 Squadron swung on take-off, hit a hangar and caught fire, killing the three RAF and five Army men. The GPEU moved to Chilbolton in January 1943 but returned with all other 38 Wing units (295, 296 and 297 Squadrons) on April 1 for an inspection by King George VI. With the crews getting restless, Army Co-operation squadrons were allowed to take a more active part in operations, six aircraft of the resident 295 Squadron being despatched on a *Nickel* raid over France on April 4, followed by a bombing attack on a power station at La Theil.

No 295 Squadron moved to Holmsley South on May 1 for conversion to Halifaxes. It was replaced by the Heavy Glider Maintenance Unit and the return of the GPEU, now using Tiger Moths, Masters and Hotspurs for the essential task of keeping the Glider Pilot Regiment in Flying practice. It was during such a practice that Hotspur *HH369* crashed into the GPEU hangar on May 31.

On June 21 1943 Army Co-operation Command was disbanded and Netheravon was transferred temporarily to 10 Group, while the Tactical Air Force got itself organised and took over 38 Wing units. The frequency of exercises and their scale gradually increased with Netheravon often in use as the LZ because of its general resemblance to the expected operational terrain, and the ease with which gliders could be retrieved. Aircraft and gliders of the Wing had been involved in operations in Sicily, and although the airborne assault was little short of disaster, the Wing element had acquitted itself well. It was realised, however, that the next task—the invasion of Europe—would need considerably more planning and on November 11 1943 the Wing became 38 Group, its HQ remaining at Netheravon.

The GPEU continued to be shuttled about airfields in the area, but by the end of 1943 it had left Netheravon for good, and the units in residence were the Operational Refresher Training Unit, 1 Heavy Glider Maintenance Unit, 235 MU and the RAF Regiment. Early in 1944 the Air Transport Tactical Development Unit moved in from Tarrant Rushton with a variety of aircraft and in March 1677 (TT) Flight formed with Martinets to give

Fairey Battle of 1 SFTS at Netheravon during the severe winter of 1940 (R. Godden).

training to the air gunners in the new four-engined glider tugs now in use by 38 Group.

Two days after the demonstration for the King on May 19, a 46 Group exercise was held, 75 Horsas making tactical landings on the south airfield. The main effort of the unit then became the preparation of Horsa and Hamilcar gliders in readiness for the invasion of the Continent. The invasion itself was almost anti-climax at Netheravon, and it was not until August that work increased as glider parts returned from France for refurbishing, followed by 39 complete Horsas snatched from their landing sites in Normandy. During September 1944 38 Group moved into airfields vacated by the USAAF in East Anglia and on October 12 the HQ left Netheravon. Flying activity fell to an all-time low with just the ATTDU plodding on with trials work which mainly concerned glider snatch and pannier drops by Dakotas and Halifaxes. More unlikely aircraft were Buckingham *KV365* and *'369*, undergoing tests as high-speed couriers in February 1945.

In the first week of March, 150 gliders were ferried out from Netheravon to various 38 Group airfields in preparation for Operation *Varsity*, the crossing of the Rhine. While this was going on the IXth US Troop Carrier Command detached 12 Dakotas to Netheravon and in five days dropped 8,000 troops on the Divisional DZ. There were the usual crop of broken legs, sprained backs and other more minor injuries, but on March 12 the rigging lines of Lance Corporal Phillips, 6th Airborne Division, caught on the tailwheel of C-47A *42-92736* and he was left spinning helplessly in the buffeting slipstream. While the pilot flew as slowly as he dared, the jump instructor, Sergeant Beamish, hitched together several nylon strops and tied a kitbag on the end. This lifeline was played out to the parachutist. Somehow he managed to cling to it while the remaining men in the stick hauled him back to the door against the slipstream—believed to be the first time this type of rescue had been successful.

After their drop on March 24 and 350-mile march to the Baltic coast it seemed only justice that some 3,000 of the 6th Airborne should be returned to Netheravon by Transport Command in a slightly more comfortable fashion—albeit the webbing seats of a noisy Dakota.

In the middle of 1945 Transport Command took over 38 Group and the ATTDU was renamed the Transport Command Development Unit, continuing trials on the York, Buckingham and even the Mosquito, as well as equipment tests on older transport types. The advance part of the unit started a move to Harwell on September 13, but two days later the TCDU provided a Dakota, Liberator, York, Stirling, Halifax, Mosquito and Master for Netheravon's static display at the first Battle of Britain open day. For present-day visitors to this annual RAF display such a line-up of aircraft would be mouth-watering, but with so many stations open and transport so difficult, only 859 civilians and 150 soldiers went to that first show.

An Army Beaver in front of one of the 'A' Type hangars at Netheravon in September 1976.

The old 'A' Type hangar from across the airfield. On the left is the old First World War hangar used for parachute drying during World War 2.

During September new segregated, and wire-enclosed, WAAF quarters were built and personnel were allowed to wear civilian clothing when off duty—peace had arrived! Despite the poor airfield surface its position ensured that Netheravon remained open after the war, and it continued with its task of training the Glider Pilot Regiment, the Royal Army Service Corps Air Despatch Company and the Parachute Regiment. The Dakotas of 53 Squadron arrived in November 1946 and stayed until replaced by the specialist Transport Support Training Unit a year later. Such training was stopped in 1948, however, when all available crews and aircraft went to Germany for the Berlin Airlift.

On November 30 1950 Netheravon became the HQ of the RAF Police. They remained until 1962 when better accommodation became available at Debden and the airfield was then closed, apart from the married quarters, which were retained as overspill accommodation for Upavon and Old Sarum, and the domestic area of the camp was used by Army units in transit. The airfield buildings, including the famous Cathedral hangar, fell into disrepair. In 1963 the Army Free Fall Parachute Association flew two DH Rapide biplanes sponsored by the cigarette firm, Rothmans. Southern Command formed a gliding club and the Royal Artillery Aero Club arrived, all using the hangar accommodation and wide open spaces of the airfield.

Meanwhile the Army Air Corps, which had formed in 1957 with its HQ at Middle Wallop, was in a state of flux having outgrown its original concept and accommodation. It was decided that HQ 2

Wing, responsible for nearly all Army Aviation in the United Kingdom and Mediterranean, would be based at Netheravon. The HQ was established in the old control tower duirng 1966 and administered the units attached to 3 Division. When the small Air Troops and Platoons were re-formed as squadrons Netheravon became HQ Army Aviation Strategic Command, responsible for all operational Army aircraft. The whole of Netheravon camp was taken over by the Army Air Corps and a programme of refurbishing the many 1914-18 War period buildings and the construction of some new ones in the lower camp was commenced.

The 1976 Defence Paper cuts resulted in 3 Regiment being disbanded on June 30 1977 and further reorganisation meant that by the end of 1978 Netheravon was operating 658 Squadron of 8 Field Force and 7 Regiment with 6 and 8 Flights. Two grass surface runways, the longest 3,582 ft (1,092 m) in length, were maintained to allow fixed-wing aircraft of the light communications type to land, but the main acitivity was by helicopters.

In recent years the airfield has only once been opened to the public when the display showed what an ideal location Netheravon is for helicopters. The rolling grasslands and small copses so typical of Salisbury Plain provide Army pilots with ample opportunity to practice their skills, especially that of approaching unobserved. If the Army hold another display at Netheravon pay a visit. After all, there are not many airfields which have been in almost constant use since 1913, and on which one can still see original buildings.

The wartime wooden huts in the copse at the north end of New Zealand Farm LG. These were in use by the A&AEE out-station in the 1950s (MoD(PE) A&AEE).

New Zealand Farm (Lavington), Wiltshire

ST967505. 5½ miles SW of West Lavington

Yet another of the Relief Landing Grounds established on Salisbury Plain by the CFS Upavon, New Zealand Farm, briefly known as Lavington, was opened on October 9 1940, and used mainly for night flying. A near circular copse provided excellent natural camouflage for the Nissen huts which provided sleeping accommodation and messing facilities for the groundcrew who went out from Upavon for a week at a time on flarepath and refuelling duties. With a couple of bowsers, storage for the gooseneck flares and a fairly large piece of rough Chevell Down, this was the sum total of the RLG. During the winter of 1940/41 the personnel had a miserable time at the Farm.

The Oxfords or Masters used to arrive from Upavon during the late afternoon and commence flying as soon as it was dark. Once the flarepath was laid the groundcrew had to stand by to move it if the wind changed, or dowse it if a raid warning was issued—and this meant being out in bitter winter weather with no protection from the elements.

Despite these precautions a single bomber, doubtless attracted by the flarepath, attacked the RLG on April 14 1941 while night flying was in progress. Ten bombs were dropped, but only one landed on the airfield and did no damage apart from shaking up the groundcrew and duty pilot.

Acidents were really surprisngly few, a fatal occurring on the night of April 30 when both instructor and pupil were killed

in a Master, and again on September 16 when Oxford *V3502* crashed. Beam approach equipment was installed in 1942 and more accommodation built in the copse as the strength of the unit gradually increased—it had reached 76 in July 1942. Meanwhile the parent unit had changed. The CFS disbanded on April 1, part staying at Upavon as 7 Flying Instructors School. It made little diference to the work at New Zealand Farm except that the emphasis changed to multi-engined instruction and the Oxford reigned supreme.

In January 1943 an operational Wellington crash-landed on the strip and in March two Oxfords crashed, one while landing on the newly installed sodium flarepath. During June 7 FIS decided that each course would stay at New Zealand Farm for the 7th and 8th week of the course while they concentrated on night flying. This scheme continued successfully until November 1 1943 when flying was suddenly suspended and all personnel returned to Upavon. The reason for this, only three months after a Darky beacon had been installed, was the Army's increasing use of the Imber range and their expansion plans. The RLG was closed and transferred to the War Office on December 17 1943.

After the war New Zealand Farm became an out-station of Boscombe Down and was used for weapons trials. Observation points, some of them virtually underground strongpoints, were built and the accuracy of weapon drops could be visually and photographically assessed. It was at this time that the approach road from the A360 at St Joan a Gores Church was built and the accommodation improved. Among the trials carried out were those of the Glow-worm rocket fitted to a Neptune.

It was also used occasionally as a DZ for paratroop exercises but currently the site has returned to its original use—as a landing ground for the Army. A single strip of 2,900 ft (883 m) is available for light aircraft visiting Imber range. It is within the range danger area and cannot be approached past Littleton Down.

North Stoke, Gloucestershire (now Avon)

ST717687. 3½ miles NW of Bath

No doubt good racing men winced when they heard rumours of Landsdown racecourse being used as an airfield—though perhaps they had other things on their minds in 1943! On a fine day, with a light wind, it was doubtless a superb spot, but it could also be cold and with the sharp escarpment to the west and the wind funnelled between trees the air could be turbulent, and the site more suitable for gliders than aircraft.

All this was doubtless taken into account when Wing Commander Gosnell, the commanding officer of 3 Flying Instructors School, visited on May 4 1943. He also probably reflected upon the well-drained turf and the fact that his students were comparatively experienced pilots when deciding to accept the racecourse as a RLG for his unit at Castle Combe.

With the track railings removed a good east/west runway was laid out, and it was also possible to land in other directions with a reasonably strong wind. The students of 3 FIS were soon practising circuits in their Oxfords and the rumble of Cheetahs throttled back for the approach became a familiar sound.

Few additional buildings were necessary at North Stoke, as the RLG was named, for the aircraft were flown over from Castle Combe daily and the racecourse facilities were very adequate. In view of the wind shear which must have been a frequent hazard there were few incidents though an Oxford was badly damaged on March 7 1945 during a landing.

With the disbandment of 3 FIS in July 1945 North Stoke was handed over to 7 FIS Lulsgate Bottom, but not for long, for on August 22 it ceased to be available as an RLG. Since the end of the war Landsdown racecourse has been returned to its former state and has resumed its place in the racing calendar. It has

retained its association with aircraft, however, for like most racecourses it is used by light aircraft, and increasingly by helicopters, during race meetings.

Oatlands Hill, Wiltshire

SU095408. 4 miles W of Amesbury on A303

Built as a satellite of Old Sarum, this grass airfield occupied an exposed site near Stonehenge, just south of the A303. It was opened in June 1941 when Tomahawks of 239 Squadron used the landing ground and from September No 41 OTU trained pilots there for the fighter-reconnaissance squadrons of Army Co-operation Command.

Considerable efforts were made to conceal the presence of a landing ground at Oatlands Hill, the domestic accommodation being widely dispersed around the perimeter, close to woodland or farm buildings. The only technical buildings were four Blister hangars. By March 1942 Harvards were in use for course flying and in the following month both Tomahawks and Mustangs were operating. For these fighter aircraft Oatlands Hill was marginal and there were a number of spectacular accidents, Mustang pilots having an unhappy tendency to collide with other aircraft on the ground.

Two bombs were dropped just to the west of the airfield on September 29 1942 but were probably just strays and in any case 41 OTU was starting to vacate the site, finally leaving in November. Oatlands Hill was then used intermittently for fighter-reconnaissance and AOP squadrons undergoing field training until 43 OTU was moved in from Old Sarum on February 17 1944. They found the camp spartan after the old-fashioned comforts of old Sarum for it was in poor shape with insufficient accommodation for a unit operating 30 Austers.

After an inspection by the AOC 70 Group, 43 OTU was moved out as soon as space became available at Andover. They gratefully departed on August 10 1944 and Oatlands Hill was reduced to Care & Maintenance but used occasionally to accommodate AOP Austers to relieve the pressure on Old Sarum, 665 Squadron spending a month there early in 1945.

Transferred to 11 Group on July 10 1945, the airfield continued to be parented by Old Sarum until finally closed down on May 13 1946 when it returned to

One of the two Blister hangars alongside the wood on the south side of Oatlands Hill airfield—now all farmland.

agriculture. The only evidence of its wartime use are two well preserved Blister hangars on its southern boundary. They are in use for the storage of farm machinery and produce.

Okehampton (Folly Gate), Devon

SX575970. 1½ miles NW of Okehampton on A386

Anyone who has toiled up the hill to the castle, looked at the impressive bulk of Dartmoor to the south, or across the hills and valleys to the north might be excused if they found it difficult to imagine an airfield in the Okehampton area.

Army Co-operation aircraft, certainly those before the Tomahawk and Mustang, were designed for operation from small fields, however, and it was for these machines that Okehampton was established in 1928. A large flat field at Folly Gate, it was used annually as a landing ground during artillery practice camps on the Dartmoor ranges from May until September. 13 and 16 Squadrons using Bristol F2B, Atlas and later Audax aircraft were the units usually involved on these exercises, the personnel living in tents on the airfield. These detachments continued up to the summer of 1939 by which time they had Lysanders, but there were still no facilities of any kind on the landing ground.

Following the outbreak of war Okehampton/Folly Gate remained unused until August 1940 when a reformed 16 Squadron arrived from Cambridge with Lysanders after their traumatic experiences in France. On August 9 they started dawn and dusk coastal patrols covering Lyme Bay and a stretch from Portishead to Barnstaple, checking for any suspicious movement. The HQ and A Flight moved to Weston Zoyland a few days later but patrols continued from Okehampton until autumn weather forced the squadron to move its forward operating base to Roborough. 225 Squadron, also flying Lysanders, used Okehampton briefly during November for artillery observation training, but it was then deserted for the winter.

In May 1941 the airfield became a satellite for Weston Zoyland and was used by both 16 and 225 Squadrons as a base while co-operating with Army units during Corps exercises. These detachments continued until April 1942 when a flurry of excitement was caused when a Whitley V of 58 Squadron, Chivenor, attempted a forced landing after engine failure, hit an obstruction and was badly damaged.

Meanwhile it had been decided to use the site as a Forward Holding Unit for aircraft spares and 73 MU was formed in March 1942, becoming active on December 15. The opening-up party moved into A Site in Folly Gate village pending the completion of B Site in the north-west corner of the airfield, while the nearest of a row of bungalows was requisitioned as officers' quarters and Mess. The Forward Holding Unit (C Site) itself was built in Abbey Ford Wood to the east of the airfield and consisted of two large sheds and a number of large Nissen huts.

WAAFs started to replace airmen in February 1943 when 73 MU was supplying aircraft spares and equipment to most of the south-west of England. Aircraft movements were few, and some of these were unexpected, like the USAAF Tiger Moth which crash-landed in April 1943, fortunately without injury to the pilot. Piper Cubs from the 227th Field Artillery Battery, 29th Field Division, US Army, were attached for a short period late in 1944. On July 24 1945 the MU was ordered to close, responsibility for its task being transferred to 7 and 225 MUs in August, though clearance took longer than expected and was not completed until October.

The airfield remained in occasional use by AOP Austers until the early 1950s, but the wooden buildings were sold and the old WAAF site is now occupied by new bungalows and the village hall (which is an ex-WD hut). The concrete bases of the HQ and airmens' accommodation remain in the corner of the airfield, the area being used as a smallholding, and the only complete building is a derelict Davis hut on the southern side, originally a pump house. The Forward Holding Unit storage site is now the property of the Forestry Commission.

Old Sarum (Ford Farm), Wiltshire

SU153335. 2 miles N of Salisbury

For 24 years Old Sarum was synomonous with the School of Army Co-operation and there could have been no better place for it, right on the edge of Army country! Indeed its affiliation with land warfare lasted much longer, for the school remained using a succession of names until 1979—a total of 59 years.

The pasture between the Portway (an old Roman Road) and Ford village was acquired by the War Department in 1917 and Ford Farm airfield was built on the land. A double line of 1917-style hangars was built alongside the Portway together with many wooden huts and in August 1917 98 and 99 Squadrons moved in, followed by 103 the following month. Day bomber squadrons, they trained at Ford Farm before leaving for France in the spring of 1918, by which time the airfield had been renamed Old Sarum. They were replaced by 11 TDS which remained until the end of the war using Avro 504K, DH 4 and DH 6 aircraft.

Old Sarum was one of the airfields retained by the decimated RAF after the war. The School of Army Co-operation was formed in 1920 and ran courses for Army officers and the RAF pilot/observers of the Army Co-operation squadrons, concentrating on artillery spotting and tactical reconnaissance. From April 1924 a number of Army Co-op squadrons were based at Old Sarum, among them 13, 16 and 59, all attached to the School. 16 Squadron was still in residence in September 1939, its Lysanders remaining until February 1940 when it set out for France to join the other tactical recce units of the AASF.

The School of Army Co-operation was operating Hectors, Lysanders, Ansons and Blenheims in September 1939, though the airfield was not really suitable for the latter and they were flown from Andover and Boscombe Down and re-formed as No 2 School of Army Co-operation in October. With the difficulties experienced in France because of communication problems, 1 S of AC became interested in a new idea, the use of light aircraft directly under the control of the local Army commander. A variety of aircraft were tested during late 1939/early 1940 including such oddities as the GAL Cagnet, Arpin A-1 and the Dutch Scheldemusch, but it was the Taylorcraft Model D which proved the most effective and which formed the initial equipment of D Flight, formed in February 1940 for field trials. This unit left for France in April but following the German breakthrough returned to Old Sarum without having had the opportunity to prove itself.

The first RCAF unit to reach the United Kingdom, 110 Squadron, arrived at Old Sarum with its Canadian-built Lysanders in February 1940. It joined 110 (AAC) Wing in March before exchanging places with 225 Squadron at Odiham. The latter squadron, also Lysander-equipped, carried out dawn and dusk anti-invasion coastal patrols from Selsey Bill to St Albans Head from Old Sarum until the end of the month, when it moved to Tilshead.

The airfield was largely ignored by the Luftwaffe but on October 21 1940 a Ju 88A-5 of KG51, unable to find its briefed target, strafed Old Sarum from low level. It was chased and shot down near Lymington by two Spitfires of 609 Squadron, Middle Wallop. During the night of May 11/12 1941 another enemy aircraft dropped incendiary and HE bombs, burning out one hangar, the Sergeants' Mess and Signals Section, but these remained isolated incidents.

The vulnerability of the Lysander during tactical recce work behind enemy

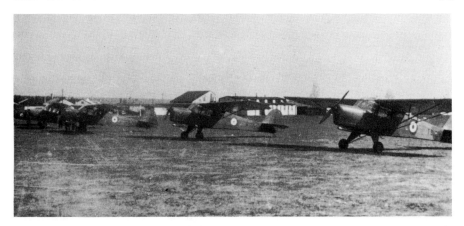

Top *The aircraft of D Flight at Old Sarum just before leaving for France in April 1940* (Museum of Army Flying). **Above** *The one-off GAL Cagnet with D Flight at Old Sarum in February 1940* (Museum of Army Flying). **Below** *The First World War hangars at Old Sarum still in good condition in April 1980.*

Old Sarum on July 26 1956. The First World War hangars can be seen grouped on the northern side of the grass airfield (DoE).

lines led to the introduction of fighter-recce aircraft, initially Tomahawks. On September 20 this element of 1 S of AC was re-formed as 41 OTU with an establishment of 28 Tomahawks plus Harvards, Magisters and a small number of target-towing aircraft. The school then concentrated on the elementary phases of Army Co-op work using Lysanders, and on the formation of new Air Observation Post squadrons for the Army. 651, the first of these, formed at the beginning of August 1941 with Auster AOP 1, followed by many more during 1942 and 1943.

In November No 41 OTU was moved to Hawarden but immediately replaced by 43 OTU which had been formed at Larkhill the previous month with Auster AOP 1s. The much improved Mk III Auster started to replace the early aircraft in May 1943, but during February 1944 the unit very reluctantly transferred to the wilderness of Oatlands Hill for no very obvious reason, and Old Sarum was left with just the school in residence. Changes were afoot, however, for in December the S of AC became the School of Air Support which brought in the Royal Navy and their contribution to seaborne assault. The unit was divided into two wings, the Offensive

Support Wing and the Transport Wing, and relinquished its flying training role concentrating on classroom and battlefield demonstrations. In May 1947 the name was changed again, becoming the School of Land/Air Warfare but continuing to give four-week courses to officers from all three services.

The only postwar flying concerned the Ansons, Dominies and Chipmunks of Station Flight and gliders of 622 Gliding School, ATC. On June 29 1956 Salisbury conferred the Freedom of the City on RAF Old Sarum, and on November 5 1962 granted the unit a signal honour—that of incorporating part of the city coat of arms into the station badge.

The School of Land/Air Warfare was amalgamated with the Amphibious Warfare School, Poole, on April 1 1963 with the new title of Joint Warfare Establishment. The Joint Helicopter Tactical Development Unit worked in liaison with the JWE and had the distinction of operating the last Whirlwind HAR 7 in service. Known as the 'Iron Chicken' it was also the unit's only aircraft for several years before finally retiring on July 22 1976.

Meanwhile the RAF transferred Old

Sarum to the Army Department on December 15 1971. The JHTDU was disbanded in October 1976 but flying continued until November 1978 when 622 Gliding School left for Upavon. The station was finally closed as a military base in 1979 but some of the buildings remained in use by the Department of the Environment and the airfield was retained as an unlicensed landing ground for light aircraft. A Tiger Moth was based there in 1980 and it appears that Old Sarum will be allowed to fade away gracefully—fondly remembered by many thousands of RAF personnel for its pleasant position close to Salisbury and its easy access to the fleshpots of London and the south coast.

Overley, Gloucestershire

SO965046. 4½ miles NW of Cirencester

The problem of storing reserve aircraft so that Maintenance Units did not make tempting targets for the Luftwaffe was finally solved by the introduction of Satellite Landing Grounds. These were chosen in places where aircraft could be hidden by trees, and the site disturbed as little as possible to disguise its use as an airfield.

Late in 1940 MUs in 41 Group were instructed to find suitable sites for SLGs, and one chosen by 20 MU Aston Down was near Overley Wood. It was approved in January 1941 and by late April had been designated as 14 SLG and work, expected to cost £7,000, had been started. Grading the runways and preparing dispersals continued throughout 1941 and the site was declared ready at the end of January 1942 when the contractors were withdrawn. After some rectification the MAP accepted Overley on March 1 and aircraft deliveries commenced shortly

afterwards.

With aircraft widely dispersed under trees around the landing area north-east of Park Corner, they proved difficult to keep safe from the curious and malicious and Army guards had to be provided. These guards were not completely successful and in April 1942 anti-sabotage dog patrols were introduced. Unfortunately they had to be withdrawn for priority tasks after two months and replaced by humans.

Considering the largely unprepared state of the ground and the lack of the usual airfield clues, there were few problems with take-offs or landings, though a Hampden did graze the trees on the approach on April 16 1942. In June Oxfords of 3 SFTS started to use the strip as a RLG and continued such landing practice throughout the rest of the year. Meanwhile, dispersal of four-engined aircraft was approved in July 1942 and plans to extend the north/south strip across the road were made, work by the contractors starting in October. Some additional accommodation was also built on the SLG, designed to look like civilian property, the HQ being in the form of a bungalow near Park Corner, while a Super Robin hangar, which resembled a farm shed, was transferred from Kemble.

In April 1944 10 MU Hullavington also dispersed a number of aircraft at Overley, followed by 27 MU Shawbury in July, but they had both withdrawn by September leaving 14 SLG to 20 MU for the rest of the war. With Germany's capitulation the aircraft were withdrawn and the site abandoned in October 1945 after the lifting of some 16,000 sq yds of steel mesh track. The only visible signs remaining are the sadly dilapidated bungalow and another building across the road which was probably used for storage.

Little is now visible of Overley SLG, but this derelict bungalow was the HQ and Guard Room—compare with Barnsley Park building on page 34.

Perranporth, Cornwall

SW740528. 1½ miles SW of Perranporth on B3285

During the evening of July 1944 a small German convoy leaving harbour at St Peter Port, Guernsey, under escort by three armed trawlers was sighted by an 850 Squadron Channel patrol. The aircraft peeled off to attack the two merchantmen with 500 lb bombs, scoring five direct hits on the leading vessel. It belched flame and smoke, and an hour later was seen beached north of the harbour—a total loss. One of the Avengers was bit by flak but was landed safely on an American airfield in Normandy. The others returned to their base at Perranporth on the north Cornish coast. What FAA aircraft were doing at this RAF fighter base is just part of the Perranporth story.

Perranporth opened in April 1941 as a satellite for Portreath. Intended for use by one fighter squadron, the facilities were sparse, just one 'T2' and a number of Blister hangars. The three runways were joined by a perimeter track off which were blast pens, each able to shelter two aircraft. An old explosives factory provided a MT section, but the only other buildings were the watch office and flight huts, for the domestic sites were all off the camp. At 300 ft (92 m) on top of the cliffs and exposed to the full vagaries of the Cornish weather, Perranporth was a bleak and often dangerous place—it was not well liked.

No 66 was the first squadron at Perranporth, moving in from Exeter with Spitfire IIs for coastal defence and patrols over the south-west approaches. They also escorted St Eval-based PR Spitfires over Brest and on occasion flew up-country to support bombers over northern France. This set the pattern for the stream of Spitfire squadrons which followed, though as time passed the Portreath sector went over to the offensive.

Fighter sweeps were introduced in 1942 when 19, 130 and later 234 Squadrons occupied Perranporth. Sergeant G. Eames of 602 Squadron suffered engine failure and ditching during a shipping recce on April 11 1943 and created something of an unenviable record—he survived in his dinghy for nearly two weeks on the contents of his ration pack! With three squadrons often based at Perranporth the facilities had to be improved. A new briefing room was completed in March

1943 and small extensions to the runways were made. 412 (RCAF) and 610 Squadrons arrived in April, the latter being used to escort Whirlwind fighter-bombers over the Cherbourg peninsula, while both units went on numerous *Ramrods* and sweeps using forward airfields. The Luftwaffe was also active during the spring of 1943 and some inconclusive scrambles were made following hit and run attacks on coastal towns.

Probably the first four-engined aircraft to land at Perranporth was a USAAF B-17 carrying eight special couriers from North Africa on June 1 1943—it had accidentally overflown Portreath! It left the following day and later in the month, 132, 412 and 610 Squadrons were replaced by a Polish Wing, 302 and 317 Squadrons. Prior to their arrival a system of centralised servicing had been in use, but because of language difficulties the Poles retained their own maintenance Flights—with consequent accommodation problems.

The buildings near the Cligga mine at the northern end of the airfield were demolished in July because they were a hazard to aircraft using the short north/south runway. Further improvements were the erection of an earthwork buttress to prevent overruns into the Trevallas Coombe valley, and the opening of a new control tower.

Up to September 1943 Perranporth units had all been equipped with Spitfires but then 183 Squadron arrived with Typhoons to carry out fighter-bomber operations over the Brest peninsula. Unfortunately the runways were too short for bomb-carrying Typhoons and they had to use other airfields for ops, and soon left for Predannack. More activity by the Luftwaffe provided some success for 453 Squadron in October, five Bf 110s being destroyed on the 8th for the loss of two Spitfires, and 66 intercepted four Fw 190s during a search over the Ile de Batz for survivors from a British ship. Two '190s were shot down without loss but this success was marred when two Spitfires collided on return to the Perranporth circuit. During the autumn two French Spitfire squadrons, 340 and 341, arrived and on January 20 1944 formed 145 Wing, at the same time re-equipping with Spitfire IXs. They were joined by 329 (French) and all three squadrons worked up on convoy patrols and *Insteps* prior to leaving for Merston in April as 145 Airfield.

Above *Perranporth taken by a Victor of 543 Squadron in June 1967* (DoE).

On April 15 came a major upheaval. Perranporth was transferred to 19 Group, Coastal Command, and Captain Norwood, RN, assumed command! The station was to accommodate three FAA squadrons for operations against E-boats during the invasion build-up and reinforcement period which was expected to be the most dangerous stages of Operation *Neptune/Overlord*. The briefing room became an operations centre and the old Cligga mine workings were hurriedly converted into a bomb storage area. Operations commenced on April 30 when six Avengers of 849 and five of 850 Squadron went on an offensive sweep of the French coast, while Swordfish of 816 Squadron flew a line patrol. The workload gradually increased as D-Day approached and by June 4 18 Avengers and six Swordfish were flying continuous 24-hour patrols. These were maintained until the end of July though bad weather interfered on several days. There was generally little action, though on July 20 an Avenger of 850 Squadron sighted two He 177s, attacking a group of destroyers off Ushant. *850/R* waded in, and claimed one He 177 damaged.

The FAA squadrons dispersed in August 1944, the airfield being reduced to

A Spitfire Vb of 234 Squadron flown by Pilot Officer Farmiloes and almost certainly operating from Perranporth (via M. Garbett).

Care & Maintenance on September 1 and transferred to 46 Group on November 23. It was used to accommodate Transport Command Staging Post personnel awaiting despatch to the Continent. There were eight SPs on the airfield during February 1945, but the majority left by air before the end of March. On May 1 Perranporth returned to C&M, parented by St Mawgan. During May and June the airfield was cleaned up and ATC gliding commenced, 95 Gliding School using a single Blister hangar. There were no more military aircraft movements apart from a forced landing by a Boston and a crash landing by a Wellington. The airfield was inspected by the Army in January 1946 but rejected despite its closeness to Penhale Camp, and after nominal transfer to 44 Group in February Perranporth was closed by the Air Ministry on April 6 1946.

Following a tentative restart of scheduled civil flights into St Mawgan in 1950, the Air Ministry dropped a bombshell on Newquay Council by refusing permission for the 1951 season. The council turned their attention to Trevallas, as Perranporth airfield was known locally, and within four weeks had got the site de-requisitiond and re-licensed for aircraft up to 10,000 lb (4,536 kg) weight. Murray Chown reopened their Staverton-Newquay-Guernsey route using

a Proctor in May 1951 and also commenced joy-riding, while Fingland flew a weekend service from Manchester. Traffic figures were poor, however, and the operation closed down at the end of the 1952 season.

The airfield was again returned to agriculture and dereliction until 1957 when the combination of prevailing westerlies and the 300 ft (92 m) cliffs led the Cornish Gliding Club to establish themselves in the old dynamite store. Their expansion was rapid and in 1958 they were second only to Lasham in the number of certificates gained during their summer courses. The club still operates at Perranporth alongside a number of private aircraft which live in a lock-up hangar.

During 1979 Pattern Recognition Ltd started investigation into the use of the airfield for freight movements, and offered to purchase the airfield from Sir Charles Milner-Haigh, Bt, if planning permission could be obtained for a factory on the site. The company faced the usual environmental protests and the project was dropped in 1980. There is still plenty of evidence of the airfield's wartime past. The derelict tower sits squarely in the middle of the field, which is dotted with air raid and two-bay aircraft shelters, and the remains of the flight huts.

Below *Double blast pens on the southern side of Perranporth, still largely complete in April 1979.* **Bottom** *The derelict tower at Perranporth in April 1979.*

Plymouth (Roborough), Devon

See Roborough

Poole (Hamworthy), Dorset (Marine)

See Hamworthy

Portland, Dorset

SY682746. 3 miles S of Weymouth

The Isle of Portland is unique in many respects and one of them is undoubtedly its airfield. How many runways are there, tarmac-surfaced with full high intensity lighting and precision approach radar—and only 720 ft (220 m) in length? But then HMS *Osprey* is a rather special Fleet Air Arm base.

The slaughter of coastal shipping by U-boats during the First World War caused the Admiralty to establish a series of RNAS seaplane bases around the coast of Britain. The harbour at Portland was a natural choice, approval being given for a Flight of four Short floatplanes on September 28 1916. Surface forces also began to use the harbour and in 1917 a shore establishment, HMS *Sereptia* was built on the Isle.

The Portland-based seaplanes had little positive to show for their efforts but doubtless forced the submarine commanders to keep their heads down. Amongst the few attacks made was the first on a submarine by a United States naval aviator when Ensign J.F. McNamara bombed a U-boat and was 'apparently successful', in the words of the official report. With the formation of the RAF in April 1918, RNAS Portland was transferred to the new Service and 241 Squadron was formed in August. It continued as part of 10 Group until disbanded in June 1919.

Portland was the main anti-submarine base for the Royal Navy after the war. It was little involved with aircraft, however, until 772 Squadron was formed in September 1939 as a Fleet Requirements Unit flying Swordfish. These floatplanes were used for a variety of tasks, including target towing for ships' anti-aircraft gunners. Following the fall of France the naval base became a prime target for the Luftwaffe and became untenable as an Anti-Submarine School. It moved to Dunoon and 772 went too, transferring to Campbelltown in July 1940.

For the remainder of the war the seaplane facilities at Portland were on a Care & Maintenance basis and it was only when the school returned to its old home in 1946 that aerial activity revived, this time in the form of Sikorsky R-4B helicopters which were used for development work from the naval base slipway. This activity continued with newer choppers and when it was decided to replace fixed-wing anti-submarine aircraft by helicopters a major rebuilding programme commenced at Portland. The naval base playing fields were taken over as a landing ground and two hangars erected below the old Fleet canteen, which was itself converted into the SHQ, operations centre, workshops and control tower. RNAS Portland commissioned as part of HMS *Osprey* on April 24 1959, and the Air ASW School moved in from Eglinton and 737 Squadron re-formed with Whirlwinds to provide airborne training.

No 771 (Helicopter Trials) Squadron arrived in July 1961 to carry out pre-service tests on new helicopters and equipment, followed by 829 Squadron formed during March 1964 as the parent unit for Wasp Ships' Flights. The latter absorbed the SAR and aircrew rating training role of 771 Squadron, which then disbanded on December 1 1964.

An expansion of the facilities became essential in the late 1960s, and a five-year redevelopment programme costing £2.3 million was started. To increase the size of the helicopter area, more ground had to be found and 12 acres was reclaimed from the harbour using fill-in. New hangars and workshops were built along the southern edge of the maintenance area near the fuel storage tanks, and the approaches to the runway were cleared up.

No 829 Squadron became larger as more Ships' Flights were commissioned and 771 was re-formed again in 1967 to take over part of the training task. 829 lost the remainder of its training commitment in January 1972 when 703 Squadron re-formed, and with work on the base completed during 1973 the RN Pilotless Target Aircraft Squadron transferred from the dockyard to the air station in 1974. On September 6 772 Squadron re-formed by splitting 771 in two, the latter moving to Culdrose, leaving 772 with the local Portland SAR commitment.

The situation has changed little since though 737 Squadron now have elderly Wessex HAS 3s, 772 have re-equipped with the twin-engined Wessex 5 and at the end of 1980 Wasp helicopter training was running down.

Above *Swordfish floatplane of 771 Squadron flying from Portland prewar when the station was little more than a slipway in the harbour* (via R. Sturtivant). **Below** *Portland helicopter base soon after completion of the runway and enlarged helicopter parking area* (FAA Museum).

Portreath, Cornwall

SW670460. 1 mile NE of village on minor road

Portreath—the name will be familiar to many wartime Allied aircrew. It was their departure point for the Middle or Far East, and the start of a flight into the unknown. Often short of fuel, they were faced with uncertain weather and usually the horribly short runway at Gibraltar.

Many of these flights were hazardous but none more so that Operation *Beggar*, the ferrying of Horsa gliders to North Africa in readiness for the invasion of Sicily. 295 Squadron were given the task and after tests of a Halifax/Horsa combination showed that they could just reach the North African coast, the squadron started moving the gliders to Portreath during June 1943. With the Halifaxes loaded to capacity, the first four combinations left for Morocco on June 3. Only two got there, one returning with an unserviceable glider and another breaking the tow rope, the crew being rescued after ten hours in their floating Horsa. For the next fortnight the deliveries went smoothly, 14 gliders arriving at Sale despite crossing the dreaded Bay of Biscay in daylight, and within 100 miles of Luftwaffe bases in France. On the 14th a combination met up with two Fw 200 Condors returning from a shipping strike. The glider had to be cast off and the tug, despite gallant efforts by the rear gunner, was shot down. Altogether two Halifaxes and four Horsas were lost, and another of the 27 gliders which reached Sale crashed on landing. The operation was a tremendous feat of physical endurance by both tug and glider crews—just imagine the strain on those inexperienced glider pilots, sitting at the end of a tow rope with nothing but sea from horizon to horizon for hour after hour.

Authority to requisition the airfield site was given in July 1940 and Portreath was opened on March 7 1941 as a 10 Group station to replace St Eval. It was unusual in having four tarmac runways, though only the main one was long enough for anything larger than a single-seat fighter. The usual double blast pens were dispersed around the perimeter track together with four Blister hangars. These were later supplemented by four 'T2' hangars on the technical site.

The first aircraft at Portreath were Whirlwinds of 263 Squadron used to defend convoys in the western approaches. They were soon replaced by Spitfires of 152 Squadron, who tried some night sorties but reverted to day convoy patrols after losing two aircraft in accidents. Meanwhile the Luftwaffe discovered that Portreath was open and two attacks were made during April, both on a small scale with no damage or casualties. On May 9, however, a more determined attack resulted in the death of one airman and wounding of three. Two aircraft were destroyed and three damaged. Two days later the Sector Operations Room, previously at St Eval, started work from Tehidy Barton Farm, some two miles from Portreath airfield. The station was then upgraded, becoming responsible for the satellite fields at Perranporth and Predannack.

The first of many Blenheims appeared at Portreath early in May when 2 Group squadrons started using it as an advanced base for raids on France. Typical was a detachment by 82 Squadron for an attack on St Nazaire. Eight Blenheims were despatched to make their bombing runs against heavy flak defences. One hit was scored on a 2,000-ton ship in the harbour, but two Blenheims were lost and another crash-landed on return due to battle damage. These attacks, always hazardous, became more so as the German anti-aircraft and fighter defences improved, and by July most were given fighter escort. For some of these, like the attack on Brest by 18 Hampdens on July 24, seven fighter squadrons were gathered under control of the Portreath sector. Flying from several bases, including Predannack and Portreath, the fighters provided close support resulting in the destruction of four Bf 109s for the loss of two 152 Squadron Spitfires.

No 130 Squadron was formed at Portreath on June 20 and worked up on Spitfire IIs, becoming operational in September. With 313 Squadron they were used on convoy escort and offensive sweeps providing cover for bomber Blenheims withdrawing from raids on French ports.

The build-up of Axis forces in North Africa during 1941 required action against their shipping and the only aircraft available were the unfortunate Blenheims of 2 Group. Thus the desperate expedient of flying the aircraft out to Malta, already tested by the Overseas Air Delivery Flight from Kemble, was introduced for whole squadrons. The geographical position of Portreath made it a natural jumping-off

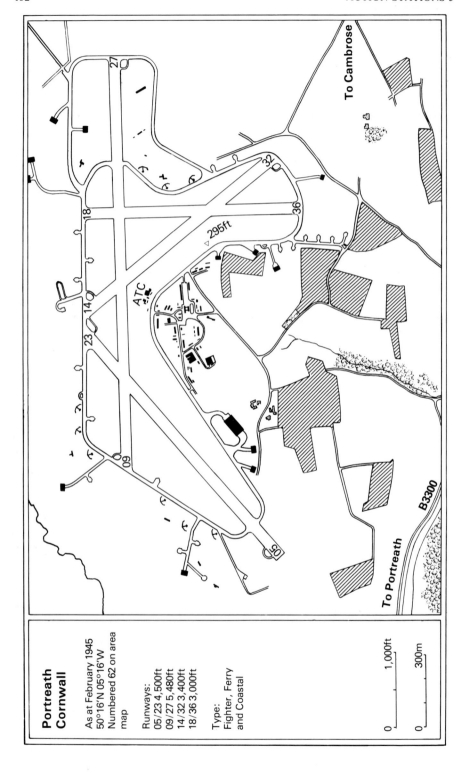

Portreath
Cornwall

As at February 1945
50°16′N 05°16′W
Numbered 62 on area
map

Runways:
05/23 4,500ft
09/27 5,480ft
14/32 3,400ft
18/36 3,000ft

Type:
Fighter, Ferry
and Coastal

To Cambrose

To Portreath

B3300

295ft

ATC

27

32

36

18

14

23

09

05

1,000ft

300m

0

0

point and the base was soon involved, 82 Squadron leaving for a five-week detachment in June 1941. The main runway was only just long enough for a heavily loaded Blenheim and many heart-stopping take-offs were made, the aircraft disappearing over the cliffs to reappear, seemingly minutes later, struggling for height over the sea. They then faced a 7½-hour flight over the Bay and around the Iberian Peninsula to Gibraltar. They had no diversions and no spare fuel for their total endurance was about eight hours.

The early ferry flights were organised by the crews themselves with help from station staff, but with the formation of the Overseas Air Despatch Unit at Honeybourne in October 1941 a detachment was set up at Portreath. Among their first customers were four RAF B-17C Fortress 1 crews who left Portreath on October 28 for Egypt to operate as a long range bomber force. The influx of crews during these ferry operations quickly overwhelmed the available accommodation and they had to use a colony of bell tents set up on the hillside. With their flights often delayed by weather, much misery was experienced by the crews, both in their tents and on their way to the inhospitable messes, or to the briefing rooms.

Meanwhile fighter units came and went. Among major efforts by the Portreath Sector were the two Operation *Veracity* daylight attacks on the *Scharnhorst* and *Gneisenau* at Brest during December 1941. During the second, made on the 30th by three Halifax squadrons, six German fighters were shot down and another 11 claimed damaged. The two Lysanders which had arrived for air-sea rescue during 1941 soon proved their effectiveness. On January 7 1942 a Wellington of 15 OTU ditched two miles off Portreath and the Lysanders made four searches. Less than two hours later a PRU Anson ditched and in under eight minutes a Lysander was airborne and had soon located the floating aircraft. This was a busy day, but not unusually so, and the 276 Squadron detachment became the recipients of a stream of congratulatory messages.

In October 1942 Portreath was cleared for Operation *Cackle*, the supply of aircraft for *Torch*. 234 and 276 Squadrons were moved to Perranporth and a USAAF detachment arrived to administer American aircraft movements. On November 6, 66 transients arrived, the first batch of 20 C-47s, loaded with paratroopers, leaving the next day for North Africa. Already stretched to the theoretical limit, Portreath found itself with 19 B-17s of the 306th BG diverted off a raid on St Nazaire on the 9th when there was a total of 107 aircraft dispersed on the airfield. Amongst the many types despatched were P-38F Lightnings and P-39 Airacobras. The latter had to wait for a tailwind, and some were delayed at Portreath for over a fortnight.

There were accidents, nine men being killed on December 8 1942 when a Hudson and a Beaufort flew into cliffs after take-off, but considering the difficult conditions, with inexperienced crews operating overweight aircraft, such losses were surprisingly light. The Germans naturally attempted to interfere with this traffic, and some aircraft were lost to their long-range fighters over the Bay. But many that did not arrive at Gibraltar or in North Africa made forced landings in Portugal. In an effort to provide some protection 400 (RCAF) Squadron, equipped with long-range Mustangs, detached six to Portreath during December but they were not very effective.

The first half of 1943 saw Portreath almost entirely committed to ferry operations, with 1 OADU despatching a steady stream of aircraft. Amongst the units which passed through were 23 Squadron with their Mosquitoes and the 44th, 93rd and 389th BG, USAAF. The latter move involved 124 Liberators en route to North Africa during June for the Ploesti oil refinery raids.

The Perranporth squadrons often used Portreath as well and in May the 78th FG brought in 46 P-47 Thunderbolts to add weight to the escorts provided for the continual bombing of Brest and other French western ports. With German fighter activity in the Bay area again causing trouble, two more Mustang squadrons, 414 and 613, provided detachments to escort Coastal Command aircraft through the worst areas. A new Sector Operations Centre was opened on Tregaea Hill in July, but it was little concerned with operations from Portreath which now mainly concerned coastal strike and anti-fighter operations over the Bay of Biscay using 143 and 235 Beaufighter Squadrons. They left in February 1944 but were replaced by 248 Squadron, newly equipped with Mosquito VIs, for fighter support to strike

Top *A 235 Squadron Mosquito VI makes a belly landing at Portreath in July 1944. In the background are other Mosquitoes, Blister hangars and Maycrete buildings* (B.H. Quelch). **Above** *The same Mosquito grinds to a halt on the grass at Portreath* (B.H. Quelch).

squadrons. Operations commenced late in February and on March 10 came the first real action when four Mk VIs escorting two Mosquito XVIIIs (6-pdr gun equipped) intercepted a German naval force a few miles off northern Spain. The ships were accompanied by ten Ju 88s and a number of individual combats ensued, resulting in the fighters destroying two '88s, while the XVIIIs attacked the convoy and also shot down another German aircraft—all without loss and very little damage.

No 248 Squadron was joined by 235 in April, the latter still flying Beaufighters, and they formed 153 (GR) Wing in 19 Group, Coastal Command, in readiness for D-Day. On April 11 the squadrons took on four ships and eight Ju 88s escorting a U-boat and in the battle two '88s were destroyed—for the loss of two Mosquitoes. Throughout May operations continued at a furious rate, reaching a peak on D-Day itself when 248 Squadron

mounted five separate missions. On the last of these ten Mosquitoes covered 31 Beaufighters on a *Rover* over the Bay of Biscay. Three destroyers were attacked by the Beaufighters and the Mosquitoes claimed an escorting Ju 188. Late in June 235 Squadron also received Mosquitoes and joined 248 on strikes and Beaufighter escorts off the French coast, from Brest to the Gironde river.

When the Royal Navy started operating in these waters the Mosquitoes had the additional task of looking after their air defence. In appalling weather on July 21, 235 Squadron was provided protection for a destroyer escort group off Ushant when glider bomb-carrying Do 217s were sighted. One was already under attack by another Mosquito (of ADGB) so the two Portreath-based aircraft intercepted the second, set it on fire before going after the other one, which blew up after several bursts of cannon fire.

Another four Do 217s carrying

Henschel 293 glider bombs were intercepted on August 9 by 12 Mosquito VIs of 235 and two XVIIIs of 248 during a Biscay patrol. Two were promptly shot down and the others damaged. The final sorties over the Bay were on September 7 but activity was now slight, and the coastal squadrons were transferred to Banff in Scotland, 153 (GR) Wing disbanding on September 18.

Portreath was left to the ASR squadrons and 1 OADU. The Warwicks, all capable of carrying a lifeboat, were transferred from 276 to 277 Squadron in November but remained at Portreath with a Walrus detachment of 275 Squadron— until February 1945 when both units left. Diversions of both Lancasters and Fortresses continued to be handled, but with the OADU the only flying unit now at Portreath, the station was transferred to 44 Group at the beginning of May. During that month over 200 replacement aircraft were delivered overseas and a Transport Command Briefing School was established.

The overland route to the Middle and Far East was now available and with Portreath unable to handle transatlantic traffic, movements rapidly declined. Following the move of 76 Squadron Dakotas to the Far East during August/September 1945, the OADU elements were transferred to St Mawgan. The Briefing School left on October 8 and the following day air traffic control was closed down.

In December the station was reduced to Care & Maintenance, transferring to Technical Training Command in July 1946 for use by 7 (Polish) Resettlement Unit. When this unit moved out the airfield was abandoned until taken over by the Ministry of Supply in May 1950 as a sub-station of the Chemical Defence Establishment. Then named Nancekuke, it was made inaccessible to the general public by high wire mesh fences and the closing of all approach roads. It remained the subject of secrecy and much local rumour until the CDE moved out in 1978 and after considerable discussion concerning its future was taken over by the Ministry of Defence as a GCI radar station. No 1 Air Control Centre arrived from Wattisham early in July 1979 and after a work-up period commenced operation early in 1980. The station was formally reopened as RAF Portreath on October 1 1980.

Predannack, Cornwall

SW685162. 2 miles S of Mullion on A3083

Intruding was always an exciting business but never more so than on the night of June 20/21 1943. Led by their CO, Wing Commander Allington, four crews of 264 Squadron set off from Predannack in their Mosquito NF IIs for Lake Biscarosse, south-west of Bordeaux. This was the home of 1 (F) 129 which flew the Bv 138 three-engined flying boats which were making a nuisance of themselves over the Bay of Biscay. Despite poor weather on the outward flight they found the base, shot down two Bv 138s in the circuit, and then set about other boats on the lake. Smoke and flame indicated some success but in the early dawn light it was difficult to make detailed claims. Confirmation came later that two Bv 138 and two of the huge six-motor Bv 222 flying boats had been destroyed on the water and hangars and other installations left on fire. All the Mosquitoes returned safely from an operation which made up for many earlier disappointments and put Predannack firmly on the night fighter map.

The airfield, built on the bleak Lizard peninsula using 780 acres of rough heathland, was opened in May 1941 as a satellite for Portreath. 247 Squadron arrived on June 18 and found things very primitive with most of the accommodation incomplete and the airfield a sea of mud and confusion. At first there was very little action for the Hurricanes but in August the squadron commenced sweeps over France. 247's first confirmed victory came in September when an He 111 was destroyed at night, but the main task remained intruder operations on which it was joined by 118 Squadron in December.

Accommodation had been a terrible problem during 1941 when the 'Polurrian Hotel' was used as an officers' mess and most of the personnel were dispersed in billets all over the peninsula. Good weather during the autumn enabled progress to be made with camp buildings, however, and in November the communual sites alongside the Helston-Lizard road were completed.

During the same month an unusual night fighter unit arrived. This was 1457 Flight which flew Havocs fitted with a Turbinlite searchlight in the nose, intended to illuminate the target while a single-seat fighter, in this case a Hurricane

Predannack on June 13 1967 taken by 543 Squadron. The helicopter landing spots on the runways used by Culdrose units can be plainly seen, but the airfield is basically as it was during the war (DoE).

of 247 Squadron, attacked it. The first operational patrol was made on January 29 1942, but the first contact was not until June 30 when a Ju 88 was illuminated, but evaded by stall turning. Another was contacted on August 4 but was again lost before the Hurricane could get into firing position. The use of another squadron to act as attacker proved unsatisfactory and a Hurricane Flight was added to the unit strength just before it became 536 Squadron and left Predannack.

The Luftwaffe also tried its hand at intruding, the first attack being made on October 12 1941 by a Ju 88 which followed a Beaufighter on the approach and shot up the airfield. On December 14 two aircraft on the airfield were damaged during another raid.

After several detachments at Predannack, 600 Squadron moved in completely during December for anti-shipping sorties and interception of reconnaissance aircraft. Numerous other fighter squadrons used Predannack as a forward base for *Rhubarbs* and bomber escort duties. The latter supported daylight operations against the *Scharnhorst, Gneisenau* and *Prinz Eugen* which absorbed 37 per cent of Bomber Command's effort between December 10 1941 and January 20 1942.

Three 1,000 lb (454 kg) bombs were dropped during January but caused no casualties or damage. Much more difficult to deal with was the severe weather which badly damaged some of the Blister hangars providing the only aircraft protection at Predannack. On March 7 a 600 Squadron crew found an He 115 floatplane just off Lizard Point and quickly despatched it, but things were not so easy for Pilot Oficer Harvey and Flying Officer Wicksteed (later a *Daily Express* columnist) on June 7 when they shot down an He 111 but were then forced to ditch after accurate return fire. They got themselves in a dinghy and finally reached Portreath beach under their own steam. 600 Squadron left suddenly for Church Fenton in September and was replaced by 406 (RCAF) Squadron which saw little action during its three-month stay, their Beaufighters being used mainly for search and rescue work.

The forward position of Predannack made it a natural place for emergency landings, and it provided a haven for many heavies during 1942. On October 20 a Liberator of 224 Squadron crash-landed after being damaged by its own depth charges during an attack on a U-boat. It burst into flames on touchdown but the crew were dragged out safely.

The geographical location of the airfield also resulted in it being used as a jumping-off point for North Africa during November/December 1942. The sheer volume of traffic overwhelmed the normal ferry despatch unit at Portreath and all the larger airfields in the south-west, however unsuitable, were pressed into service. Thus part of the 60th TCG, their C-47s carrying paratroopers, staged through on November 7, and the majority of the 81st FGs P-39s were refuelled at Predannack before the long flight across the Bay and around Spain and Portugal, made at the turn of the year.

Meanwhile a detachment of 263 Squadron Whirlwinds from Warmwell arrived for anti-shipping strikes. They had started using bombs in September and rapidly built-up a reputation on *Roadsteads*. In December 604 Squadron moved in for Bay patrols and 248, a special coastal Beaufighter squadron, also arrived to help combat the flak ships which were causing so much trouble to torpedo strike aircraft. Although the station remained in 10 Group during 1943 nearly all operations were maritime-orientated, and when a Wellington of 304 Squadron made a hasty landing on February 9 after being damaged by Ju 88s, four Beaufighters of 248 took off, chased the enemy and shot down all three.

No 141 Squadron, commanded by the famed Wing Commander Bob Braham, DSO, DFC, arrived with night fighter Beaufighters tasked with escorting shipping strikes, intruding and *Insteps*. Not overawed by this fighter presence, 248 continued to maraud over the Bay, destroying a Ju 88 on March 10 and an Fw

200 Condor two days later. After the first of these combats the Beaufighter suffered an engine failure but the Free French pilot, Lieutenant Maurice Guedj, flew it 200 miles (322 km) back to base—a considerable feat, for the number of aircraft lost due to engine failure far outweighed those lost by enemy action. There were other reasons too, high spirits or over-confidence leading to the loss of *X7751* of 141 Squadron on April 26 when it lost a wing after hitting a hut during an airfield beat-up.

No 263 Squadron's Whirlwinds returned for convoy patrols in March and in April 264 Squadron brought in the first Mosquitoes. They were used for shipping recce over the western approaches and on night *Rangers*, the sortie rate gradually increasing, 248 and 264 flying over 1,100 hours in May. Detachments from 307 and 456 Squadrons arrived in June as more and more *Insteps* wee flown to try and keep the Bay of Biscay clear of the Luftwaffe.

The increasing numbers of American bombers operating over France in daylight resulted in many unannounced visitors. Usually they arrived in ones or twos, but on May 1 1943 the 306th BG was badly mauled as they withdrew from St Nazaire and 15 B-17s put down at Predannack, three of them badly damaged and carrying dead and wounded. One of the aircraft of 423 Squadron received several hits with resultant fires in the radio compartment and the tail. Senior Sergeant Maynard Smith, finding his ball turret guns inoperative climbed out just in time to see two other gunners and the radio operator bale out. Smith, however, stayed to fight the fires, gave first aid to the badly wounded tail gunner, and even found time to fire the waist guns at Fw 190s still attacking the formation. Escaping oxygen fuelled the fires and ammunition boxes started to explode—he threw them out through a gaping hole—and for 90 minutes continued to fight the fires as the aircraft headed for the English coast. First Lieutenant Lewis P. Johnson put the badly damaged aircraft down at Predannack and the wounded were rushed off to hospital. A few weeks later Sergeant Smith was awarded the Legion of Honor—America's equivalent of the VC—the first to a living member of the VIIIth Air Force.

During 307's stay at Predannack HMS *Sheffield* was used as a radar picket ship to extend fighter control further into the Bay. It soon brought results, the Pole' destroying five and damaging six out of the 12 aircraft intercepted. Five crews of 618 Squadron, a special Mosquito unit, were posted in during October and were absorbed by 248 which had just received its first Mosquito XVIIIs. This was an anti-submarine version of the aircraft, equipped with a 6-pdr (57 mm) gun capable of punching a hole through a submarine's pressure hull. Operations with the aircraft started on October 24 and a fortnight later a U-boat was found on the surface. Several shells struck the base of the conning tower causing a rapid crash dive, but despite the good performance of the guns in service no submarine was sunk by the 6-pdr during 248 Squadron service.

Other changes made late in 1943 resulted in Typhoons of 183 Squadron arriving at Predannack to roam over the Brest peninsula, and Mosquito IIs of 157 replacing 307 on shipping patrols over the western approaches. They soon drew blood, claiming a Ju 290 four-engined maritime reconnaissance aircraft on November 20, together with one of the four Ju 88s escorting it. Eleven days later three Ju 88s were shot down for the loss of a Mosquito and crew. But with the New Year came bad weather and a reduction in activity, both 157 and 183 Squadrons leaving soon afterwards.

The runways were extended during 1943 and this enabled continuous operation by larger aircraft. 304 Squadron moved out of Davidstow Moor in December and spent nearly three months operating Wellington XIVs from Predannack. Bad weather reduced U-boat sighting opportunities but during January 1944 the squadron destroyed one of the three attacked. The Leigh Light Wellingtons were replaced by Liberators of 311 (Czech) Squadron in February. They were equipped with rocket projectiles for operations against U-boats making the final run home on the surface. Unfortunately the enemy was now extremely cautious and opportunities to use this specialised equipment were few.

No 151 Squadron brought its Mosquito XIIIs from Colerne in March and started shipping attacks during which its total score reached 100 aircraft on April 11 when seven German aircraft were destroyed for the loss of two Mosquitoes. At the end of April 1944 Nos 1 and 165 Squadrons formed a Spitfire IX Wing at Predannack for *Instep* operations designed to catch Ju 88s attacking

shipping in the south-west. They were frequently scrambled but communications delays prevented any interceptions. Shipping recces were also flown and on May 19 resulted in a strike being mounted on four merchantmen off Ushant. The Spitfires escorted coastal Beaufighters and tried to draw the flak as the attack went in. One destroyer escort was sunk and two merchantmen were damaged for the loss of two Beaufighters.

In May the Leigh Light Wellingtons of 179 joined 311 Squadron and invasion rumours grew stronger as the month progressed. The Spitfire Wing was ordered to give continuous cover to a convoy assembling near Falmouth on June 4 and were amazed to see the size of it. For the next two days it continued to grow, and at dawn on the 6th eight 1 Squadron aircraft on their way to Brittany found themselves over a never-ending stream of ships—the invasion was on. During the following week operations were hampered by low cloud but several road convoys were strafed and, with the Luftwaffe noticeably absent, the Spitfires were armed with 500 lb bombs and sallied out to attack radar installations on the French coast. On June 15 they attacked shipping in St Peter Port, Guernsey, before leaving for Harrowbeer four days later.

Both 179 and 311 Squadrons were fully occupied with *Cork* patrols, designed to block off the English Channel and Irish Sea to U-boats. On the evening of the invasion 15 U-boats left Brest but an hour later *U-415* was attacked by a Wellington of 179 Squadron and badly damaged. Unable to dive she limped back to Brest with *U-256*. They were luckier than the *U-955* and *U-970* which were sunk during the night by other 19 Group aircraft.

The U-boat war moved away from the Channel area in the summer of 1944 and with it went 179 and 311 Squadrons. 152 (GR) Wing was disbanded on September 7 and Predannack became a rest and re-equipment base for fighter units. The first cusomters were 264 and 604 Squadrons of 142 Wing which arrived late September from the Continent. They left early in December and 33 and 222 Squadrons flew in to convert from Spitfires to Tempest Vs.

From a peak strength of 3,600 the numbers had again dropped to below 2,000 and nearly everyone was accommodated on the base. In February 1945, 349 (Belgian) and 485 (RNZAF)

Squadrons started re-equipment with Tempests but serviceability problems delayed the work-up so much that the latter unit was given Typhoons and then sent back to the Continent in April with Spitfires!

VE-Day was celebrated at Predannack without any flying units, but immediately afterwards the Mosquitoes of 151 and 406 Squadrons returned. With the abrupt end of the war against Japan 406 disbanded, leaving 151 to linger on until the end of May 1946 when it left for Exeter. Meanwhile the Battle of Britain display on September 15 produced over 4,000 visitors to this isolated station. They were treated to the usual varied display including a flypast by nine Mosquito XXXs of 151 Squadron returning from a mass formation over London.

On June 1 1946 the airfield was reduced to Care & Maintenance parented by Exeter and it seemed certain that it would soon be returned to heathland. It did indeed lie abandoned for several years, but its very isolation was the reason for rekindled interest. Barnes Wallis had been conducting experiments with variable geometry models for Vickers and Thurleigh and by 1951 was ready for more extensive testing, including free flight. Predannack was selected and a launching track built across the airfield alongside 06/24 runway. Trials were due to start in September 1947 but constant delays were experienced with the *Wild Goose* test vehicles and launching gear and it was not until April 1952 that a flight was made. Control dificulties resulted in the model hitting a building and being wrecked, but tests continued and altogether 31 powered flights were made, at least one by an updated version, the *Swallow*, before Vickers stopped work on the project. Predannack was abandoned in October 1954.

Four years later, with helicopter training expanding at Culdrose, a relief airfield was needed and Predannack proved ideal. It was taken over by the Fleet Air Arm on December 15 1958 for elementary training of helicopter pilots away from the main airfield. The 06/24 runway was cleared and resurfaced in 1971 to enable fixed-wing aircraft to land and several were flown in for the RN Fire Fighting School which was established on the airfield.

The airfield is still in use by Culdrose, a new administrative block and control tower having been built in recent years.

Evidence of the wartime airfield abounds, with shelters and crumbling dispersals visible on the eastern side of the A3083, and a mixture of derelict and refurbished buildings on the airfield side. Some of the latter are in use as holiday villas and self-catering chalets, while another houses the Hervan Road riding stables.

Roborough (Plymouth), Devon

SX503605. 3½ miles NE of Plymouth off A386

The Allied collapse in France during June 1940 threw Fighter Command plans into confusion. Suddenly the south-west of England was in the front-line and the ports, especially the naval base at Devonport, in real danger from air attack. The newly-formed 10 Group desperately searched for airfields, and with Exeter already overloaded their choice fell on the small grass airfield at Roborough (Plymouth Airport). Suitable aircraft were another problem, solved by taking over the Gladiators of the Sumburgh Fighter Flight on the Shetlands. They started the long journey south on July 23, became 247 Squadron on arrival, and were operational as a dockyard defence force on August 13 with 12 aircraft, some of which were kept at St Eval.

Roborough was first used for flying in the autumn of 1923. The original Plymouth aerodrome at Chelson Meadow had proved unsuitable and Roborough Polo Ground was rented for an experimental service between Plymouth, Birmingham, Manchester and Belfast. Unfortunately it did not attract enough customers and was soon closed down. Some years later the Plymouth & District Aero Club started using the same field and when the Corporation decided to open a civic airport Roborough was chosen. The polo ground and adjoining fields were purchased, and the aerodrome was officially opened on July 15 1931. Great Western Railways started a regular air service to Cardiff in April 1932 and were quite successful, but in common with most internal services closed for the winter. Railway Air Services became the major operator, later joined by a number of small airlines, including Jersey Airways.

The RAF used Roborough for the occasional exercise and communications flight from 1935 onwards and in June 1939 15 Group Communications Flight formed there with single examples of

Above *Gladiator* N2306 *of 247 Squadron at Roborough in 1940.* **Below** *Night fighter Hurricane of 247 Squadron dispersed in front of houses on the north-west side of the grass airfield in 1940. The houses are still there alongside the A386.* **Bottom** *Chipmunks of the Royal Naval College Air Experience Flight lined up at Roborough in October 1978. The bungalow to the right in the background is also in the Gladiator photo.*

Magister, Vega Gull and Envoy plus two Walrus amphibians.

With the outbreak of war scheduled passenger services ceased and the airfield was requisitioned by the Admiralty, later becoming part of HMS *Drake*. Communications flights increased and in November No 2 AACU started using landplane Sharks to tow targets for the Gunnery School at Devonport. This continued until April 1940 when the Shark detachment moved to St Eval and Roborough then saw little activity until the arrival of the Gladiators late in July. August was fairly hectic for, in addition to 247 Squadron, a detachment of Lysanders from 225 Squadron, Tilshead, was carrying out daily dawn and dusk coastal patrols for the Army's Southern Command. They covered the coast from Lyme Regis to St Eval looking for signs of unauthorised landings—the invasion scare was at its height. At the end of September 225 was replaced by 16 Squadron whose Lysanders combined the coastal patrol with air-sea rescue in the English Channel. It was the start of a long, but intermittent, association with 16 Squadron for the rescue detachment continued until taken over by 276 Squadron in October 1941, and the airfield was still being used in 1942 for Lysanders taking part in live shoots on the Okehampton ranges.

Meanwhile, 247 Squadron had its first combat on October 28 when Pilot Officer Winter intercepted an He 111. Nine days later the same pilot claimed an He 111 damaged, but following replacement by Hurricanes in December there was little action and the squadron HQ moved to St Eval in February 1941, leaving a detachment at Roborough. The airfield was awkward for Hurricanes and when Portreath became available in May 1941 the whole squadron moved there.

With the formation of HQ 19 Group, Coastal Command, at Mount Batten, its communication flight replaced the 15 Group unit on February 14 1941. In the following June 2 AACU returned, now equipped with Hectors and the odd Gladiator, but easily the biggest aircraft seen at Roborough during the war was Fortress I *AN523* which made a crash landing on the airfield after repeated attacks by seven Bf 109s on August 16 1941 during a raid on Brest. When the fighters broke off, some 30 miles (48 km) from the south coast, it had the starboard outer on fire, flaps inoperative, ailerons damaged and the bomb doors drooping.

The aircraft overran, hit a tank trap, broke up and was destroyed by fire.

In May 1942 Roborough was transferred from Admiralty to Air Ministry control, parented by Mount Batten, but it made little difference to activity on the airfield—the towing by the AACU still being concerned with the Gunnery School. C Flight, 2 AACU, became 1623 Flight in February 1943 with Gladiators, Defiants and Battles. There was supposed to be a Roc available for dive bombing demonstrations, and in September this duty was taken over by two Barracudas, a very unusual aircraft for an RAF unit to have on strength. 1623 Flight became 691 Squadron in December 1943 when Hurricanes and Oxfords arrived for gun-laying exercises, while Defiants continued to drag drogues up and down the ranges. The squadron finally left in February 1945 but a detachment of No 3 Armament Practice Camp remained with Martinets until the following May.

With the end of the war in Europe activity rapidly declined. 19 Group Communications Flight remained, now using Ansons and Dominies and 82 Gliding School was formed for ATC flying.

Civil flying resumed in 1946, the airport being operated by the Plymouth & District Aero Club (Straight Corporation) on behalf of the City Council. In addition to flying training, the club carried out some charter work using a Messenger, and later a Gemini. Jersey Airlines began services into Plymouth in April 1952 using DH Rapides and other companies tried their luck with schedules to Roborough but they were usually shortlived.

Early in 1961 the Britannia Royal Naval College Air Experience Flight was formed at Roborough to provide flying for Dartmouth officer cadets and to grade those aspiring to become pilots in the Fleet Air Arm. Operated by Airwork Services Ltd, the Flight used Tiger Moths until replaced by Chipmunks in 1966, and these are still current. Airwork also took over the operation of the airport which was modernised by the building of a restaurant and clubhouse to join the old hangar built in 1931. The contract was transferred to Brymon Airways on May 1 1975, and as their services built up they transformed Roborough from a backwater into the centre of a network embracing Cork, the Channel Islands, Morlaix, Cherbourg, Exeter, Newquay and the Scillies.

In the meantime, the Air Troop of 41 Commando, RM, arrived in April 1967 with three Sioux helicopters. They moved into a new hangar opposite the airport terminal and were joined by 45 Commando in an adjacent hangar during December. Both units spent a lot of time on detachment and room was found for three Sioux of Air Troop 95 Commando Light Regiment, RA, in August 1968. Further rapid changes saw 8 (Interim) Squadron AAC and 666 Squadron based here for short periods but they had all left by early 1972 when the Marines started to use heli-pads at their Coypool base just to the south of Roborough.

Since the arrival of Brymon many changes have been made at Roborough. The old air traffic tower, precariously perched on the roof of a hangar, has been replaced by a smart wooden building, more hangarage has been built and most important, a 2,480 ft (756 m) SW/NE tarmac runway has been laid, complete with lighting. The increased activity, currently involving Twin Otters and the Dash 7 four-engined STOL airliner, has resulted in a proliferation of prefabricated buildings which unfortunately has reduced the view from the public enclosure drastically—but on the other hand there is now something to see.

Rollestone, Wiltshire

SU088439. 1 mile E of Shrewton village

Another of the nebulous collection of small airfields on Salisbury Plain, this grass strip was closely associated with the much older Rollestone Camp on the other side of the B3086 road.

The War Office site had been in existence since No 1 Balloon School, Rollestone Camp (Larkhill), was formed in July 1916 to train personnel in the use of observation balloons. The unit survived the wholesale cuts in the Services of 1919-22 and, renamed the RAF School of Balloon Training, continued in operation throughout the 1920s and most of the 1930s. For many years the balloons, usually two Type R of 35,000 cu ft capacity, were kept in Bessoneaux hangars, but these large canvas structures were easily damaged by strong winds and in 1932 a large double shed was completed, capable of holding two inflated balloons.

Things changed little at Rollestone, except names, for it became No 2 Balloon

Training Unit and transferred from 22 to 24 Group, Training Command, in December 1936. The unit moved to Cardington on February 1 1939 when additional accommodation was built and the camp reopened in June as the RAF Anti-Gas School.

This unit provided anti-gas training for specialist RAF personnel and all unit and flight commanders throughout the war. A number of grass fields between the A360 and B3086 were requisitioned at the beginning of the war, graded to produce a landing ground, and used from September 1939 by aircraft to spray exercise gas on the courses under training. Initially the aircraft were provided by 1 FTS Netheravon, supplemented by the Special Duty Flight at Boscombe Down and the Chemical Defence Experimental Station, Porton. From March 1940 the spraying was carried out exclusively by the latter units, but 1 FTS continued to use the LG for night flying, the ground personnel being transported from Netheravon prior to each session—an unpopular duty!

Early on May 12 1941 an enemy aircraft dropped eight bombs on the LG and then made a low run over the camp area, and was engaged by a machine-gun post. No damage was done except to windows which were shattered.

The spraying of chemicals from aircraft was to provide trainees with experience of gas warfare under realistically simulated conditions. The problem was that the wind, notoriously strong on Salisbury Plain, tended to disperse the gas too quickly. The solution was truly Heath Robinson in concept. A canvas screen said to stretch the full 4,500 ft (1,371 m) length of the LG, some 60 ft (18 m) high and of wedge-shaped cross section, was built alongside the farm track from Rollestone village to Middle Farm. This amazing structure was intended to deflect the wind and appears to have worked for it was retained until late 1942 and possibly into 1943. Then the Glider Pilot Exercise Unit started using Rollestone as a LG until it was put under Care & Maintenance in August.

With the end of the war in Europe the size of the anti-gas course dropped dramatically and in October 1945 the unit moved to Sutton-on-Hull to amalgamate with a fire-fighting training school. The same month the LG was put back into operation and used by AOP Austers, 657 Squadron arriving on December 16 and remaining for six weeks.

Rollestone again reverted to C&M and the LG closed on July 25 1946. The camp was transferred to the Army and they still use it, little changed from its wartime state, with the balloon shed towering over dreary lines of wooden Handcraft huts. Postwar, some flying from Austers and Beavers has taken place, but from a strip to the east (SU096454) not the wartime LG which has reverted to farmland.

St Eval, Cornwall

SW873685. 6 miles NE of Newquay

Even the usually taciturn Group Captain was rushing about clutching the attack photographs. For during the night of June 8 1944 the crew of Liberator *224/G* had sunk two U-boats in the space of 22 minutes; and had the evidence on film. Captained by Flying Officer K.O. Moore, the crew were on a *Channel Stop* sortie patrolling between the Scillies and Ushant looking for U-boats trying to attack the mass of shipping crossing from England to France. Suddenly the radar operator reported a contact 12 miles ahead. In bright moonlight the pilot slowly descended the aircraft and at three miles a surfaced submarine was sighted. As the Liberator ran in to attack it came under fire which was returned. At 50 ft (15 m) a stick of six 250-lb depth charges was dropped as the aircraft tracked over the target. It was a perfect straddle, three charges on either side, and the submarine was seen to break up amongst the explosions.

Jokingly, Moore said, 'Now let's get another one', and they did just that! 20 minutes later the radar operator picked up a contact six miles away. Again they ran in, sighting a small U-boat at 2½ miles. It was a duplicate of the first attack, with the same results. St Eval remained an operational station for all the 20 years it was open. There were many successes during that time, but none more outstanding that this double kill.

When the RAF Expansion Schemes of the 1930s started, the planners rightly concentrated on the development of fighter and bomber operations. But with the Anson general reconnaissance aircraft entering production, thoughts turned to the needs of the newly-born Coastal Command. To provide anti-submarine patrols around the Cornish peninsula an airfield was needed and during 1937 a number of possible sites were surveyed. The choice finally fell on the parish of St

Eval though it was not without opposition for the destruction of a small hamlet was involved and it was rumoured that the church would also be demolished. In fact it remained a landmark, and survived to become the centrepiece of the station badge. The airfield was designed as a standard Expansion Scheme station, accommodating two general reconnaissance squadrons. It was to have four large 'C' Type hangars on the eastern side with adjacent barrack blocks, administrative and technical buildings, and a large married quarter area.

Work started in 1938 and by September 1939 the airfield area had been cleared of dry stone walls and foundations for the hangars laid. The contractors had made little progress with the station buildings, however, and wooden huts soon sprouted all over the place in the usual haphazard fashion. As soon as a few huts were complete, RAF personnel started to move in and St Eval officially opened on October 2 1939 when Ansons of 217 Squadron arrived from Warmwell. They quickly became a familiar sight as they plodded their way out to sea on convoy protection and anti-submarine patrol work. They were joined by a unit called 6 Coastal Patrol Flight. Equipped with ex-civil Hornet Moth biplanes, they were used to discourage U-boats from surfacing close to the coast—virtually the same job as their forebears, the DH 6 and DH 9 did from neighbouring Padstow during 1918. They also had little better performance, and their engines turned out to be just as unreliable!

Meanwhile Whitleys from Bomber Command arrived on short detachments. With a far greater range and capable of carrying much heavier loads, the Whitley was potentially a tremendous improvement on the Anson but suffered from a lack of role experience amongst the crews, and aircraft unserviceability. The latter had long since lost the bloom of youth.

Dual control Beauforts heralded a role change for 217, but training on these torpedo bombers lasted many months while the Ansons continued their monotonous patrols around the convoys. With the fall of France fighters appeared at St Eval, Spitfires of 234 Squadron giving inshore convoy protection from the Luftwaffe. Much stranger shapes appeared on June 20 when a Farman 222 and a Potez 540 landed. They were followed in July by several Martin

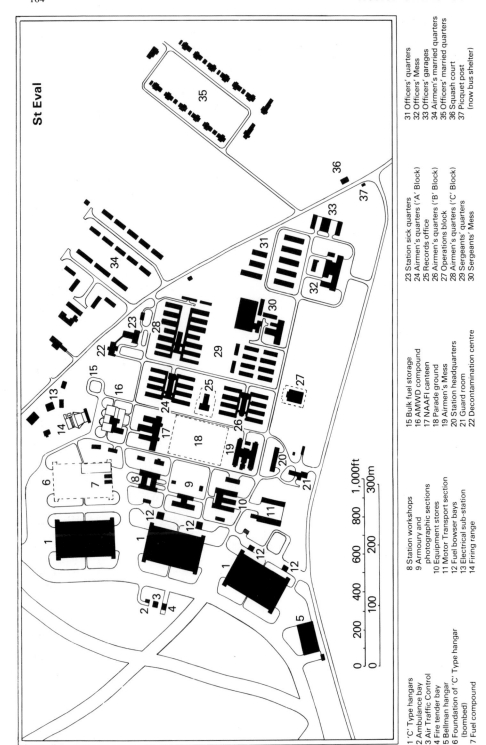

St Eval

0 100 200 300m

0 200 400 600 800 1,000ft

1 'C' Type hangars
2 Ambulance bay
3 Air Traffic Control
4 Fire tender bay
5 Bellman hangar
6 Foundation of 'C' Type hangar
  (bombed)
7 Fuel compound

8 Station workshops
9 Armoury and
  photographic sections
10 Equipment stores
11 Motor Transport section
12 Fuel bowser bays
13 Electrical sub-station
14 Firing range

15 Bulk fuel storage
16 AMWD compound
17 NAAFI canteen
18 Parade ground
19 Airmen's Mess
20 Station headquarters
21 Guard room
22 Decontamination centre

23 Station sick quarters
24 Airmen's quarters ('A' Block)
25 Records office
26 Airmen's quarters ('B' Block)
27 Operations block
28 Airmen's quarters ('C' Block)
29 Sergeants' quarters
30 Sergeants' Mess

31 Officers' quarters
32 Officers' Mess
33 Officers' garages
34 Airmen's married quarters
35 Officers' married quarters
36 Squash court
37 Picquet post
  (now bus shelter)

167 bombers, all carrying escaping Frenchmen.

The Admiralty were very concerned about the German Navy's use of the Biscay ports and two Spitfires of the PRU were sent down to carry out daily photo runs over the ports, especially Brest. This soon became a very dangerous occupation, for the Germans were quickly aware of these regular visits and determined to stop them. Various strange colour schemes were tried, to merge the Spitfires into the sky including green, white and pink before the standard PRU Blue was universally adopted.

Increasing air activity by the Germans forced 234 Squadron to start night flying, but the Spitfire was quite unsuitable, and after several accidents they were replaced by Hurricanes of 238. Shortly after a sector operations room was established on the station, a series of air raids started, a hangar being destroyed on August 21. The next night the Luftwaffe came again and scored a lucky hit on the pyrotechnics store. The result was startling, all manner of flares and rockets exploded, and the bomber crew must have thought they had destroyed the station.

Little damage was done on the night of August 26/27 because a dummy flarepath had been lit on the Q site, some three miles to the north-east, the area around the decoy being subjected to attack for several hours. No defence was offered against this raid but Bofors and machine-gun positions were now in place and arrangements made for a detachment of black-painted night fighter Hurricanes of 247 Squadron to be flown in each evening from Roborough.

Work on runways, two of 3,000 ft (914 m) and a main one of 3,600 ft (1,097 m) was begun in the spring of 1940 with flying going on around the construction. These improvements were not a moment too soon for great difficulty was already being experienced with heavier aircraft because of a soft strip across the middle of the airfield.

During the autumn the airfield was used as a forward base for attacks on Biscay ports, even the Ansons of 217 Squadron being thrown in against barges assembled at points along the French coast. In December 217 Squadron completed conversion to Beauforts and the aircraft was soon engaged in bombing, sea mining and anti-submarine work; practically anything except its intended torpedo bombing function.

That St Eval was a thorn in the side of the Reich was made evident by constant references to its imminent destruction by Lord Haw Haw in his broadcasts from Germany. With the completion of the runways and construction of the 'C' Type hangars well advanced, almost nightly attacks, using one or two aircraft, started in January 1941. On the 25th one of the seven 250 kg bombs dropped scored a direct hit on a shelter near the watch office and 21 were killed. As the attacks intensified hotels and guest houses in the area were requisitioned and as many as possible lived off the airfield. 'Watergate Bay Hotel' later became RAF property and was used for many years by St Eval, first as an officers' mess and later as married quarters.

The inshore convoy patrols were forcing the Germans to use long range Fw 200 Condors to attack shipping further out to sea. A detachment of 263 Squadron Whirlwinds arrived in February 1941 to attempt interceptions of this dangerous adversary, but it was not very successful because of navigational problems and aircraft unserviceability.

The presence of the German capital ships in Brest harbour caused increasing anxiety at the Admiralty after PRU photos on April 5 showed that the *Gneisenau* had left dry dock. It was decided that a torpedo strike should be attempted by the recently arrived 22 Squadron, on the following day. The CO, Wing Commander F.J. St G. Braithwaite, could only provide six crews, and of these only three were properly torpedo-trained. The operation started badly for heavy rain had swamped St Eval and two of the bomb-carrying Beauforts got bogged. The one that did get off lost his way in heavy cloud, as did one of the torpedo carriers. The other two, flown by Flight Lieutenant Hythe and Flying Officer K. Campbell, reached Brest and waited for the bomb explosions which were the signal for their attack, unaware of the other aircrafts' problems. As it became light Campbell decided to go in alone and made a near perfect approach and attack, dropping his torpedo as he crossed the mole of the inner harbour. The flak started as he turned away and he was hit immediately, the aircraft falling into the harbour. The *Gneisenau* was severely damaged and eight months later was still under repair. When news of this gallant effort filtered through to London in March 1942 Campbell was posthumously awarded the

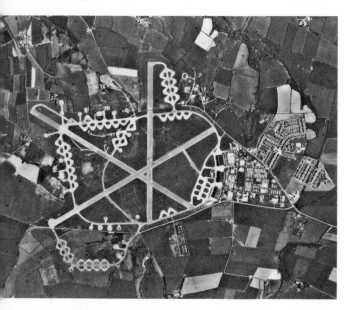

The steady enlargement of St Eval over the years can be seen in this photo taken on June 13 1967 (DoE).

Victoria Cross.

Two particularly heavy raids in May resulted in the destruction of three Blenheims and damage to over a dozen other aircraft. The officers' and sergeants' messes were virtually demolished and two hangars were so badly damaged that canvas Bessoneaux units were set up inside the shells.

Meanwhile the effectiveness of the aircraft at St Eval continued to increase. Hudsons of 206 Squadron scoured the Bay of Biscay to find targets such as blockade runners for the Beauforts of 217, who were again joined by 22 Squadron in October 1941. They managed to torpedo a large tanker off Cherbourg, but at the end of the year 22 Squadron was warned for overseas, the strength of the strike force being maintained by the arrival of 86 Squadron. 206 was relieved by 224 Squadron, and in January 1942 502 arrived with Whitleys to fly anti-submarine patrols.

This was the scene in February when the daily PRU sorties over Brest indicated that the *Scharnhorst* and *Gneisenau* were about to break out. The problem was— which way would they go, into the Atlantic or up the Channel? The C-in-C Coastal had both possibilities covered with *Stopper* patrols and on February 9 all leave for the strike Beaufort crews was cancelled and six experienced 22 Squadron crews were recalled to St Eval to help man the 13 serviceable aircraft. 19

Group was ready, but even the best-laid plans have flaws. During the night of February 11/12 a Hudson on *Stopper* was intercepted by a Ju 88 and forced to switch off the ASV radar during evasive action. When switched on again it did not work. The aircraft returned to base, the crew changed aircraft and went back on patrol but bad weather had forced the early return of another aircraft on the barrier, and yet a third was scanning in the opposite direction for the vital few minutes when the crew might have spotted the ships. They had slipped out of harbour under cover of darkness and remained undetected for 12 hours. By this time the St Eval strike force was wrong-footed.

With the threat to the Atlantic convoys from U-boats reaching a new peak in the spring of 1942, 53 and 58 arrived at St Eval and in August the first detachment of 10 OTU Whitleys arrived. Flown by student crews whose inexperience made their effectiveness suspect, these aircraft were better than nothing, and certainly prevented the U-boats from spending much time on the surface. The OTU was involved in many incidents, inevitable with newly trained crews on a busy operational station. In retrospect, one of the more amusing occurred while a Supply Dropping Unit was on detachment at St Eval, also with Whitleys. An OTU crew accidentally took one of their aircraft for a bombing exercise and on reaching the

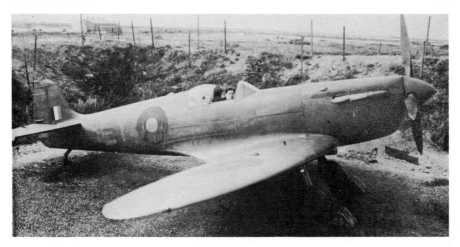

Top *PRU Spitfire at St Eval in August 1941 with the gymnasium in the background* (M.C.B. Anderson). **Above** *St Eval would not be complete without its famous church— or without a 224 Squadron Liberator during the latter stages of the war.*

range opened the bomb doors, and released the stores. The area was deluged with a strange variety of articles, from machine-guns to tinned food. The crew were surprised by the result of their efforts, and later considerably shaken to find that a full scale invasion alert had been called.

B Flight of the PRU became A Flight of 543 Squadron in October 1942 but continued to maintain a wary eye on activities in Western France. During the same month Liberators of the 409th Squadron, 93rd BG, USAAF, arrived from Alconbury to gain experience in the anti-submarine role. This was the start of an influx of American units, the 409th being replaced after a month by the 1st Anti-sub Squadron (Prov), USAAF. A second squadron arrived early in 1943, both leaving for North Africa in March 1943, having achieved one definite kill *(U-519)*.

The invasion of North Africa in November 1942 produced a tremendous strain on the whole station, with up to 72 aircraft on the airfield at times. To relieve the pressure most anti-submarine aircraft were detached to Beaulieu and Holmsley South, but continued to use St Eval as a forward base. By the end of the year things had settled down and 502 Squadron, now with the very successful GR Halifax, returned, followed by 58 Squadron in March 1943.

In July the 479th Anti-submarine Group (4 and 19th Squadrons), USAAF, arrived on the station with Liberators, but just a month later they were replaced by a series of US Navy patrol squadrons using the PB4Y-1 version of the Liberator. As in 1942, the Americans used the opportunity to work with 19 Group to gain experience, but they were also a valuable addition to the AS forces over the Bay at a time when the U-boats were again a serious threat.

Extensions and improvements to the airfield by Canadian construction engineers during 1943 did nothing to reduce the hump in the main runway and it remained the reason for many heavy landings and several accidents. One of the worst occurred just before the last 10 OTU detachment left in August 1943. A Whitley on take off collided with a Liberator which was taxying across the runway, hidden from view until the 10 OTU aircraft reached the top of the rise. The Whitley caught fire, the depth charges cooked and finally went off with a tremendous explosion, destroying both aircraft.

During September very hush-hush GCA equipment was moved in from Davidstow Moor for trials which were successful, though cut short when it left for Hinton-in-the-Hedges at the end of October. Meanwhile the installation of FIDO had been approved and work went ahead throughout the winter. Although having twice the capacity of other installations, it was still not able to cope completely with the combination of low stratus and high wind which characterises Cornish coastal weather. The first operational use was by a Wellington of 304 Squadron which made a single-engined landing in April after diversion from Chivenor.

The station started 1944 with three Liberator squadrons, 53, 224 and 547, in residence, some of the aircraft fitted with Leigh Lights. 206 Squadron joined the Wing in April and as D-Day approached the number of patrols increased, 5,135 operational hours being flown from St Eval during June, resulting in 14 U-boats being attacked and three sunk.

Activity in the area decreased as the Germans abandoned their Biscay bases and by the end of September all four Liberator squadrons had moved north. They were replaced by 282 Squadron, equipped with ten Warwicks carrying airborne lifeboats. During this slack period the runways were resurfaced, 282 spending most of October at St Mawgan, and when the station reopened 179 Squadron moved in with Wellington GR XIVs, soon replaced by the troublesome Warwick GR Vs. In March 1945, 304 (Polish) Squadron joined 179 and they carried on patrols after the end of the war in case any U-boats had not received, or chose to ignore, the surrender message.

The Polish unit left in July but was replaced by the Liberators of 224 Squadron, and during the same month 282 was disbanded, its SAR task taken over by 179 Squadron. The roomy Liberators were stripped of their operational equipment and used for trooping from India at the end of the Japanese war. In February 1946, 179 Squadron received its first Lancaster IIIs and on June 1 was split in two, Y Flight becoming 210 Squadron. With continued retrenchment 179 Squadron was disbanded in September and the following month 224 relinquished its much-loved lend-lease Liberators, receiving Lancasters instead.

No 203 Squadron arrived from Leuchars in January 1947 and despite difficulties with continual changes in personnel, the three Lancaster squadrons settled down to their peacetime role, the major task being SAR with meteorological flights and fleet exercises thrown in for good measure.

During the early spring a joint RAE/Vickers team arrived at St Eval with a Mosquito B XVI and started trials on transonic rocket models which lasted for 18 months. They were intended to test the aerodynamics required for flight above Mach 1 and had been developed to replace the cancelled Miles M52 piloted test vehicle. A range was established off the Scilly Isles and the Mosquito took off with the first model slung under its belly on May 30 1947. Unfortunately the model was lost when the aircraft inadvertently flew through thunderclouds and succeeding tests were also unsuccessful until the very last on October 9 1948, which resulted in a speed of 1.38 Mach being attained.

Meanwhile, 224 Squadron had been temporarily disbanded in November 1947, and the other squadrons found it difficult

Cierva C.30A radar calibration autogiro over a bomb-blasted 'C' Type hangar at St Eval in August 1941 (M.C.B. Anderson).

to maintain their tasks due to a serious shortage of personnel. Despite this some overseas exercises were successfully completed though by the end of 1951 the Lancaster, always a stopgap maritime aircraft, was overdue for replacement.

This started at St Eval in November 1951 when the newly formed 220 Squadron arrived from Kinloss and their Shackleton MR 1s took up residence near the Station Church. 42 Squadron re-formed in June 1952 followed by 206 in September, and when 203 and 210 Squadrons left for Topcliffe, St Eval was completely Shackleton-equipped.

For some time the station had been one of the 12 Master Diversion airfields, always open to receive aircraft diverted by weather or emergency. These varied from 40-odd Canberras diverted one afternoon from Lincolnshire, to large civil airliners when Heathrow fogged in. The civilian passengers were always a problem, some being accommodated in Newquay hotels, but latecomers had to make do with the floors of the NAAFI and Officers' Mess.

More married quarters were completed early in the 1950s and the patch took on the appearance of a small town, though the usual facilities were missing, the present Post Office/Store and the NAAFI being the only shops. The latter was extended to become one of the first NAAFI Social Clubs in the country.

As more experience was gained on the Shackletons, their activities were extended and they made many overseas flights, especially after the introduction of the Mk 2 aircraft, the first of which joined 42 Squadron in January 1953. All three squadrons provided three aircraft and crews for the Coronation Review flypast over Odiham in July 1953, the complete 18 aircraft element operating from St Eval. For one rehearsal and on the day 20 Shackletons lined up and took off in stream—an unforgettable sight—and noise!

In April 1954 a reorganisation took place which resulted in 42 Squadron being fully equipped with the Mk 2 while 206 and 220 soldiered on with the Mk 1s. The Wing was completed by 228 Squadron which re-formed on July 1 and received new Mk 2s. After trials by 42 Squadron had proved that up to 33 troops could be carried—albeit in great discomfort—every available Shackleton was sent to Blackbushe in January 1956 for Exercise *Encompass*, the uplift of 1,200 troops of the 16th Parachute Brigade to Cyprus to combat EOKA terrorists. Yet more roles were discovered for the aircraft when 42 Squadron became a colonial policing unit which involved training in medium-level bombing, and 206 Squadron provided two aircraft for the atomic bomb trials from Christmas Island. They ferried stores and flew meteorological flights.

In December 1956 220 Squadron moved to St Mawgan in preparation for the Shackleton Mk 3 which was considered too heavy for operational flying from St Eval and, at the beginning of 1957, 42 Squadron commenced the colonial policing role in the Middle East. On January 10 1958, 206 Squadron followed 220 to St Mawgan and the rundown of St Eval was really underway.

When 42 Squadron returned to the United Kingdom in September it was transferred to St Mawgan and St Eval was closed down on March 6 1959, the disbandment parade of 228 Squadron being held on the same day. The airfield reverted to Care & Maintenance, the quarters being retained for St Mawgan-based personnel.

The Air Training Corps used the airfield for winch-launched gliding until 1964 but then two of the taxiways became public roads and for some years the runways were a popular rendezvous for learner drivers. They were also used as motor cycle and car race tracks while the grass areas reverted to farmland. In recent years, however, most of the airfield has been fenced in for Ministry use and the racing has ceased.

The single remaining hangar and the church are visible on the skyline for miles. The latter has been a landmark since the 15th century, a welcome sight to seafarer and aviator alike. It contains many items of aviation interest including numerous wall plaques from squadrons which have served at St Eval, the last ensign flown from the station, and a rough wooden cross which once marked the grave of a Shackleton crew member who lost his life in a crash in the Far East.

Hudson of 233 Squadron landing on Runway 02 at St Eval in August 1941 (M.C.B. Anderson).

St Just (Lands End), Cornwall

SW375292. 5 miles W of Penzance

Considering the desperate need to push fighter cover out into the south-west approaches during 1940-41, it has always been a mystery to the writer why Lands End Airport was not used for Hurricanes, or even Spitfires. A flat grass field, it had adequate runs in most directions and, although prone to sudden weather deteriorations, its record was no worse than anywhere else on the north Cornish coast.

Its history goes back to 1935 when Captain Olley of Olley Air Services saw the possibilities of a regular air service between the Scilly Isles and the mainland. He purchased some ground between Sennen and St Just later in the year and made several proving flights using twin-engined Dragons during the next 18 months. The field was opened as Lands End Airport in September 1937 and a scheduled service using a Westland Wessex monoplane started by Channel Air Ferries. This cut the four hours taken by the *Scillonia* ferry boat to 20 minutes, and during the summer months was a great success.

During 1939 the Great Western & Southern Airlines was formed to operate the service and, using two DH Dragon aircraft, they steadily increased the number of schedules. On May 5 the service was extended to Plymouth and Bristol, three days before Western Airways started a Swansea-Barnstaple-Newquay-Penzance (St Just) route. All the services were suspended on September 3 but the need for quick communication between the Scillies and the mainland soon became evident and the short sea leg was reopened, the only internal air service in the south of the country. During the winter of 1939-40 the frequency was reduced to three flights per day, resulting in one Dragon being withdrawn and used for searchlight co-operation flights from St Just. Unfortunately, poor night flying facilities forced the authorities to find another base for *G-ADDI* early in 1940 although, as the military installations on the Scillies increased, so did the demand on the service, resulting in the remaining Dragon sometimes flying ten return flights in a day.

Military aircraft landed occasionally, amongst them 16 Squadron Lysanders during their anti-invasion coastal patrols

Lands End Airport (St Just) soon after the war. The hangar on the left is now used for the construction of flying replicas.

from Roborough, while an Army exercise in April 1941 resulted in A Flight moving in to provide air co-operation.

On June 3 1941 the Dragon *G-ACPY* disappeared after leaving St Mary's for St Just and was presumed to have been intercepted by a Luftwaffe aircraft. The service was immediately suspended, reopened in October, but then stopped by the Air Ministry on November 4. The airport was closed and the landing area obstructed with chicken coops and poles until the end of the war, though a B-17 is reported to have crash-landed there on September 16 1943. In May 1945 the Great Western & Southern resumed normal services on the route with Dragon Rapides, these aircraft continuing in service when British European Airways absorbed the company and the route on February 1 1947. They flew the ageing Rapides until they were replaced by Silorsky S-61N helicopters in 1964. These moved to the new heliport at Penzance in May 1964 and the revenues of St Just took a steep dive.

The Lands End Aero Club took over the running of the airfield and, with additional revenue from gliding courses, managed to keep the enterprise financially viable. In August 1971 Westward Airways (Lands End) was formed and application made for scheduled services to the Scilly Isles. The licence was not granted, however, and in January 1972 the company purchased a Rapide and used it for parachute drops and pleasure flying. *G-AIYR* became the last DH 89 to fly commercially in the United Kingdom, continuing in operation until withdrawn and replaced by a Cessna 172 in 1978.

The appearance of St Just aerodrome has hardly changed since its early days, and the original hangar often contains surprising objects—a World War One

A DH 89A of BEA gets airborne at St Just in 1953. The buildings are still there but modified in appearance by an ATC tower (Aeroplane).

fighter, or even a Schneider Trophy seaplane. These are replicas of the aircraft, lovingly constructed to order by Mr Vic Bellamy's small team of engineers. Several of the machines now at Thorpe Park were built and flown at St Just, and a peep through the windows of the hangar alongside the road may be very rewarding. In recent years the Flying Club has undergone a revival in its fortunes and it now holds an annual open day which is well attended—definitely worth a visit.

St Mary's, Scilly Isles

SV922104. 1 mile E of Hugh Town

When the red flare went up there had only been time to refuel one of the six Hurricanes. Pilot Officer I.J. Badger climbed into the CO's aircraft and was off. About five miles away he sighted an He 115, which immediately made off south. Despite violent evasion by the floatplane, Badger got on its tail and fired four short bursts from close range. The He 115 turned steeply and dived into the sea. The Hurricane pilot landed back at St Mary's just a quarter of an hour after the alert and within a couple of hours of 87 Squadron's arrival on the Scilly Isles. There can rarely have been such a quick return from the opening of a new fighter base.

The first military aircraft in the Scilly Isles were floatplanes and flying boats which operated from Port Mellon and Tresco during the First World War on

Top *Hurricane 1s of 87 Squadron at St Mary's on the Scilly Isles. The table in the foreground is supported by a propeller case and the tent is the pilots' rest room* (via N.L.R. Franks). **Above** *The famous Dragon G-ADDI of the Great Western and Southern Airlines close to the passenger reception at St Mary's.*

anti-submarine patrols. Occasional visits were made by other flying boats during the 1920s but it was not until 1929 that the first landplane touched down—on the golfcourse! The same fairways were used for the first scheduled air service between Penzance (St Just) and St Mary's, which started on September 15 1937. Operated initially by a Wessex and later by Dragons of Channel Air Ferries, the service was timed to connect with the 'Cornish Riviera Express' train at Penzance.

In 1938 the Duchy of Cornwall leased some land to the east of Hugh Town to a newly formed company, Great Western & Southern Airlines. They took over the route early in 1939 using the same Dragons. Following the outbreak of war the service was one of the few in the British Isles which was maintained, the twin-engined Dragon biplanes plodding back and forth with amazing regularity, despite the often appalling weather and poor conditions at St Mary's, where the aerodrome had a steeply sloping surface and a maximum run of about 1,350 ft (411 m). It was difficult enough in wet conditions for experienced pilots of Great Western but the plan to extend fighter coverage by detaching Hurricanes there seemed bizarre in the extreme.

However, after preliminary practice on a marked strip on their airfield at Charmy Down, six Hurricanes of 87 Squadron, led by the CO, Squadron Leader Ian Gleed, successfully flew in during the evening of May 19 1941. The squadron was soon ready for action, connected by telephone to observation points around the islands. It came on the 24th when the CO and

Sergeant Thorgood were the duty pilots. They were returning empty-handed when a Do 18 flying boat suddenly appeared directly ahead of Gleed. Both pilots fired at it and saw it crash into the sea.

But not every intruder was reported, and it was assumed that Dragon *G-ACPY*, which disappeared between the Scillies and St Just on June 3, was the victim of one. The service was suspended until October, reopened for a few days, but again stopped on November 4 by the Air Ministry.

At this stage the facilities on the airstrip were minimal with the groundcrew living in tents by the dispersals on the south side of the field, while the pilots were accommodated in Hugh Town. Long-range tanks were fitted to give the Hurricanes more time on patrol but after the initial successes little happened until July 18 when an He 111 was destroyed. On August 16 a Ju 88 was shot down but, although further interceptions continued at intervals, boredom crept in. To relieve this some Army Co-operation exercises with local troops were carried out in January 1942. Unfortunately one pilot flew too low and hit HT cables—the first RAF casualty on the islands.

In April 1942 the detachment became 1449 Flight, retaining six Hurricanes, six pilots and 33 groundcrew. Enemy activity remained low but the Flight was often engaged in escorting crippled RAF and USAAF bombers. It also decided to improve the airfield and work started on a tarmac extension at the easterly end of the main grass strip. A building programme resulted in the construction of a Blister hangar, wooden watch tower, HQ block and three Nissen huts, all near the original civil terminal. These were ready for occupation in October 1942 when most operations were in support of Walruses of 276 Squadron engaged in rescue work. The few interceptions of German aircraft proved inconclusive.

On August 12 1943, whilst escorting the RMS *Scillonia*, a Hurricane hit the foremast and crashed into the sea, but even more spectacular were the attempts at emergency landings by large aircraft on the still very inadequate airfield. The first of these was a Whitley V of 10 OTU with engine failure—it overshot and crashed on January 27 1943. Just over a year later a battle-damaged Liberator tried a landing, but skidded into a wall and the pilot was killed, though his crew of eight survived the impact.

Following the landings in Normandy, the war moved away from the Scillies and on September 17 1944 1449 Flight was disbanded. A week later St Mary's was reduced to Care & Maintenance parented by Portreath and at the end of the year became the responsibility of the Air Ministry Works Department.

In June 1945 Great Western & Southern Airlines restarted scheduled services to the Scillies using camouflaged Dragon Rapides. During the same year Island Air Services was formed at St Mary's with two Proctors, but this soon foundered and it was British European Airways which took over the route in 1947 and operated the airport until August 1949 when the Ministry of Transport & Civil Aviation became responsible. A control tower and improved terminal facilities were then provided and the number of passengers on the route steadily increased. The journey from Penzance to St Just remained a deterrent, however, and as soon as a practical helicopter became available BEA started a direct Penzance-St Mary's service. This was in May 1964, since when the annual passengers carried has doubled. A number of other operators have tried services to St Mary's, notably Mayflower, Westward and Brymon. The latter company has made a success of it, flying Islanders and now Twin Otters from Plymouth and Newquay.

With a smart new terminal building and control tower opened in 1975 and daily services throughout the year by equally smart S-61N helicopters, St Mary's seems assured of a steady future. Like the whole of the Scillies it is well worth a visit—especially if you go by air.

St Mawgan, Cornwall

SW870646. 3½ miles NE of Newquay

The small airfield of Trebelzue (qv), perched high on the cliffs above Watergate Bay, proved a disaster. It was operationally unusable and soon after Ferry Command took it over as No 2 Overseas Aircraft Despatch Unit the C-in-C took a major decision—to completely rebuild it by taking more land further inland and constructing new runways better orientated in direction and very much longer. The new airfield engulfed the hamlets of Trenoon, Deerpark and Mawgan Cross, and cut the access road from St Columb to Watergate Bay.

Work started in 1942 and was sufficiently advanced by February 24 1943

Above *St Mawgan in 1945 seen from the east. In the background are the old runways of Trebelzue which were used as dispersals* **Below** *Spitfire PR XIs of 541 Squadron at St Mawgan in 1944, on detachment from St Eval (J. Olver).* **Bottom** *Seen from the rear turret of a Lancaster GR III in September 1952, St Mawgan was still in its wartime state with the perimeter track dividing the tower and Building 2 from the technical site (via Chaz Bowyer).*

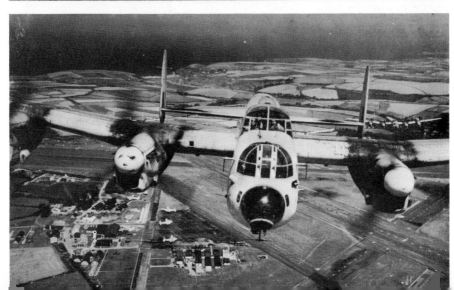

for the name to be changed to St Mawgan. At this time a detachment of Henleys from 1 AACU, Cleave, was using the old Trebelzue runways and a small ferry overflow from Portreath was being despatched, mainly Beaufighters and Wellingtons. They were joined by a detachment from 297 Squadron, Thruxton, which arrived during May for field exercises. They lived under canvas or in their Horsa gliders, using their own equipment and rations. But there was little general activity until June when personnel of the 491st Base and Air Base Squadron, Air Transport Command, USAAF, arrived and took over a large Secco building alongside the ATC tower. The first of the new runways was opened on July 1 and the first landing made by a B-24 Liberator, followed closely by a B-17. A month later the other runways were in use and Trebelzue became a parking area. There was a tremendous increase in movements, the list of aircraft despatched to North Africa during August, September and October for the USAAF alone making St Mawgan one of the busiest airfields in the country.

During October the unit was informed that two USAAF Met Flights with eight B-17s would be accommodated for three months. They arrived on November 5 and during the same month 2 OADU deliveries started to slow down, this being offset by arrivals from the States which steadily increased, and BOAC/KLM who started to operate some of their Whitchurch schedules through St Mawgan. After 2½ weeks the USAAF Met Flights departed amid general relief, for the transit aircraft were using all available dispersals. During December there were two nasty accidents involving Liberators. On the 21st a USAAF B-24 crashed two miles east of St Columb, killing four, and seven days later a war-weary PB4Y-1 of the US Navy went over the cliffs and into the sea after a fully loaded take-off en route to the States. The 13 'tour-ex' crew and passengers were killed and five USAAF men from St Mawgan lost their lives when they were cut off by the incoming tide during a brave rescue attempt.

In February 1944 the last of the personnel still accommodated at Trebelzue were moved to St Mawgan sites but an increasing number of hotels in Newquay were taken over to provide transit facilities. The arrival of 169

American aircraft during February 17 alone, requiring beds for 600, gives an indication of the size of the problem. During March the hardstandings on St Mawgan were taken over from the contractors, and work on the extension to the main 32/14 runway was completed in May together with a new control tower, operations room and met section. The airfield was at last without major construction work for the first time since it opened.

Meanwhile the first southbound Transport Command passenger service had left on March 1 and the station was just settling down to a steady traffic flow, with enough dispersals and accommodation, when a Warwick of 525 Squadron on the Port Natal/Algiers service crashed into the sea after take-off, killing all 16 passengers and crew. With routes across France open again BOAC moved its services to Hurn on November 1 but the total movements for the year still amounted to a staggering 16,110. At the end of 1944, 1529 (Radio Aids Training) Flight re-formed at St Mawgan with six Oxfords, the first unit to provide training on the SBS51 Instrument Landing System. Installed by the Americans, the ILS at St Mawgan was one of the first in the country.

Several large-scale Bomber Command and VIIIth Air Force diversions were handled during 1945 for St Mawgan and the other smaller coastal airfields in Cornwall were regularly the only open airfields in England during the last winter of the war. With the collapse of Germany St Mawgan became Transport Command's No 1 Diversion Centre and the UK departure point for heavy aircraft reinforcements to the Far East. At the same time USAAF aircraft started to return to the States and another mass movement in June 1945 was that of 165 Lancasters of 6 Group, RCAF, on their way home to Canada. During July No 1 Air Traffic School opened and in August the USAAF handed over their facilities at St Mawgan to the RAF at the end of a very efficient Allied combined operation. The next month Portreath closed and its traffic was transferred to St Mawgan, many of the aircraft used to rebuild the French Air Force being despatched at this time.

With the completion of such deliveries, the traffic level declined. In July 1946, 16 Lancasters of 35 Squadron arrived from Graveley on the first leg of their flight to the American continent. They returned at the end of August after a very successful tour of the USA and Canada and proved to be the highlight of the year. The airfield was reduced to Care & Maintenance on July 1 1947, and quickly fell into disrepair.

In 1949 local rumour suggested that St Mawgan was to be reopened for Convair B-36 operations and it was later confirmed that the airfield was being retained by the Air Ministry and that the public roads through the station might have to be closed. The Plymouth Aero Club operated pleasure flights during the 1949 season using the western end of the main runway and in 1950 the use of the airfield included a weekend service by Fingland Aviation from Manchester. This enterprise was quite successful but at the end of the season the Air Ministry told Newquay Council that the airfield was to reopen for military operations and that the civil facilities could no longer be provided.

In the face of much local opposition St Mawgan *did* reopen in April 1951, but not for B-36s. An advance party from the newly formed School of Maritime Reconnaissance arrived and flying started in June using Lancaster GR 3 aircraft though only the bare minimum of airfield and domestic services were available. The school was joined by the Air Sea Warfare Development Unit and later by 744 Squadron, FAA, which were also engaged in development work. The station was still in a terrible state, the refurbished Nissen and Secco huts barely weatherproof, and during the first winter personnel had to be moved into Newquay hotels because their accommodation was condemned.

No 22 Squadron was the first to be permanently based here, the HQ arriving from Thorney Island in June 1954. Their Whirlwind helicopters were serviced at St Mawgan but operated by detached Flights and it was June 1956 before the two operational aircraft of A Flight started SAR work from St Mawgan.

The year 1956 was one of change for the station. At the end of September the S of MR disbanded, its task taken over by the Maritime Operational Training Unit at Kinloss, and in December maritime squadrons arrived. These were 220 and 228 Squadrons from St Eval, the former soon re-equipping with the first Shackleton MR 3s which required the longer runways at St Mawgan for operations at maximum weight. 206

Squadron moved in from St Eval to become the second Shackleton MR 3 unit, supplanting 228 in January 1958, and the build-up continued with the formation of 1360 Flight during the same month. A few weeks later they became 217 Squadron and took their Whirlwinds to the Far East late in 1959.

Small civil aircraft started to use St Mawgan and late in 1959 Starways Ltd of Liverpool made arrangements to start summer tourist services. This was the start of a long series of attempts by various companies to run viable services to and from Newquay. Most failed but by 1962 the number of passengers had outgrown the RAF facilities and Newquay Council persuaded the Air Ministry to allow the construction of a small terminal on the north side of the airfield, near the village of Carloggas. The arrival of British Midland Airways on the scene in 1969 started a decade in which civil operations into St Mawgan finally stabilised, particularly following the take-over in 1977 of their London-Newquay route by Brymon Airways.

Meanwhile, 220 became 201 Squadron in October 1958, and 42 moved over from St Eval during the same month to establish St Mawgan as the premier operational station in 19 Group, Coastal Command. A Flight of 22 Squadron moved to Chivenor in November and the station then settled down to its surveillance task covering the south-west approaches and Atlantic areas. In addition many overseas detachments were made for operational, humanitarian and goodwill reasons and St Mawgan's Shackletons could be seen in almost any part of the western world. With the closure of St Eval came confirmation of a long-term future for St Mawgan. Plans were made for the replacement of many dilapidated wartime buildings, the work starting in 1962, and the airmens' Dining Hall was opened in June 1963 followed by most of the other major buildings on the station, both domestic and technical.

Changing priorities brought a requirement to strengthen the air maritime forces in Scotland. In March 1965, 201 Squadron moved to Kinloss, followed by 206 in July and in the opposite direction came the MOTU with its Shackleton T4s. No 42 Squadron stayed in the south and on July 14 1966 was presented with its Standard by Her Majesty the Queen. She opened the new officers' mess at the same time.

The large hangar which dominates St Mawgan was built for the Nimrod, the first of which arrived in October 1969 to enable the newly re-formed 236 OCU to start the task of converting Shackleton crews.

On May 1 1970, 7 Squadron was re-formed with various versions of the Canberra to provide targets for Army and Navy units all over the country. 42 Squadron was re-equipped with Nimrods in April 1971, sharing its aircraft with the OCU under a centralised servicing system, though at times various aircraft have carried the squadron badge on the tail.

One of the major airfields in the country, St Mawgan has a 24-hour, 365-day a year Master Diversion task and enjoys a reputation for being open when most of the country is weatherbound. Conversely, its location means that it sometimes suffers from a phenomena all its own—gale force fog! Only a few old buildings, incuding a couple of hangars, remain at St Mawgan, but the flavour of wartime accommodation can be experienced by anyone—by a visit to Treloy Farm Tourist Camp. This uses many of the buildings of a dispersed site on the approach road to the RAF station, with the interiors brought up to modern comfort standards.

At the end of 1981 the Canberra-equipped 7 Squadron was disbanded, and during 1982 the OCU was due to move to Kinloss, leaving just 42 Squadron based at this large airfield.

A good view of the flying at St Mawgan can be gained from the civil airport, and another popular spectator spot is the western end of the main runway where the ground is slightly higher than the airfield and there is some parking space.

St Merryn, Cornwall

SW889714. 3 miles SW of Padstow

In 1937 a small aerodrome was developed on a site at Treginegar, St Merryn, under the direction of W. Rhodes Moorhouse, a famous name in aviation circles. By October a large hangar had been built and the 52-acre field was being promoted as Cornwall's first public airfield—though in practice it was little used.

During 1939 the site was surveyed by the Admiralty and in December the original airfield and adjoining fields were acquired and work commenced on St Merryn Naval Air Station. Contracts were signed for the laying of four 3,000 ft (914 m) runways, diversion of roads and the erection of four hangars. The airfield commissioned on August 10 1940 as HMS *Vulture*, four months after the first aircraft had landed—a Shark from Roborough which mistook St Merryn for St Eval! 792 Squadron was formed with Rocs and Skuas as an air target-towing unit, and 774 Squadron arrived from Evanton with Swordfish and Rocs to provide telegraphist air gunner training. These two units were the main occupants of St Merryn until late 1943, but a series of front-line squadrons spent short periods for work-up training. Accommodation was a major problem and hotels at Padstow, St Merryn and Harlyn were requisitioned, while the sick bay was established at Woodlands, Treator, near Padstow.

It was not long before the Luftwaffe showed interest in the airfield, a Bf 110 causing slight damage on October 3, two Do 215s bombing on the 9th and two He 111s machine-gunning the camp on the 14th. On November 11 an He 111 made a low-level attack, badly damaging two hangars and injuring two people.

Fighter units appeared early in 1941 with 809 Squadron forming with Fulmars at St Merryn on January 15 and 801 arriving from Hatston four days later. The latter was intended for dive bombing attacks on shipping in the Channel and a daylight assault on the *Scharnhorst* and *Gneisenau*, while these ships lay in the port of Brest. The Skua crews included many untried pilots and practice attacks on targets off Trevose Head from St Eval

HMS Vulture *(St Merryn) being rebuilt in 1944 with a Mainhill hangar under construction* (FAA Museum).

Above *Seafire IIcs of 895 Squadron at St Merryn in 1943. Behind is a Skua of a Fleet Requirements Unit* (R.K.L. Yeo). **Right** *Barracudas, Avengers and Swordfish of 736 Squadron on their dispersal at St Merryn, and well supplied with Mains hangars* (FAA Museum).

showed they had little chance of hitting the ships. Wisely the operation was called off.

After a lull of several months the Luftwaffe returned in April 1941, a low-level attack causing some damage, while on May 5 in the worst raid experienced by St Merryn, six bombers dropped HE and incendiaries, damaging 22 aircraft and injuring two ratings.

By the middle of 1941 the unit was entirely devoted to fighter training, operational squadrons disembarked from carriers spending about a month on air-to-air and air-to-ground gunnery. Amongst them was 809 Squadron which disembarked from HMS *Argus* after helping to fight through the famous Malta convoy of August 1942. At St Merryn they became the first FAA squadron to be specially trained on Army Co-operation work, this involving some flying with an early form of napalm—probably more of a hazard to the user than the opposition. Another unit was 897 Squadron which arrived from Lee with ten Seafires on May 5 1943 for an air firing programme and two weeks' work-up—a typical schedule.

Meanwhile, 748 Squadron formed in October 1942 to operate as a Fighter Pool for Seafire pilots, and the following year the airfield was virtually rebuilt to accommodate the School of Air Combat. This involved the construction of numerous Mains hangars, additional office and domestic accommodation and the lengthening of the main runway. The school started work in September 1943, 736 Squadron arriving from Yeovilton as the flying element, initially with Seafires and Masters, but later receiving Fireflies and the odd Barracuda. The school was responsible for all fighter combat training and also commenced courses for weapons specialists known as air combat instructors. As the task expanded, new specialised training squadrons were formed, 719 for weapon training, 709 for ground attack work and 715 as an additional air combat unit.

During 1944 another rebuilding programme got under way and by August an imposing new ATC tower was nearing completion and two 'T2' hangars were among the many new structures. The work was largely complete by April 1945 and thus, as on so many other airfields, it was never fully utilised.

In December 1944 the emphasis had changed and training concentrated on

Pacific Ocean operations, the students being given the benefit of experience gained by the FAA and USN during the initial offensive against the Japanese. The unit was renamed School of Naval Air Warfare and 719 Squadron was disbanded. The types of aircraft became even more varied, however, for the school was now responsible for strike and torpedo squadron training as well as fighters. These intensive courses continued right up to the end of the war with Japan. St Merryn then suffered a period in limbo but it was decided that the range facilities were too good to waste and 725 (Fleet Requirements Unit) and 748 (Fighter Pool) Squadrons arrived in September 1945. They did not last long, however, and it was left to 736 Squadron to keep the flag flying, joined by 741 (Operational Flying Training) Squadron in July 1946, both units equipped with Seafires. In November 1947 the Telegraphist Air Gunner School was re-established at St Merryn with 796 Squadron as the flying unit, equipped with Firefly FR 1s and Barracuda IIIs.

The School of Naval Air Warfare was still operating, but now concentrated on the specialised training of potential squadron commanders and senior pilots. This course lasted three months and was one of the most intensive and competitive in the Navy. The flying was designed to bring students up to date on gunnery, rocket-firing, bombing and tactics, while the ground school dealt with flying operations and strategy. In March 1948 the school went to Culdrose and merged with the Naval Air Fighter School. It was replaced by the Air Armament School in June, this unit taking over most of the equipment of the Air Gunnery School, Whale Island. The new school trained both ground and air officers and ratings, the Air Weapon Officers also flying with 736 Squadron.

In February 1950, just as the Sea Fury started to replace the Seafire, 736 Squadron moved to Culdrose, thus ending 6½ years affiliation with St Merryn. During the early 1950s the new RNVR squadrons started using St Merryn for their annual weapons training. Some 50 Seafires from the three RNVR squadrons flew in during June/July 1951 and carried out extensive cannon, rocket-firing and dive bombing training on the ranges. The largest, 1832 Squadron, sent 24 aircraft and fired 470 rockets and more than

45,000 rounds of ammunition during their two-week stay.

Air Weapons Officer courses ceased in 1952 and the Air Armament School closed down. 796 Squadron had become rather unwieldy and in February 1952 the Barracuda element was hived off as 750 Squadron, the two units remaining at St Merryn as No 2 Operational Flying School. These Barracudas proved very unreliable and the course schedule was only maintained by the introduction of four Ansons while awaiting Sea Princes, the first of which was delivered in February 1953. Firefly T7s re-equipped 796 Squadron in April and at last the unit had a full set of new aircraft which it took to Culdrose starting in November as part of *Solitaire*, the rationalisation of the Fleet Air Arm.

The station was paid off as HMS *Vulture* on October 14 1953 but was immediately renamed HMS *Curlew* and the School of Aircraft Maintenance arrived, followed by the Naval Air Ordnance School from Yeovilton. Both trained naval ratings in the artificer trades. 750 Squadron moved to Culdrose in March 1954 and after little more than two years both technical schools moved out and the station was placed on Care & Maintenance in June 1955 while a decision was made on its allocation to another service. It finally closed as a naval base on January 10 1956.

Newquay Council was still looking for a satisfactory site for an airport and expressed interest in using St Merryn but on December 8 1955 the Air Ministry announced that the station would be reopened early in 1956 as a training camp for the RAF Regiment, and the regional depot in place of Watchet. In fact neither of these plans materialised any more than a proposed take-over by the Army in 1959, and in October 11 Main hangars and 63 acres were sold, the start of the disposal of the whole site.

In the 1960s parts of the old airfield and buildings were developed into a holiday camp while the majority returned to agriculture. A light aircraft was kept in one of the buildings and occasionally flew at weekends, but there was little aerial activity for more than 20 years. Then in 1979 a number of home-built single-seat autogyros started flying, but were soon in trouble with local residents because of the noise they made. Greater local sympathy was expressed when the Cornwall

Parachute Centre moved in during May 1979. They applied for planning permission for the use of an airstrip and buildings at St Merryn for their Cessna 182, and after some delay this was granted. Regular parachuting took place during the summer of 1980 when a Spitfire was also being rebuilt in one of the old hangars.

Part of the old airfield is fenced off for flying and a large number of buildings are in use for farming purposes. Others are owned by a plant hire firm and the bases of dismantled hangars are used by a caravan site. St Merryn can be visited with permission, but beware the 'sleeping policemen' on the entrance road—they are vicious!

Sandbanks, Dorset

SZ044877. 3 miles SW of Bournemouth

A small marine base was established during 1940 by the Admiralty on the north-west side of Sandbanks, the narrow promontory which forms the eastern side of Poole Harbour. It was commissioned as a satellite of HMS *Daedalus* (Lee-on-Solent) on May 15. A single hangar, capable of accommodating 14 folded Walrus amphibians, was erected and a concrete apron extended down below the waterline for use as a slipway. The only other facilities were an electrically driven winch, 1,000-gallon fuel tanks and a small workshop.

Operations commenced as the Basic

Above *Walrus of 765 Squadron coming up the slipway at Sandbanks in May 1942* (via R. Sturtivant). **Below** *A 765 Squadron Seafox approaching the Sandbanks slipway in May 1942* (via R. Sturtivant).

Seaplane Training School (otherwise Seaplane Training Part I), 765 Squadron moving in from Lee in June 1941 with Walrus amphibians which were usually moored inside the harbour. Occasionally, however, they were beached on the sea side of the peninsula (SZ045875) and used Poole Bay for flying operations. The squadron later received a number of Vought Kingfisher floatplanes which were also flown from Sandbanks, pilots then going on to Lawrenny Ferry to complete Seaplane Training Part II.

During July 1943 700W Flight was formed with six Walruses at Sandbanks and four Swordfish at Lee-on-Solent. Its purpose was described as 'Special Service' which is vague enough to cover most things. It moved to Machrihanish at the end of the month.

The congestion in Poole harbour, used by the RAF and BOAC flying boats as well as shipping, made training difficult and as soon as alternative arrangements could be made 765 Squadron was disbanded and the Fleet Air Arm paid off Sandbanks on October 15 1943.

Shrewton, Wiltshire

SU076460. 1 mile N of Shrewton

A large, roughly triangular, field, the relief landing ground at Shrewton was first used in July 1940 by the Harts, Hinds and Audaxes of 1 SFTS, Netheravon. The school was very busy and on a good day that summer the air was filled with the sound of Kestrels (the Rolls variety) buzzing round the circuit. They were joined in 1941 by Battles which used the field for night flying, it having a much better surface than the very undulating home base a few miles to the north-east.

Army Co-operation units also used Shrewton, the Lysanders of 16 and 225 Squadrons being regular visitors during exercises with the Army. In June a detachment of 225 Squadron Lysanders carried out night flying, and the whole unit was in residence during July while Tilshead underwent repair. Inevitably, training pressures and night flying from a gooseneck flarepath brought a spate of accidents. Though wasteful and occasionally spectacular, as on November 11 1941 when two Battles crashed on the RLG in separate incidents, there were remarkably few fatalities or serious injuries.

The new year brought great changes to Salisbury Plain and its airfields. The Glider Pilot Regiment was formed in January 1942 and the Glider Exercise Unit, soon renamed 296 Squadron, moved into Netheravon and its Hector tugs and Hotspur gliders became the main users of Shrewton RLG in April when 1 SFTS was disbanded.

The first unit actually based at Shrewton was the Heavy Glider Conversion Unit which formed on June 29 1942. To be equipped with Whitleys and Horsas it was quickly obvious that Shrewton was unsuitable for the HGCU and its stay was very short. It moved to Brize Norton before any aircraft had been delivered! Meanwhile it was becoming apparent that it was no use training pilots, dispersing them to Army camps on Salisbury Plain for months on end, and then expecting them to fly safely on operations. Continuation flying was required and so the Glider Pilots Exercise Unit was formed in August 1942. Shrewton reverted to its old use as a night flying RLG—with Hinds and Hectors again towing Hotspurs. A tragic accident in November, resulting from a tow rope break at low level, killed Colonel Rock, one of the most forceful glider protagonists. There were other accidents, but the piloting standard improved.

No 43 OTU brought in its Austers from Larkhill in November but during the following month it was decided to develop the airfield. The Night Flying Flight of the GPEU moved to Chilbolton, and on December 21 1942 Shrewton was handed over to the Air Ministry Works Directorate.

Three Blister hangars were built along the north-eastern boundary of the field and Laing put up timber barrack huts and a combined ranks' mess on an adjacent site. Shrewton reopened as an emergency landing ground in March and was used for Horsa landing practice and demonstrations. When Army Co-operation Command disbanded on June 1 1943, the airfield was transferred to Fighter Command, but it was little used until taken over by 38 Group and brought up to a full RLG standard during the summer. The GPEU then returned, the Tiger Moth Flight in October, followed by Masters and Hotspurs in November. The unit was renamed the Operational & Refresher Training Unit in March 1944 when the HQ moved to Hampstead Norris, leaving the Tiger Moths at Shrewton until the Flight disbanded on

November 11 1944.

With the end of the war Shrewton was put on Care & Maintenance parented by Netheravon. Though virtually abandoned in April 1946, it was retained as an ELG for 38 Group for some years and was occasionally used by A&AEE Boscombe Down when carrying out trials on the Larkhill ranges. It is now a large grass field with no sign of its wartime use except a few foundations by the road in the north-east corner.

Staverton, Gloucestershire

SO887218. 3 miles NE of Gloucester

The present Gloucester/Cheltenham Airport is the progeny of an airstrip opened at Down Hatherley by the Cotswold Aero Club in September 1932. It proved impossible to extend this field and when proposals for a public aerodrome were put forward they concerned ground on the other side of the main Cheltenham-Gloucester road, then the A40. The Gloucester and Cheltenham councils finally agreed to a joint purchase of 160 acres in March 1934 and work started on the site the following November. An operating licence was received on November 18 1936 and its first scheduled air service started when Railway Air Services called in on their Birmingham-Bristol route.

With the RAF expansion in full swing, the Air Ministry became interested in the airport during 1937. After lengthy discussion it was agreed that they could use the airfield for training purposes for 12 years in return for improvements to the facilities. The cost of adding 25 acres was investigated and the Air Ministry provided night flying equipment and erected buildings for its planned reserve flying school.

No 31 E&RFTS, operated by Surrey Flying Services, was formed on September 29 1938 with Tiger Moths. It was joined by the Airwork Civil School of Air Navigation in May 1939. This unit moved in from Shoreham to provide elementary training for RAF observers using Dragon Rapides. A month earlier Rotol Ltd had established a Flight Test Department on the airfield, a Wellesley arriving on April 17, the first of nearly 90 aircraft, ranging from Gauntlets to Halifaxes, which flew on Rotol trials during the war.

The Airwork organisation became 6 Civil Air Navigation School on August 6 and with war imminent 31 E&RFTS

closed down to provide aircraft for other schools and to allow more room for the navigators. The airport was officially renamed RAF Staverton on September 10 1939 and soon afterwards the main unit was renamed 6 Air Observer Navigation School. By the end of 1940 most of the Rapides had been replaced by Ansons which flew 2½-3-hour exercises, each aircraft carrying three students who each did a leg navigating, map reading and taking bearings under the control of the staff pilot. A staff wireless operator kept in touch with base and assisted with bearings if the aircraft became lost.

On August 3 1940, 2 EFTS arrived from Filton and Tiger Moths became a familiar sight flogging round the Staverton circuit. With the demand for instructors reaching a peak in 1941 the EFTS became 6 (Supplementary) FIS in November and Staverton continued to be alive with Tigers until they moved to Worcester in April 1942.

Meanwhile, Folland Aircraft's flight test department had been instructed to leave the south coast and with components being manufactured in Cheltenham they chose Staverton, arriving at the end of 1940 and sharing a hangar with 6 AONS. Their main task concerned the Folland 43/37 series of engine testbeds, one of which disintegrated near Gloucester, the pilot parachuting to safety. They were joined by Gloster who established a flight test centre in 1941 to relieve the strain on Brockworth, and it was soon possible to see as many as 60 aircraft in primer paint lined up awaiting their first flight.

No 6 AONS continued to expand, having 63 Ansons and 240 pupils by the summer of 1941. It had outgrown Staverton and from August established detached Flights at Moreton Valence and Llanbedr. The main servicing load was still carried at Staverton, however, aircraft being allocated to Flights as required by the task. Yet more title changes occurred, it becoming 6 Air Observer School on January 17 1942 and 6 (O) Advanced Flying Unit 18 months later. From June 1942 it was completely RAF-manned.

Flight Refuelling Ltd was the next manufacturing company to arrive. During 1942 they shared a hangar with Folland but in 1943 moved into a new Bellman which enabled them to work on their larger aircraft under cover. They were responsible for a whole series of

Opposite page, top to bottom *Staverton viewed from the south-east on April 29 1941. The main technical site is on the northern perimeter with the Rotol works on the far side of the Gloucester-Cheltenham road* (IWM). *A Hurricane with an experimental four-blade propeller under test at Staverton* (Dowty-Rotol). *Lancaster* ND648 *of Flight Refuelling at Staverton in 1945* (Flight Refuelling Ltd).

interesting experiments including anti-icing tests, flame-damping, self-sealing tank development and the towing of fighter aircraft by Wellingtons to explore the practicality of ferrying them to Malta in this fashion. But they also continued work on the loop-line system of flight refuelling and after years of disinterest by the Air Ministry suddenly received a contract in February 1944 to develop equipment for 600 Lancaster tankers and 600 receivers—required for projected Far East operations.

With losses in bomber crews not as high as anticipated, a surfeit of aircrew was evident by late 1944, and in December 6 (O) AFU was closed down, dramatically reducing the RAF flying from Staverton. 44 Group Communications Flight remained active during 1945 but most of the flying was by Dowty, Gloster and Flight Refuelling Ltd. The short runways were very tight for the refuelling trials Lancasters and there were several incidents. In August 1945 one overran and finished up in Bamfurlong Lane and even more embarrassing was a similar incident on October 11 after a demonstration refuelling flight witnessed by the Minister of Aviation.

No 44 Group Communications Flight closed down in August 1946 and Flight Refuelling left for Tarrant Rushton later in the year leaving Staverton to Rotol and a number of small civil operators. Some of the hangars were used by 7 MU Quedgeley as a sub-site but the main RAF presence was provided by the Police Guard Dog Training School and, from June 1948 by No 1 RAF Police Wing.

Staverton was de-requisitioned on September 29 1950 and, with no one organisation in overall control, the airfield and buildings rapidly deteriorated. In March 1953 Cambrian Airways were invited to take over the management and when Smiths Aviation Division moved in the situation started to improve, though facilities were still spartan and the only aid was a beacon. Unfortunately, Cambrian found their low key operations at Staverton uneconomic and were forced to withdraw in 1956. Dowty having closed down their test department in 1954, Smiths had little alternative but to take over the airport and they provided the Manager, Fire Section and air traffic control until 1962 when it was transferred to the joint Gloucester and Cheltenham councils.

The year 1963 saw the establishment of the Skyfame Museum in the Bellman hangar previously occupied by Flight Refuelling, and the formation of Glosair. This company was formed to provide local aircraft maintenance, an aircraft sales outlet and a charter organisation. In 1965 it became the UK agent for the Victa Airtourer and later started assembling them from imported parts.

Skyfame and Glosair both played their part in putting Staverton on the map but, like many other small organisations at the airfield during the post-war years, financial problems defeated them. On the airline scene Derby Airways/BMA replaced Cambrian on summer services to Jersey, introducing Viscounts in February 1967. Three years later a reorganisation of the company resulted in them withdrawing services from Staverton and for the 1971 season Intra, a Jersey-based airline, commenced schedules using DC-3s. Subsequently they also introduced Viscounts but the services have now ceased.

Despite a general tidying up and a few new buildings, Staverton looks much the same as it did during the war. Following more stringent security regulations introduced by the CAA during recent years, the apron is now much more difficult to approach but a small viewing terrace can be reached through the airport terminal building. Aircraft landing on the SW runway can be seen to advantage from the coach park. Car parking space is limited and beware the sleeping policemen—they are a menace.

Stoney Cross, Hampshire

SU246125. 7 miles NE of Ringwood

Set in a heavily wooded area of the New Forest just north of the A31 (T) road, Stoney Cross was originally planned as a secret airfield, a landing ground deliberately devoid of any of the usual facilities and with camouflaged hides for

Left *Stoney Cross on July 26 1956 taken from an 82 Squadron Canberra* (DoE).

Below *B-26 Marauder 295930 of the 387th Bomb Group flying from Stoney Cross in 1944.*

Right *Stirling V PK143 of 242 Squadron at Stoney Cross in 1945* (IWM).

aircraft. Later it was decided to develop the emergency airfield into an advance base for both fighters and bombers and work started on the necessary buildings in 1942.

Stoney Cross was opened by 38 Wing, Army Co-operation Command, on November 9 1942 in an incomplete state, and with the contractors still occupying most of the airfield. It was not fit for the planned move of 170 Squadron but after Sommerfeld tracking had been laid over soft ground 239 arrived on January 13 1943—in gliders towed by 296 Squadron. A month later 123 Airfield HQ set up camp to the north of the airfield, joined two days later by Mustangs of 26

Squadron and at the beginning of March by 175 Squadron. With the runways cleared and Ashby Walk bombing range restricted in use, Stoney Cross was considered ready for action. 123 Airfield commenced operations during Exercise *Spartan*, a large scale Army Co-operation exercise.

Transport and Coastal Command representatives visited early in April but both turned Stoney Cross down. Wimpey, the contractors, were still finishing the runways, perimeter tracks and dispersals, and as if to emphasise its unsuitability a collision between a Mustang and a contractor's lorry occurred the following day, resulting in the death of three

civilians. It was then offered to 38 Wing who agreed to use it for 295 Squadron but to delay the unit's arrival until the middle of May to enable Wimpey to complete their work. 123 Airfield units moved out early in April and with 295 going to Holmsley South instead the airfield was without flying units.

With the disbandment of Army Co-operation Command on June 1 1943, Stoney Cross was transferred to 10 Group, Fighter Command, while construction work continued. B-17 Fortresses of the VIIIth Air Force, USAAF, started to appear in increasing numbers from June onwards, bringing in American aircrew for rehabilitation at Broadlands, the Mountbatten family home at Romsey.

The airfield was at last fit for regular operations when 297 Squadron arrived from Thruxton in August 1943 with a mixed strength of Albemarles and Whitleys. More Americans appeared to herald fresh developments but they were only concerned with the erection and towing out of Waco Hadrian gliders. Meanwhile, 297 Squadron had dropped units of the 12th Commando at St Valerie (they were retrieved by the Navy) in September and had been threatened with re-equipment with Venturas. Then, on November 4 the squadron was split up, B Flight becoming the nucleus of 299 Squadron at Stoney Cross while C Flight moved to Tarrant Rushton to perform the same service for 298 Squadron.

No 299 Squadron received the Venturas and together with 297 was soon busy on intensive training with the Airborne Division on such oddly named exercises as *Try Again*. At the beginning of 1944, 299 Squadron re-armed with Stirling GT IVs while 297 carried on with the Albemarle on almost non-stop exercise paratroop drops by day and night. These exercises gradually got larger and more involved, 14 Albemarles of 297 Squadron taking part in the drop of 1,500 troops of the 3rd Parachute Brigade Group on February 6.

Supply drops over France were made by 297 Squadron during February, and by both squadrons in March. The whole station was beginning to work well when both squadrons were suddenly moved out of Stoney, 297 going to Brize Norton and 299 to Keevil. The USAAF took it over on March 13 1944 and P-38 Lightnings of the 367th FG, IXth AF, arrived on April 1. The three squadrons (392, 393 and 394) immediately commenced training, having arrived direct from the States. From their first combat mission on May 9 operations were almost exclusively aimed at airfields, rail junctions, road bridges and French coastal batteries in preparation for *Overlord*.

After D-Day the Lightnings roamed over France interdicting, operations which continued when the Group moved to Ibsley on July 7 and Stoney Cross returned to RAF control. Only very briefly, however, for on the 27th the Marauders of the 387th BG (556-559 Squadrons) arrived from Chipping Ongar. Operations were against communications in France but the BG was only waiting for landing grounds on the Continent to become available before they moved forward on September 5. The RAF element had warning of a take-over by Brize Norton units—but this was cancelled and a detachment of No 1 Heavy Glider Servicing Unit, Netheravon, arrived instead. They took over two hangars and a workshop and repaired assorted glider parts retrieved in France and brought over to Southampton docks by landing craft.

On October 7 the airfield became a satellite of Ibsley. Nine RAF Regiment squadrons moved in to use the accommodation whilst in transit, and a month later 116 Wing, Transport Command, took over the unit. A large influx of personnel in November heralded the formation of two Wellington transport squadrons, 232 and 242. Four of the established 25 Wellington C XVIs of 232 Squadron had arrived by the end of the month and training commenced, but a change of plan brought re-equipment with Dakotas in January 1945, and the Wellingtons were handed over to 242 Squadron.

No 46 Squadron re-formed on January 9 1945 with the first Stirling C Vs to reach an operational unit and the training role of Stoney was accentuated by 52 Squadron (Long Range Flight) which was attached for six weeks to convert part of 232 Squadron to C-87 Liberators. Two days after the LR Flight left, four aircraft of 232 were despatched to Karachi and more went later in the same month. At about the same time the Dakota element of the squadron moved to Merryfield and became 243 Squadron, the remnants of the unit remaining at Stoney Cross to convert to C-54 Skymasters later in the year.

This confusion and turmoil was only increased when 242 Squadron exchanged its Wellingtons for Stirling Vs and, using mainly ex-Bomber crews, started training flights to North Africa. 46 Squadron flew their first route service on March 3 and from early April were operating to India. They were just about to be joined by 242 Squadron when the latter was told it was to receive 15 Avro Yorks. By May 1 242 had three Yorks, 18 Stirlings, one Wellington and an Oxford, while 46 Squadron had 24 Stirling Vs on strength.

The MAP took over No 2 hangar (at the southern end of the airfield) during May and a party of Bristol Aeroplane Co personnel moved in to modify Stirling IVs to the trooping role. Much to 242 Squadron's disgust, these were delivered to them to replace their Mk Vs, the latter having already supplanted their Yorks which had suddenly been withdrawn in July. Despite these many changes the amount of flying increased during August with 46 Squadron shouldering extra tasks while other squadrons used Stoney as their route departure point.

A new passenger and freight building complete with a large hardstanding came into operation in September, just in time for the large trooping commitment at the end of the war with Japan. During

December 242 Squadron moved to Merryfield but 46 continued services to India on a reduced scale, and in February 1946 they were told that they were to re-equip with Dakotas. They slowly completed the changeover in April and then flew services to the Middle East.

With the move of 46 Squadron to Manston in October 1946 Stoney Cross was rapidly run down and transferred to Care & Maintenance. Retained as an inactive site, it finally closed in January 1948.

The easterly perimeter track was taken over as a minor road to Lynhurst and later the NE/SW runway was similarly used as the base of a road to Linwood. The three 'T2' hangars were still present in 1956 but after the Forestry Commission took over they were removed together with the remaining concrete runways, perimeter tracks and dispersals except on three camping sites. These use the foundations of the main barrack area on the edge of Kings' Garn Gutter Inclosure (SU250129), the Janes Moor Pond site (SU246136) and Ocknell Inclosure (SU250120) where aircraft dispersals were employed. The whole airfield has been successfully converted into a public recreation area by the Forestry Commission.

Tarrant Rushton, Dorset

ST946058. 3 miles E of Blandford Forum

Tarrant Rushton had a somewhat chequered career but undoubtedly its greatest moment came when the serried ranks of Halifax tugs and Hamilcar gliders started to move off down the runway carrying elements of the 6th Airborne Division to Normandy. What a night that must have been!

Development of the airfield on a plateau to the east of the River Tarrant started in May 1942 and right from the start it was intended for the airborne forces of the newly formed 38 Wing. It was handed over on May 17 1943 but the slow build-up of glider towing squadrons delayed its opening until October. Compared with most of the Group's airfields, Tarrant Rushton was well situated and had good surfaces so it was decided to use it for operations with the very large Hamilcar glider. Capable of carrying a small tank, the Hamilcar required a four-engined tug and it was with an initial establishment of 17 Halifax Vs and seven Horsa gliders that 298 Squadron formed at Tarrant Rushton on

November 4.

Bad weather and servicing problems delayed progress until February 1944 when a third Flight increased the strength to 40 Halifaxes and crews. On March 16 the unit was split and 644 Squadron formed, but because of accommodation problems at Tarrant much of 644's practice flying was from Chelveston. The training reaching a peak in April when a display was laid on for General Eisenhower, six Halifax/glider combinations taking off from Tarrant Rushton in three minutes and, after release, the gliders approached in line astern to demonstrate their ability to land close together.

Meanwhile Stirling IVs from 190, 196 and 620 Squadrons used Tarrant Rushton as a forward base for night supply drops to the French Resistance during February. These SOE operations could be extremely hazardous. Not only did the aircraft have to fly over the DZ as low as 200 ft (61 m) but they also suffered attention from the many anti-aircraft gun batteries scattered around France.

For Operation *Neptune*, the airborne phase of *Overlord*, the Tarrant squadrons had three tasks. For the first, six specially trained crews were to tow Horsa gliders to two bridges so that they could be captured intact. They were over the targets just before midnight on June 5/6 and very successful, most of the gliders landing on the bridge approaches, a covering diversion being provided by the tugs which bombed a cement factory near Caen. For Operation *Tonga*, the main glider operation, both units sent 17 Halifaxes towing two Hamilcars and 15 Horsas. One aircraft and five gliders did not make the objective, but four of the Horsas landed safely in England, while for the final phase, Operation *Mallard*, 298 and 644 each towed 15 Hamilcars and one Horsa with complete success, though a second Halifax was lost to flak. Re-supply continued until June 27, after which the squadrons reverted to training interspersed with SOE, SAS and tactical bombing operations.

General Montgomery's imaginative thrust across the natural barriers of the Maas, Waal and Lower Rhine rivers was the occasion for the next major airborne operation, *Market Garden*. With the involved business of marshalling aircraft and gliders completed all was ready for the drop at Arnhem on September 17. The combinations left at 45-second intervals, 298 Squadron towing seven Hamilcars

and 13 Horsas and 644 a further seven Hamilcars and 14 Horsas. They met little opposition but the re-supply on the two following days suffered from bad weather and intense flak.

Immediately after Arnhem the Tarrant Rushton squadrons re-equipped with Hercules-powered Halifax IIIs and returned to SOE operations, some as far away as Norway. For the last mass glider operation of the war, the Rhine crossing, they moved to Woodbridge with their 60 Halifaxes. On return to Tarrant Rushton the squadrons were again on SOE work over Norway and Denmark, culminating in the landing of 1st Airborne Division at Copenhagen on May 8 1945, the day hostilities ceased. This was followed by Operation *Doomsday* which involved the movement of 7,000 troops and their supplies to Norway to occupy Oslo and other major towns.

No 298 Squadron left Tarrant Rushton for the Far East during July and was followed as far as Palestine by 644 in November. 190 Squadron moved in from Great Dunmow and within a fortnight was towing Hamilcars on training sorties. But policy changes were almost continuous and on 28 December it was disbanded. Before this could take full effect it was decided that a heavy glider tug squadron was required after all and the personnel and aircraft were re-formed on January 21 1946; but as 295 Squadron.

No 644 Squadron's mail service, which had used Earls Colne as the UK terminal, transferred to Tarrant Rushton in February, and in April 297 Squadron was re-formed, using the crews of 295 which had been disbanded yet again on March 31. All these machinations left Tarrant Rushton with just 297 Squadron, and when room became available at Brize Norton in September 1946 the unit moved.

The airfield was immediately put on Care & Maintenance and then declared 'surplus to requirements' in December 1947. It lay abandoned until Flight Refuelling Ltd arrived from Ford in June 1948. They modified four of the dispersed 'T2' hangars together with many of the wartime buildings on the north-east side of the airfield. Almost immediately the Berlin Airlift started and Flight Refuelling was given a contract to carry bulk fuel into the beleaguered city. Despite lack of personnel at Tarrant Rushton, a Lancaster left on a direct flight to Gatow on July 27 carrying 8,800 gallons of fuel

Top *A well-known photograph but it epitomises Tarrant Rushton. It shows Halifaxes, Hamilcars and Horsas lined up on the southern end of the airfield on June 5 1944* (IWM). **Above** *Seafire F 17 SP343 of 1832 Squadron visiting Tarrant Rushton in 1950.*

and the cargo volume rapidly increased as things became organised. Inevitably there were setbacks, the worst occurring when a Lancaster crashed at Thruxton in bad weather while returning to Tarrant Rushton for servicing on November 23 1948. Two complete crews plus an extra pilot were lost in the crash, but when the Airlift ended in August 1949 the company had been strengthened immeasurably. There was real interest in the flight refuelling principle at last—from the USAF. This work and a contract to run a flying training school put the company on a firm footing.

No 210 AFS was formed at Tarrant Rushton in August 1952 equipped with Meteor F4 and T7 aircraft. The

maintenance was carried out by Flight Refuelling personnel and they soon gained a reputation for always providing enough aircraft to complete the task early. With the reduced amount of training required after the Korean War, the unit was closed in June 1954, but the RAF's interest in Tarrant Rushton was not immediately diminished for it was decided to develop it as one of the series of V-bomber standby airfields spread across the country. The old dispersals near the threshold of 01/19 runway were rebuilt and strengthened to provide hardstandings for Vulcans or Victors and a loop was built at the 19 end. This enabled aircraft to backtrack the runway and eliminated the need to strengthen the perimeter track.

In practice, Tarrant Rushton remained unused by the V-Force but stayed busy as contracts for refurbishing Meteors for use as drones continued. To assist in this work a radio command station for testing pilotless aircraft was built and to further the flight refuelling side of the business a full scale fuel system test rig was built.

The cost of running an airfield has escalated over the years and in 1979 Flight Refuelling announced that they would be moving to Hurn when essential equipment had been installed in their new premises. The airfield at Tarrant Rushton was officially closed on September 30 1980 after the final Sea Vixen had flown out but light aircraft and the Dorset Gliding Club continued to use it until trenches were dug across the runways on January 26 1981.

Thruxton, Wiltshire

SU280455. 5 miles SW of Andover

The land for this three-runway airfield was purchased by the Air Ministry in 1940 from the Thruxton Manor Estate and construction was well advanced when the runways were tested by Blenheims of No 2 School of Army Co-operation on June 22 1941. The concrete surface proved too rough, resulting in three tyre bursts, and the opening was delayed until August while tarmac was laid.

Taken over by Army Co-operation Command as a satellite for Andover, 225 Squadron moved in its Lysanders from Tilshead on August 4 and did ASR work while specialised rescue units were being set up. 42 OTU operated a detachment from Andover joined by the Oxfords of 26/1526 (BAT) Flight in November.

The A303 road gave a good view of activities and an interested spectator could not have failed to see the 16 black-painted Whitleys of 51 Squadron dispersed around the field at the end of February 1942. They were there for Operation *Biting*, the first British operational paratroop drop mounted from the UK, and their objective was the Würtzburg radar station at Bruneval, near Le Harve. During the evening of February 27, C Company, 2nd Parachute Battalion, and Flight Sergeant C.W.H. Cox, an RAF radar expert, emplaned in 12 Whitleys which, led by Wing Commander P.C. Pickard, successfully found the target. Ten sticks dropped accurately and while the troops held off defenders, Cox first photographed and then, with the aid of

his sappers, dismantled vital components and blew up the rest. They withdrew to the beach, and after an anxious wait were lifted off by the Royal Navy and returned in triumph to Portsmouth with their booty.

No 225 Squadron received Mustangs in May and later moved to Macmerry, leaving the airfield clear for the next drama, the Dieppe raid of August 19. To cover this seaborne assault very strong RAF forces were gathered and Thruxton became host to Bostons of 226 and Blenheims of 13 and 614 Squadrons—all engaged in smoke-laying. Led by 13 Squadron, the smoke-layers left early in the morning and flew over the Channel to their targets, the well-positioned gun batteries flanking Dieppe. The makeshift 100 lb phosphorus bombs were very effective, producing masses of smoke, and the guns were successfully blanketed for the loss of a 13 Squadron Blenheim and considerable damage to the Bostons. With the sudden decision to withdraw the troops, the smoke-layers were again in demand and although 13 Squadron was forced to abort through escort problems the smoke was successfully laid. It was followed by a third sortie by 226 Squadron to cover the naval forces leaving the beachhead. For Thruxton Operation *Jubilee* was over.

The steady expansion of 38 Wing during 1942 brought more Whitleys to Thruxton. 298 Squadron formed in August with ten Mk Vs, but a change of plan brought disbandment again in October. The 42 OTU detachment which had operated for most of the year departed to Ashbourne and in their place came 297 Squadron from Hurn. Its Whitleys were used for paratroop exercises by day and *nickelling* over France by night. Early in 1943 these activities became more aggressive when 297 started bombing and in March Horsa glider towing was commenced. This training was put to good use two months later when Whitley/Horsa combinations started moving units from one airfield to another. These included 1481 Gunnery Flight from Lindholme to Binbrook, 460 Squadron from Breighton to Binbrook, and 88/169 Squadrons from Charmy Down to Swanton Morley.

Albemarles joined 297 Squadron in July and, fully equipped, the squadron left for Stoney Cross at the end of August. Meanwhile some excitement was caused by the sudden arrival of a USAAF B-17F

Thruxton on September 25 1945 with numerous Horsas still in open storage (DoE).

which diverted in from Boscombe Down carrying a load of gas bombs which it had been unable to drop on the range. They were very carefully unloaded by experts from Porton.

The Glider Pilots Exercise Unit moved in during September 1943 but was turfed out the following month to enable 123 Airfield (168, 170 and 268 Squadrons) to use Thruxton for winter accommodation. Meanwhile, part of 3209 Servicing Commando had arrived in September to do modifications on Typhoons. The aircraft were flown in, modified, and flown out under arrangements made by Fighter Command—the work lasting a month. 63 Squadron replaced 268 as part of 123 Airfield on November 7 and three days later all the Mustangs left for Sawbridgeworth. The GPEU returned with its Masters and Hotspurs and then became the Operational Refresher Training Unit before moving to Hampstead Norris with 1526 Flight, leaving Thruxton clear for the USAAF to take over on March 1 1944.

In fact large numbers of Americans had arrived during February, causing chaos, but all had been sorted out by the time the P-47 Thunderbolts of the 366th FG, IXth Fighter Command, landed. Commanded by Colonel Dyke F. Meyer, they flew their first operation on March 14 and gradually built up their experience in the months up to D-Day. On June 6 the first sorties were made at daybreak in the fighter-bomber role, each Thunderbolt carrying two 1,000-lb bombs—their target the coastal

batteries near the beachhead. Later they turned their attention to enemy armour and were one of the first units to move to the Continent—on June 20.

They were replaced by the Anson ambulances of 1311 Flight which had been formed at Aston Down in anticipation of numerous casualties requiring rapid transportation from bridgehead airstrips to hospitals. Fortunately the casualties were fairly light and the Flight became 84 Group Communications Squadron in July and operated alongside the Support Unit. Meanwhile, 43 OTU started using the airfield for Auster AOP flying and Thruxton was also used to house Mobile Parachute Servicing Units. With the completion of glider operations in Europe the number of Horsas in open storage on the north side of the field increased and soon exceeded 100.

By the end of 1945 the gliders were being slowly broken up and the airfield was declared surplus in 1946. The following year it was leased by the Wiltshire School of Flying, which moved in from High Post and built up a large training organisation. They also undertook the conversion of Tiger Moths into four-seat Thruxton Jackaroos. Eighteen of these aircraft were built by their subsidiary, Jackaroo Aircraft Ltd, between 1957 and 1960, the most famous of which was a specially souped-up machine for Sheila Scott.

The land was auctioned in June 1958 but had already been approved for permanent use as an airfield, and the

Wiltshire School of Flying continued to occupy it under the terms of their original lease. Soon afterwards the perimeter track started to be used as a racing circuit by motor bikes. This venture prospered and is now an established motor racing circuit complete with spectator stands and the other paraphernalia associated with the sport. The runways are now unsafe, aircraft operating from the grass, while a strong helicopter presence was built up in recent years. There is still plenty of evidence of Thruxton's military past in a variety of derelict Nissen huts and other buildings. One 'T2' hangar and the ATC tower are still in use and in good condition.

Tilshead, Wiltshire

SU021478. 1 mile W of Tilshead village

Close by one of the many Army camps in the area, Tilshead landing ground was little more than a stretch of downland in use from 1925 for Army Co-operation squadrons during annual manoeuvres on Salisbury Plain. The standard practice was to send out a small ground party who erected tents on the edge of the LG and sat down to await the aircraft, which were used for artillery spotting and reconnaissance. At first Bristol Fighters, later they were Atlases, Audaxes, Hectors, and by the beginning of the war, Lysanders. Sometimes the detachments to Tilshead lasted a month, such as those by A Flight of 16 Squadron in June 1931 and August 1932, but usually it was for much shorter periods.

During the early months of the war Tilshead was not used as an airfield, but in June 1940, with a desperate lack of places to disperse the units returned from France, it was cleared of obstructions. On July 1, 225 Squadron moved in from Old Sarum with their 12 Lysanders and set up a tented camp for 28 officers and 355 men. Their immediate task was to continue a dawn and dusk coverage of every bay and inlet from St Albans Head to Selsey Bill, to check for signs of invasion or infiltrators. They were soon providing aircraft for the Bognor Regis-Lizard sector also, usually flying from Roborough on detachment for this leg, or landing at St Eval to refuel, returning to Tilshead after the dusk patrol. It was a time of great and understandable nervousness over anything unusual and rumours abounded. Strange lights and bonfires were reported to Southern

Command by the public via the police and each had to be checked out—even a report of hedges cut into the shape of a swastika was investigated!

On July 29 a Lysander on a photo reconnaissance of Weymouth was attacked by a Bf 110 but took violent evasive action and escaped in cloud. Perhaps more surprising were the events of August 13. At 16:30 hours a single He 111 overflew Tilshead at about 3,000 ft (914 m). The guns posts were manned and shortly afterwards the aircraft made a wide sweep over the ranges, then disappeared from view to the east, before approaching at low level over the southern end of the LG. Both gun posts and the rear guns of two parked Lysanders opened fire as the He 111 dropped five bombs. One destroyed two unoccupied tents, another landed in the middle of the LG, two more fell amongst partially completed Army huts and the fifth set fire to the grass. Two Lysanders and a Tiger Moth were damaged by splinters and machine-gun fire, but there were no casualties, all personnel being in slit trenches.

With September came rain and when the tents started leaking the squadron moved into Tilshead Lodge, a requisitioned country house just to the east of the LG. A Flight was sent to

A Lysander of 225 Squadron demonstrates message pick-up—almost certainly at Tilshead (IWM).

Hatfield as a nucleus for 239 Squadron and the coastal patrols continued in worsening weather which made the location of Tilshead on return extremely difficult.

In 1941 Army exercises gradually took over from the patrol work and many detachments were carried out, as far afield as Okehampton and Staverton. A large-scale exercise during May 1941 simulated an invasion of the Weymouth area, and for three days the squadron flew tactical and photo recce sorties. Eight Lysanders and a Gladiator from 239 Squadron also used Tilshead during the month for air firing and bombing on the ranges, and in July a detachment arrived from 16 Squadron, Weston Zoyland, for more exercises.

The camp was not very satisfactory, however, and as soon as accommodation elsewhere became available it was decided to move 225 Squadron. After some indecision the chosen airfield was Thruxton and the squadron went during August 1941, leaving Tilshead to be used for exercise detachments until it was handed over to the Army Department at the end of the year to become part of an enlarged range area.

Townsend, Wiltshire

SU070725. ½ mile NE of Yatesbury village
A large field just to the north of Townsend village, this landing ground was used by the Tiger Moths of 10 EFTS Yatesbury for forced landing practice until the unit moved to Weston-super-Mare in September 1940.

Meanwhile, ever-increasing numbers of aircraft picketed out at MUs were causing mounting concern, especially after the German breakthrough in France when large-scale air attack was expected on the south of England. Dispersal was the answer and among the sites chosen by 10

MU staff in August was Yatesbury ELG, for it was obviously capable of accepting aircraft and had cover around it in the form of small clumps of trees.

The LG was taken over by 10 MU, Hullavington, in October 1940 and on November 29 three Bothas and a Wellington were delivered successfully. In 1941 the site became 45 SLG Townsend but it was not extensively used by 10 MU because of waterlogging during the winter months, and during September the aircraft were withdrawn.

In April 1942, 45 SLG was reopened and transferred to 33 MU Lyneham, their first aircraft arriving on April 18, the total increasing to 16 by the end of May. During July work started on a second landing strip and access to the dispersal fields was improved by laying tarmac and felling trees. Aircraft holdings had reached 26 by midsummer and discussions were under way about Townsend's suitability for four-engined aircraft dispersal. Then, despite all the improvements, 41 Group suddenly ordered its closure for the winter. All aircraft had been removed by October and although 45 SLG was retained until November 1944 it was not used again for aircraft storage.

The work was not wasted, however, for the graded landing strips were increasingly used by 2 Radio School, Yatesbury for staff pilot circuits and bumps on Proctors from 1943 until the end of the war; and possibly by 2 EFTS when it reformed in July 1945 until 1947.

There is now little sign of Townsend's wartime use apart from one or two Maycrete buildings close to the village. The landing ground returned to arable and pasture many years ago.

A rare photograph of aircraft on a SLG— at Townsend in August 1941. At least two Wellingtons can be seen dispersed amongst the trees (IWM).

Trebelzue in September 1947 with the main runway converted into dispersals for St Mawgan. The Blister hangar and some of the buildings on the south-west perimeter are still present.

Trebelzue, Cornwall

SW851641. 3 miles NE of Newquay

This little-known airfield had its origins in Alan Cobham's National Aviation Day touring circus which visited Newquay in the mid-1930s and used a 40-acre site high on the cliffs above Porth called Trebelzue Big Field. It was also used for newspaper delivery flights and then by Western Airways who started a twice daily service connecting Swansea-Barnstaple-Newquay-Penzance (St Just) on May 8 1939. Using a DH Dragon, they maintained the service until it was closed down with the outbreak of war.

The Big Field was requisitioned for development as a satellite for St Eval and after completion of two runways and minimal services was opened in September 1941. A detachment of 80 ground gunners moved in but there was virtually no flying until Trebelzue was transferred to 44 Group, Ferry Command, on December 30 and the nucleus of No 2 Overseas Aircraft Despatch Unit arrived from Portreath. The first batch of aircraft passed through during February on delivery to the Middle East via Gibraltar, but it quickly became apparent that the airfield was inadequate for the task. Further requisitioning of dispersal fields was undertaken but the main problems were crosswinds, short runways and poor weather.

On April 23 a conference was held to consider how to extend the airfield so that it could accept the whole of 44 Group's Middle East commitment, estimated at 100 aircraft per month. It was considered essential that three runways of at least 4,200 ft (1,280 m) be provided and that this could only be achieved effectively by building a new airfield to the east of the present one, which could then be used for dispersals.

Despatches in April totalled 14, but they were the last. Flying was then limited to the odd communications flight and the Henleys of 1 AACU which arrived in May and towed targets for the gunnery school at Penhale Army camp throughout the summer and autumn.

Work on the new runways started on August 24 1942 and this made the airfield even more difficult to use, though a number of C-47s visited briefly during October, one of them carrying out a para-troop demonstration. To counter the threat posed by German long-range fighters operating in the south-west approaches, a detachment of Mustangs from 400 Squadron was sent to Portreath late in 1942. With accommodation problems at Portreath they were moved to Trebelzue on December 23 to fly *Instep* patrols and were augmented by Mosquito IIs of 264 Squadron at the end of the month. But neither were very successful and the Mosquitoes found the airfield particularly difficult to use. 400 Squadron returned to Middle Wallop in the middle of January, and the Mosquitoes moved to Portreath on February 10 1943.

Meanwhile, waterlogging at Cleave had forced the Henleys of 1602 and 1604 Flights to operate again from Trebelzue and a small number were still in residence when the airfield was renamed St Mawgan on February 24 1943.

Treligga, Cornwall

SX047848. 1½ miles W of Delabole

First used pre-war as a gliding site, Treligga was selected by the FAA late in 1939 as a bombing and gunnery range. Because of the difficulty in carrying out an emergency landing in the surrounding area, 'wheels-up' landing strips were laid out on the actual range. This unique arrangement has led to the assertion that Treligga was used as a RLG for St Merryn early in the war, but in fact the surface, certainly until 1944, was much too rough for normal take-offs and landings. However, the confusion Treligga has caused, and its use on at least one occasion for a safe 'wheels-down' arrival, merits its inclusion.

Some 260 acres of the North Cornwall coast were requisitioned by the Admiralty in March 1940 and laid out as an air-to-ground and air-to-sea firing range. The ground targets were placed on the cliffs between Start Point and Tregannick Tail. Between the Tail and Treligga village three rough grass landing strips, each about 2,250 ft (686 m) in length, were marked out and intended for landings by aircraft suffering engine failure or richocet damage while firing on the range. The only buildings were a tall brick quadrant hut in the centre of the range and a living hut just north of Treligga village.

A satellite of St Merryn, the range was named *Vulture II*, and was perhaps unique in being run entirely by WRNS, some 20 girls being accommodated locally in Port Isaac. They operated the quadrant equipment to record angle of dives and accuracy of attacks made by aircraft from St Merryn, including the Fighter Pool (748 Squadron) and School of Air Combat (736 Squadron). Numerous operational units detached to St Merryn also used the facilities and one day in 1944 the girls on duty were surprised to see a B-17 Fortress circling the range and then put down on the strip. When the Americans stepped out of their aircraft they were amazed to find the place in the hands of females. No doubt their surprise soon changed to delight!

With the carrier war moving to the Pacific in 1944, the Treligga range was laid out to represent a typical area of Japanese-held territory—modelled on the island of Tarawa. Real and dummy tanks, a bridge and a road convoy were provided near an airstrip. Only the waving palms were lacking and by December it was being used for intensive training of squadron commanders and senior pilots of units destined for the Pacific Fleet.

After the war the Treligga range continued in operation for the School of Naval Air Warfare and for squadrons detached to St Merryn for armament practice, and was in great demand until the early 1950s. As naval use declined it was also made available to the RAF and the Shackleton squadrons at St Eval used it to give their gunners practice in air-to-ground firing at tanks fitted with recording mechanisms. From personal experience I know it was not easy to position a Shackleton so that the Bristol B17 dorsal turret could be trained on the

Only the observation tower and a quadrant hut remain at Treligga and both are derelict.

target, especially when coping with the turbulence produced by the cliffs if the wind was anything more than a light breeze.

With the withdrawal of flying units from St Merryn in 1954 and the removal of turrets from Shackletons during 1955 the range was closed at the end of the year and quickly reverted to farmland. Today little remains except for the quadrant tower standing forlornly in the middle of a large field.

Upavon, Wiltshire

SU152542. 1½ miles SE of Upavon village

The oldest active airfield in the country—though now only a shadow of its former self—the conversion of the Army training gallops high above the village of Upavon into an aerodrome began during April 1912. On June 19 the buildings already completed were taken over and the Central Flying School of the newly formed Royal Flying Corps were opened under the command of Captain Godfrey M. Paine, RN.

It was a strange place to build an airfield when one had the whole of Salisbury Plain at one's disposal. Officially it was selected because it was isolated and thus free of sightseers, was surrounded by open country, and served by a good road. This was true, but it was also on top of a hill with a sharp escarpment on the northern side and a drop to the Avon valley to the west. These combined to provide turbulent air conditions on otherwise good days, so it would appear that the needs of pre-1914 aeroplanes were the last thing considered. Despite this the airfield and the original buildings have survived, many of them almost unchanged.

With the declaration of war on August 4 1914, CFS was denuded of both men and aircraft and when revived it was very little different from other advanced training units, apart from the Experimental Flight which formed in November 1914 to evaluate new equipment. This became the famous Aeroplane & Armament Experimental Establishment on moving to Martlesham Heath in January 1917. From then until the end of the war Upavon turned out a steady stream of pilots for the voracious front-line squadrons in France, using the original airfield and another built on the north side of the Andover-Upavon road.

The Armistice caused confusion and dismay. Wholesale demobilisation and no clear policy on training lowered morale throughout the RAF and Upavon did not escape it. Little was done until the end of 1919 when plans were made for a flying instructors' school at Upavon on the lines of Smith-Barry's School of Special Flying of 1918, and appropriately it retained the name of Central Flying School. The school started operations in March 1920 and soon became a byword for the excellence of its flying instructor output. The standard trainer was the Avro 504K with the Sopwith Snipe for advanced work.

In April 1924 the CFS was joined on the south airfield by the fighter Snipes of 3 Squadron. Two years later the station came under the newly formed 3 Group, and within two months CFS started to move to Wittering. This was completed in October when 17 Squadron arrived from Hawkinge with Woodcocks to join 3 Squadron. For three years the two units operated as the sole night fighters in the RAF, but equipped with Bulldogs both moved to Kenley in May 1934 and the station became a shore base for Fleet Air Arm units.

This did not last long for, on September 1 1935, Upavon was transferred to Inland Areas as a 23 (Training) Group station. The FAA units moved to Gosport and the CFS returned to its old base. The trusty Avro 504N was replaced by the Tutor,

and the Hart (T) and Fury were supplemented by a few Ansons for twin-engined training until the first of many Oxfords arrived in November 1937. In the same month the Refresher Flight commenced categorisation of civilian instructors for the mushrooming Elementary & Reserve Flying Schools.

At the beginning of 1938 work started on improvements to the station which still consisted largely of 1914-18 wooden huts, though the original hangars had been replaced. A single 'C' Type hangar, three barrack blocks, airmens' dining hall and workshops, together with a number of married quarters were constructed in the first phase.

The old system of appending a few handling notes to the aircraft technical manual was proving unsatisfactory for the comparatively complicated types entering service and the Refresher Flight was given the job of writing *Pilots Notes* as a separate volume.

His Majesty George VI visited CFS on May 5 1938, arriving in his Airspeed Envoy. It was a relatively informal affair for, apart from a line-up of CFS aircraft, normal work continued while the King toured the camp. The pressure was now on the four training Flights for an increased output and from August 1938 the course length was reduced from ten to nine weeks and the student strength rose from 40 to 50 on each intake.

By the end of the year the *Pilots Notes* system was proving its worth though squadrons were still receiving aircraft for which they were completely unprepared. It was therefore decided that an early aircraft of each type would go to Upavon so that handling notes could be produced to a standard format by CFS. They took over the new 'C' Type hangar on its completion in April 1939 to house the very varied collection of aircraft they rapidly assembled.

On September 3 1939 all the training aircraft were dispersed around the perimeter and guarded at night by armed RAF personnel. Obviously the threat of Fifth Column activity was taken seriously and certainly Upavon was a difficult camp to make secure. Flying continued much as before though some of the courses were cut short due to the demand for new instructors and the appalling weather experienced during that first wartime winter. Early in February 1940 flying ceased completely for almost a fortnight because of glaze frost which covered

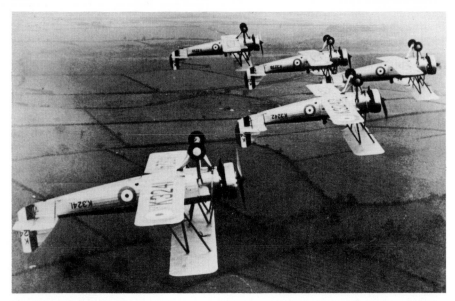

The famous Avro Tutor aerobatic team of the Central Flying School flying near Upavon prewar (Avro).

everything on the airfield.

The collapse in France caused some desperate emergency measures and Training Command Operation Order No 1 issued on May 6 1940 required Upavon to be prepared to provide Ansons to fly the personnel and equipment of 1 FTS, Netheravon, to Scampton where their Harvards were to operate as part of the anti-invasion force.

Luftwaffe intelligence services must have been very poor for they had Upavon listed as a fighter airfield—years after the Bulldogs had left. They attempted a bombing attack on August 14 during which the Geschwader Kommodore of KG55, Oberst Alois Stöckel, was killed when his He 111 was shot down.

Though some of the pressure was taken off by the formation of a second CFS at Cranwell in September 1940, both airfields at Upavon were in constant daytime use by Masters and Oxfords while much of the night flying training was being carried out at RLGs Overton Heath and later, New Zealand Farm. Meanwhile it was decided to take 40 student instructors in every fortnight, the Refresher Squadron returning to normal instructional duties while the Handling Flight left for Boscombe Down in October. The intensive flying caused

heavy rutting of the waterlogged grass and Sommerfeld tracking had to be laid, the first 3,000 ft (914 m) runway being completed in January 1942. But that did not help when it snowed, as on February 2.

The steady dilution of instructor experience and shortened courses meant that, just as in the 1914-18 War, CFS and Upavon became nothing more than another Flying Instructors' School, of which there were several. It clung on to its title for a year while the Air Ministry, feeling the need for an elite unit to maintain standards, deliberated. They finally decided to form a new unit on a new base from a nucleus of Upavon instructors and on April 1 1942 CFS disbanded and the remaining staff and aircraft became 7 FIS. Four-week OTU instructor courses were the first task of 7 FIS but in August it became an (A) FIS to carry out eight-week flying instructor courses. 21 Oxfords and all the Masters were transferred to 3 FIS Lulsgate and Magisters were allocated in place of the latter aircraft.

A 3,750 ft (1,143 m) Sommerfeld track east/west runway was completed on the south airfield and a perimeter track followed in September—the airfield was now almost weatherproof. After a spate of accidents in 1940-41 the number of serious incidents involving 7 FIS aircraft slackened considerably but a Horsa from Netheravon crash-landed on the airfield in August 1942, and the crew of a 295 Squadron Whitley was killed when it stalled whilst overshooting on January 9 1943.

In 1943 the courses were again increased in size and beam approach training was stepped up with the formation of 1537 BAT Flight in April 1943 using the Lorenz Blind Approach system installed pre-war. Whether this encouraged the crew of Oxford *LX595* to attempt a night landing in bad visibility on December 22 is not known, but it hit a flagpole and burst into flames after plunging into the roof of a hangar. 7 FIS remained at Upavon until April 1946 by which time it was completely equipped with Oxfords for multi-engined instructor training.

Three months later the HQ of 38 Group, Transport Command, moved in, and airfield activity was confined to its Communications Flight and visitors to Upavon. There had been Regiment squadrons on the airfield during the war of course, but in October 1948 No 2 RAF Regiment Wing formed at Upavon to control the air-transportable 15 and 16 Light Anti-Aircraft Squadrons and the parachute-trained 63 Rifle Squadron. 38 Group was disbanded in February 1950 and two months later HQ Transport Command arrived from Bushey Park.

When 38 Group re-formed in 1960 it returned to Upavon, but it was soon obvious that the station was not large enough for both HQs and the Group moved to Odiham. The temporary HQs were replaced by a modern building fronting the Andover-Upavon road. It was completed in 1965 when Transport Command was at its peak, controlling some 12,200 RAF and 2,600 civilian personnel and operating some 200 aircraft.

On August 1 1967, Transport became Air Support Command, and then on September 1 1972 the latter merged with Strike Command. On the same day 46 Group was formed at Upavon to control the strategic transport force, while 38 continued with the short-range tactical components. The wheel turned full circle with the amalgamation of the two Groups on November 10 1975 and 38 returned to Upavon as the largest Group in the RAF.

Since the middle of 1946 aircraft activity has been slight except for a short period during 1959/60 when 230

Squadron flew its Pioneers and Twin Pioneers from the airfield, and for a week or so around June 16 1962 when a flying and static display was held to mark the 50th Anniversary of Military Aviation in the United Kingdom. This display was attended by 75,000 spectators who saw aircraft ranging from the Avro 504K to the Harrier demonstrated. HRH Prince Philip unveiled a commemorative plaque in the partly constructed HQ building and afterwards lunched in the Officers' Mess, built in 1915 and now the oldest in the RAF.

The only permanently based flying unit now at Upavon is 622 Gliding School which moved in from Old Sarum at the end of November 1978 and occupies one of the three large hangars remaining on the south airfield; which is still open to both fixed-wing aircraft and helicopters.

Upottery, Devon

ST188101. ½ mile SW of Smeathorpe village

Known locally as Smeathorpe, the airfield of Upottery had a short career, with but one highlight—D-Day. Construction of this typical three-runway station started in the spring of 1943 on the plateau above Honiton which already contained Dunkeswell and Culmhead. The site was nominally placed under 70 Group, RAF, for administration but it was intended for the USAAF as a medium bomber airfield. To this end it was completed with a large number of dispersals and an extensive bomb dump to the north west, but with only two 'T2' hangars. A third hangar was planned but never built. The domestic sites were dispersed to the north-east, either side of the road between Smeathorpe and Churchingford, and consisted entirely of Nissen and Maycrete buildings of various types and sizes.

Upottery was opened on February 17 1944 but remained on Care & Maintenance until it became USAAF Station 462. It was to be the base of the 439th TCG (91st, 92nd, 93rd and 94th Squadrons) of the 50th TCW, IXth Troop Carrier Command, which arrived from Balderton on April 26 with its Douglas C-47 and C-53 Skytrains.

Training with Horsa and Hadrian gliders commenced immediately and on June 5 the 439th, led by Colonel Charles H. Young, took off for Normandy. His group of 81 Skytrains carried paratroopers of the 101st Airborne Division to a DZ

Upottery on May 7 1976 taken by a 39 Squadron Canberra (DoE).

near St Mère Eglise. Glider missions followed on the 7th and then the C-47s were used on re-supply tasks. The 439th continued at Upottery until September 8 though the airfield had been transferred to RAF control during August.

On October 1 it became a satellite of Weston Zoyland but was used by the United States Navy during November and December while Dunkeswell runways were being repaired. Whether this suggested the use of Upottery for anti-submarine work or it was already planned is unclear, but on January 7 1945 it was transferred to 19 Group, Coastal Command, and taken over by the United States Navy four days later.

The 107th Squadron, flying PB4Y-1 Liberators, moved in, joined later by the similarly-equipped 112th. Like the Dunkeswell units, they concentrated on Bay of Biscay patrols but sightings were very few and only one attack was made. With the end of the war in Europe the USN soon left, the Liberators flying out to the States through St Mawgan. Upottery was taken over by 19 Group at the end of July, quickly transferred to 57 Wing, 40 Group, Maintenance Command, as a sub unit of 265 MU, Collaton Cross, and used for storage. 225 MU, Warminster/Fulbeck, also used it and in November 1946 it became a satellite of 267 MU, Dunkeswell. The station was finally closed down during November 1948.

In the 1980s there is still plenty of evidence of an airfield and its dispersed accommodation sites at Upottery. Derelict Nissen huts abound to the north-east of the airfield and a caravan site uses the concrete bases of many others. On the airfield the runways are being slowly broken up, as are the dispersals either side of the road to Luppitt Common which uses the old southern perimeter track. A derelict ATC tower stands in the centre of the airfield which has largely reverted to farming except for a portion of the east/west runway which is used for stockcar, banger and hot-rod racing as the Smeathorpe Stadium.

Warmwell (Woodsford), Dorset

SY760885. 3½ miles SE of Dorchester

Built for a minor secondary role, this small airfield proved to be in the right place at the right time for two very different tasks—fighter defence during the Battle of Britain and fighter-bomber attack when 10 Group went out on the offensive late in 1941.

During the 1920s and early '30s gunnery practice had been a gentlemanly affair carried out during a camp at a landing ground specially opened each summer. It was soon obvious that this system was not going to cope with the Expansion squadrons and so a number of Armament Practice Camps, each with a permanent staff and accommodation for squadron detachments, were opened near gunnery/bombing ranges.

One of the ranges was Chesil Bank and its new airfield was sited eight miles north-east of Weymouth. It was opened on May 1 1937 for 6 APC, and named Woodsford. In July a Station Flight was formed with Tutors and Wallace target tugs and while the training organisation was getting established the airfield entertained its first visitors, 206 and 220 Squadrons arriving for the annual coast defence exercise. Soon a constant stream of operational squadrons were flying in for training over Chesil Bank, joined from January 1938 by regular attachments from Flying Training Schools. The ATC was renamed 6 Armament Training School on April 1 when it came under 25 Group and, because of confusion with the Avro factory airfield of Woodford, Manchester, the station took the name of the adjacent village of Warmwell in July 1938, when Auxiliary Squadron summer camps were well under way.

The Munich crisis saw a rush of activity and less than a year later, with mobilisation in full swing, 217 Squadron brought its Ansons to Warmwell to patrol the English Channel until St Eval was ready in October 1939. Meanwhile 10 AOS was formed on September 2 by expanding 6 ATS, the new unit having a very mixed collection of aircraft including Seals, Sidestrands and Harrows. Renamed 10 Bombing & Gunnery School on November 1, it built up to some 60 aircraft, taking on any second-line type from which a bomb could be dropped or a gun fired. The Central Gunnery School was formed from part of 10 B & GS and equipped with a selection of current bomber types for gunnery instructor training, which started on November 13 with 15 pupils on a three-week course.

By March 1940 plans were being made to extend fighter coverage to the south-west of England and these were accelerated with the German breakthrough in France and the evacuation at Dunkirk. Warmwell was chosen as a forward operating base for Middle Wallop, ideally placed for the defence of Portland naval base. It was declared operational on July 4, 609 Squadron arriving the following day, and settling into very temporary tented accommodation. Within a day or two their strength at Warmwell was reduced to a Flight which flew over from Middle Wallop at dawn, remained on 15-minute readiness throughout the day and returned home just before dusk. The first engagement was on July 9 when three Spitfires of B Flight on patrol off Weymouth were vectored on to a formation of Ju 87 dive bombers. One bomber, flown by the Staffelkapitän of 1/StG77, was shot down by Flying Officer

Crook, but B Flight was jumped by the fighter escort and Flying Officer Drummond-Hay was missing after the flight. The intended attack on Portland was broken up, however, and Warmwell had started to show its teeth.

No 10 Group, newly formed at Box, Wiltshire, took over Middle Wallop and its satellite, 10 B&GS retiring to Scotland to provide the room for Spitfires of 152 Squadron. While 152 Squadron found its feet the daily stand-bys of 609 continued but remained highly unpopular, for their dispersal was well away from the main camp and the station commander proved intractable over meal arrangements.

After several attempts the Luftwaffe finally penetrated to Warmwell on August 25. At about 16:00 hours a large raid was seen by Ventnor CH station to be forming up over the French coast. As the Ju 88s of II/KG51 and II/KG54, escorted by Bf 110s of I/ZG2, II/ZG2 and V/LG1, approached Weymouth Bay, they split into three formations and made for Portland, Weymouth and Warmwell. Twelve Spitfires of 152 Squadron took off, but it was the Hurricanes of 17 Squadron which broke up the 30-strong formation approaching Warmwell. Only seven Ju 88s got through and their bombs hit the sick quarters and two hangars on the northern side of the main camp. More problems were caused by nine unexploded bombs in the camp area, the last of these not detonating until the early morning of the 27th. Despite this there were no casualties and 152 Squadron claimed three kills and a probable off Portland for the loss of two Spitfires.

The hot summer dragged on with the Warmwell Spitfires in action from Bristol to Bognor Regis, and invasion jitters reaching a peak on September 9 when all defences were manned following a warning from Middle Wallop sector. The whole of 609 Squadron moved to Warmwell at the end of November 1940 and promptly went back under canvas—in a swamp on the northern edge of the airfield. The weather was appalling and on more than one occasion the operations marquee and crew room tentage was blown down. It was three months of misery and few interceptions before they left for Biggin Hill in February 1941. They were replaced by 234 Squadron which was used on convoy patrols and bomber escort.

When the Luftwaffe resumed their bombing campaign it was by small

numbers of low-flying aircraft. Typical was a single Ju 88 which dropped four bombs on Warmwell on March 26, and three He 111s which crossed the coast at low level and followed the railway to appear over the airfield at midday on April 1. The attack was a complete surprise and there was no time to scramble. The station workshops received a direct hit and most of the seven killed and 18 injured were in this area, though a 152 Squadron pilot was killed by a stray bullet while eating lunch in the Sergeants' Mess.

Four nights later the Q site at Knighton, 2½ miles south-west of the airfield, was bombed and with the upsurge in Luftwaffe activity plans were made to disperse all non-essential personnel each night. Before this could be completed the airfield itself was again attacked, six HE and many incendiary bombs being dropped, but though damage was caused there were no casualties. Tented sleeping sites were erected in Knighton Wood while SHQ officers were moved into Stafford

Top Hurricane IIB BE417 of 402 Squadron being bombed up on the south side of Warmwell in 1942. **Above** *Typhoon 1Bs of 257 Squadron at Warmwell in January 1944* (IWM). **Below** *Believe it or not this house was originally the ATC tower at Warmwell.*

House and the CGS staff were billeted in Conygar. The Q site again proved its worth on April 30 but in May single aircraft made two attacks. They were met by intensive ground fire from the strengthened defences but during the second raid a Wellington and Hampden of the CGS were destroyed and the airfield heavily cratered. The heaviest attack of all came on May 11 when the alert lasted most of the night and eight individual aircraft were involved. Nine bombs dropped near the watch office but the majority exploded between the northern boundary and the railway and this proved to be the Luftwaffe's last attack.

The CGS left in June, leaving the airfield clear for a new activity, the mounting of fighter sweeps. The first of these was on July 10 when 12 bombers and three fighter squadrons left Warmwell for an attack on radar sites in France.

During the autumn, 10 Group decided that the situation had improved sufficiently to re-open the Chesil Range and a target towing Flight was formed at Warmwell on November 1. Squadrons started to arrive for air-firing practice, led by 32 Squadron which spent five days early in the month on this vital training. Other squadrons used the airfield to convert to new aircraft and 402 (RCAF) Squadron arrived to pioneer the use of the Hurricane as a fighter-bomber on operations.

No 175 Squadron formed at Warmwell for the same task with the same aircraft in March 1942. Following a tragic accident when a pilot mistook the target during an air-to-ground firing demonstration and killed or wounded between 70 and 80 people, the squadron became operational on April 16. Two out of three minesweepers found off Cap de la Hague were sunk on May 15 and most of the squadron's attacks were on shipping until August 19 when they took part in Operation *Jubilee*.

They were at readiness by 04:00 and eight aircraft took off at 04:40 led by the CO, Squadron Leader J.R. Pennington-Legh—their target the four-gun *Göring* battery which lay inland from the port of Dieppe. Diving from 3,000 to 800 ft (914 to 244 m), most of the pilots dropped their two 500-lb bombs on the target, though heavy smoke prevented results from being properly observed. All aircraft returned safely, and a second mission left Warmwell at 10:05—to attack the

Rommel gun position to the east of the town. Against heavy flak they hit the target with bombs and then took on an He 111 about to attack shipping off the beachhead. The He 111, and an Fw 190 which appeared, were hit and credited as probables. Again 175 escaped without loss. The third mission of the day covered the final stages of the withdrawal, with the *Hindenburg* coastal battery to the west of Dieppe the target. They attacked in the face of intense AA fire, one Hurricane was hit and the pilot forced to bale out off the coast. He was picked up unhurt. From 175 Squadron's viewpoint the day was a great success.

Squadrons continued to spend short detachments at Warmwell for operations and training with the APC but there were also usually one or two fighter units in residence. On September 13 1942 the first of several appearances was made by the Whirlwind twin-engined fighters of 263 Squadron. These racy looking aircraft had just been converted to fighter-bombing and for the rest of the year they concentrated on *Roadsteads* before going over to night *Rhubarbs* in February 1943. Apart from short detachments to Harrowbeer, Predannack, Zeals and Manston the squadron remained at Warmwell until December 1943 when it converted to Typhoons.

The distinctive star markings of the USAAF were first seen at Warmwell in July 1942 when Spitfires of the 31st Squadron paid a short visit from West-hampnett but on September 22 1943 heavier metal appeared when P-47 Thunderbolts of the 4th FG arrived, and set off early next morning to escort 60 bombers attacking Vannes airfield in France. They refuelled after the attack before returning to base. It was a portent, for in January 1944 Americans started to arrive in force, and soon the only RAF personnel were 276 Squadron with their Walrus amphibians and a small SHQ party.

The airfield became Station 454 of the IXth Air Force in March and was used by the 474th FG (428th, 429th and 430th Squadrons). The Group carried out its first operation, a fighter sweep from Warmwell on April 25, changing to bombing and strafing attacks on targets in France a month later when the P-38 Lightnings raided Orly airfield, near Paris. The 428th and 429th bombed the airfield while the 430th flew top cover, attacking targets of opportunity on the return flight, during which they destroyed two locomotives, hit two flak towers and a number of railway trucks. The sortie rate steadily increased as D-Day approached, and continued at high intensity afterwards until the 474th FG moved to the Continent on August 6.

The Walruses of 276 Squadron were also busy. On March 25 a glider on a training exercise became lost over the Channel and C Flight went out to look for it. Finding it in the sea six miles off Swanage, the amphibian alighted and took on board 12 men. Now too heavy to get airborne, it was taxied towards the coast and 30 minutes later a rescue launch took off the survivors and the Walrus returned to Warmwell. The next month they were replaced by 275 Squadron who stayed throughout the remaining occupation by the Americans.

In August 1944 the RAF started to move back into the main camp and on the 27th 17 APC arrived from North Weald charged with providing Second Tactical Air Force squadrons with air firing practice.

Warmwell was transferred from 11 to 10 Group on November 22 and 14 APC moved in alongside its sister unit. 174 Squadron was the first to complete the 14-day course and was followed by a steady stream from the Continent which continued throughout the winter and spring of 1945, and at a slower rate after VE-Day.

On June 7, 36 Spitfires of 310, 312 and 313 Squadrons landed after escorting the King and Queen on their visit to the Channel Islands, but the station was already starting to run down and the last air-firing course was completed when 174 Squadron took its Tempest Vs out to Germany on September 19. Most of the towing aircraft left for Sylt, both 14 and 17 APCs disbanded on October 14 1945 and the station was reduced to Care & Maintenance in November.

This was the end of Warmwell as an active airfield, but at least one more emergency landing was performed on its grass surface. Following one of the innumerable engine failures suffered by the Westland Wyvern during development, Harald Penrose, the company's chief test pilot, broke cloud at 3,000 ft (914 m) to find himself in sight of Warmwell. He performed a dead stick landing between heaps of debris left on the abandoned field—no mean feat in a flying brick like the Wyvern.

The hangars were used during the early postwar years as a food depot and in 1952 the ATC tower was purchased and converted, almost beyond recognition, into a large house. Named *Egdon House*, it stands alongside the minor road which uses the northerly perimeter track as foundations. A housing development now covers the main domestic site to the east of the airfield and a holiday village nestles amongst the trees on the south side. In 1973 the airfield itself was purchased by ECC Quarries Ltd and Amey Roadstone and it is rapidly disappearing as gravel is extracted.

Weston-super-Mare, Somerset (now Avon)

ST344603. 1½ miles SE of Weston-super-Mare alongside A371

Work started on the site of Weston Airport, tucked in between the railway and the A371 road during February 1936. The airfield was sufficiently complete for services to start in May, Railway Air Services opening their Plymouth-Haldon-Cardiff-Weston-Bristol service on the 25th. The services through Weston gradually expanded and in October 1938 Western Airways started the first internal night schedules in Britain. By this time the main administrative building and the hangar were fully operational and during the same year RAF Locking opened as a School of Technical Training just a mile to the east. A Station Flight was established at Weston to provide communications and staff training facilities.

In 1939 a contract was placed by the Air Ministry with the Straight Corporation (now the owners of Western Airways) for the operation of an Elementary & Reserve Flying Training School at the airport. Equipped with Magisters and Harts, 39 E&RFTS opened on July 3 but had hardly begun to function when the outbreak of war forced its disbandment to provide additional aircraft for service EFTSs. In its place the company was contracted to provide navigation training, 5 Civil Air Navigation School being formed on September 1. Renamed 5 AONS in November, it continued flying Ansons on exercises over the Bristol Channel and Irish Sea. It absorbed 3 AONS in June but, with the expansion of the Empire Air Training Scheme to include navigator training, 5 AONS was transferred to

Top *Weston-super-Mare from the north-east in April 1941. The present Westland factory is in the foreground, while the Beaufighter assembly plant of Old Mixon is on the western side* (IWM). **Above** *Beaufighter TF X SR919—the last off the production line at Weston-super-Mare in 1945* (Bristol Aeroplane Co).

South Africa on August 22 1940.

Civil flying ceased on September 3 1939 though the airfield was taken over by the National Air Communications organisation and at the end of October a limited Cardiff-Weston service was restarted for a short time. Western Airways were used mainly for maintenance work and overhaul of the primary trainers and light communications aircraft flooding into the RAF. The airfield was transferred to the RAF on May 1 1940 and just outside the western boundary a shadow factory was built at Old Mixon, production of the Beaufighter starting in September, though deliveries were slow because of component shortages. Later a 4,200 ft

(1,280 m) SW/NE runway was laid to prevent flight testing delays previously caused by waterlogging.

Pushed out of Yatesbury by the rapidly expanding Radio School, 10 EFTS arrived at Weston on September 7 1940 and the civil maintenance personnel left at the airport when 5 AONS went abroad were absorbed by the Bristol Aeroplane Co to service the Tiger Moths. Weston was a much smaller airfield than Yatesbury and it was with relief that Lulsgate Bottom became available for circuit work, though this did not resolve the acute shortage of technical accommodation. A hurricane-force gale on November 12 1940 badly damaged 11 of 30 picketed Tiger Moths

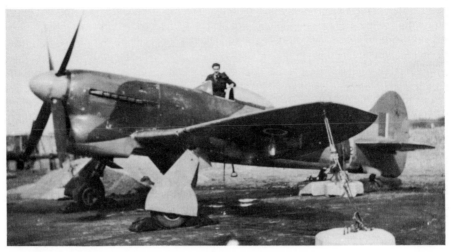

Tempest F V of the ATDU at Weston in 1947.

despite desperate attempts to manhandle them into the available hangarage and the wind was so strong that two huts were wrecked.

A Q site was set up two miles to the south at Bleadon and when a heavy bombing raid developed on the town of Weston-super-Mare during the night of January 1941 it was activated. The ignition switches failed to operate and AC2 Bright went out of the bunker and lit the dummy buildings by hand. Immediately the attack switched to the site, which was heavily cratered. Bright received a well deserved Military Medal a couple of months later. The Q site proved its value again in May when 14 HE bombs dropped on the dummy gooseneck flare-path. Several cows were killed but there was no damage to either Weston Airport or the town. Indeed, more damage was caused at the airfield when a barrage balloon was set on fire by lightning and fell on the hangar. Following the closure of Lulsgate in June 1941 Weston became very congested, forcing a move of 10 EFTS to Stoke Orchard during September.

It was over a year before the RAF reappeared at Weston, 286 Squadron moving in from Colerne during October 1942 with Hurricanes, Defiants and Oxfords. They left in April 1943 and Weston was then transferred to Technical Training Command as a satellite of Locking. 286 Squadron was soon back, returning from Zeals in July as a lodger,

and the following month the Equipment Training School moved in from Eastbourne. During December the nomadic 286 Squadron went to Weston Zoyland and the airport was left in the hands of the Bristol Aeroplane Company until March 1944, when an Air Torpedo Development Unit detachment arrived from Zoyland. Equipped with a selection of aircraft, it carried out dropping trials in the Bristol Channel until 1949.

By early 1944 Bristol was producing an average of 87 Beaufighter Xs a month and this continued until September 1945 when the last came off the line. It had been intended to build the Brabazon prototypes at Weston-super-Mare but the sub-soil was found unsuitable for the runway required and the plan was abandoned, leaving only part of the Old Mixon factory in production—making components.

Locking Station Flight was still in operation with Proctors in 1946, the year that the Cardiff-Weston schedules were resumed and the airfield transferred to the Ministry of Civil Aviation.

During 1955 all Bristol helicopter development and production was transferred to the Old Mixon factory, and the majority of the Sycamores and all the Belvederes were built there. In March 1960 the Westland Aircraft organisation took over the Bristol Helicopter Division and continued production of spares for Bristol-designed helicopters and production of new Westland designs.

Three Varsities fitted with radar were

stationed at Weston from 1959 for the Radio School at Locking. One was lost in an accident but the other two were used as flying classrooms for technicians under training until they moved with the school to Cosford in October 1966. Since then the fortunes of the airfield have declined and at the end of 1978 Western Airways relinquished their operating licence. The local council wanted to close the airfield but MoD refused to do this and instead leased the whole 350-acre site to Westland (Helicopters) Limited. Some flying will continue, including that of 621 Gliding School. In May 1978 the British Rotorcraft Museum was opened in a small enclave on the airfield; it has steadily expanded its scope through the years and now has a selection of helicopters worthy of inspection. The current renewed efforts to sell those portions of the airfield not required by Westland has again put the future of any flying, other than rotary wing, in doubt.

Weston Zoyland, Somerset

ST365344. 4 miles SE of Bridgewater

There are not many flat areas in the West Country but Weston Zoyland village sits squarely in the middle of fen-like country, criss-crossed with large drainage ditches. It is also about 19 miles from Watchet, where a large anti-aircraft gunnery range was established in the 1920s, and it was this which attracted the Air Ministry to a large field just to the east of the village. It was used by Horsleys of 100 Squadron for a summer camp in 1926 during which they co-operated with the gunners at Watchet so successfully that annual visits followed. In 1929 the Night Flying Flight, Biggin Hill, took over and, renamed the Anti-Aircraft Co-operation Flight, continued the summer camps until 1936, opening up the landing ground each May and spending the summer months under canvas.

Another change of name occurred in February 1937 and it was the Wallaces of A Flight, No 1 Anti-Aircraft Co-operation Unit which plodded up and down off Watchet towing targets, until replaced by Henleys in 1939. With the war came squadron detachments for armament practice camps but the main task of the unit remained the AA camp at Watchet. In November 1939 a detachment of Lysanders from 16 Squadron arrived for Army Co-operation, the whole unit moving in during August 1940 for coastal

patrols and work with the Army's Western Command. During the same month 8 AACU arrived from Filton for searchlight co-operation and these increasing commitments resulted in Weston Zoyland becoming a fully fledged self-accounting station on September 1 1940. Seven days later an invasion alert resulted in all personnel being recalled from leave, and on the 25th a large enemy bomber formation, reported as over 70 strong, was sighted at 16,000 ft (4,877 m), but no bombs were dropped in the immediate area.

The steadily increasing number of personnel rapidly outgrew the temporary station accommodation and airmen were billeted in Weston Zoyland, Middlezoy and Othery—some sleeping in the coach-houses and cheese rooms of large country houses. In December 1940 a detachment of the Special Duty Flight, Christchurch, arrived with two Lysanders and a Fox Moth for co-operation with the Air Defence Development Unit, this continuing for a year by which time a Henley was doing the towing.

The low-lying airfield, though prone to fog, was often open when other West Country bases were adversely affected by low cloud and early in 1941 a number of aircraft being ferried to Gibraltar had to return to the UK and were landed at Zoyland very short of fuel. This speeded up work on an extension of the main grass runway and other improvements included the take-over of Townsend House as the officers' mess and the village hall as the NAAFI canteen.

No 16 Squadron went through a bad patch in June 1941, the CO, Wing Commander Hancock, losing his life in a take-off accident at Roborough on the 9th. Squadron Leader Walker assumed command and the very next day his Lysander was attacked by four Bf 109s over Exmouth. His gunner managed to shoot down one of the fighters but this triumph was short-lived for the Germans quickly despatched the Lysander, and both occupants were killed.

It was decided that Weston Zoyland should become the major practice camp for Army Co-op squadrons and on July 6 the first unit, 239 Squadron, arrived for training. A bombing range at Steart Flats was in use and in October 1492 Flight was formed to give specialised training on the Lilstock range using Lysanders, later replaced by Masters and Martinèts.

The resident squadron started to re-

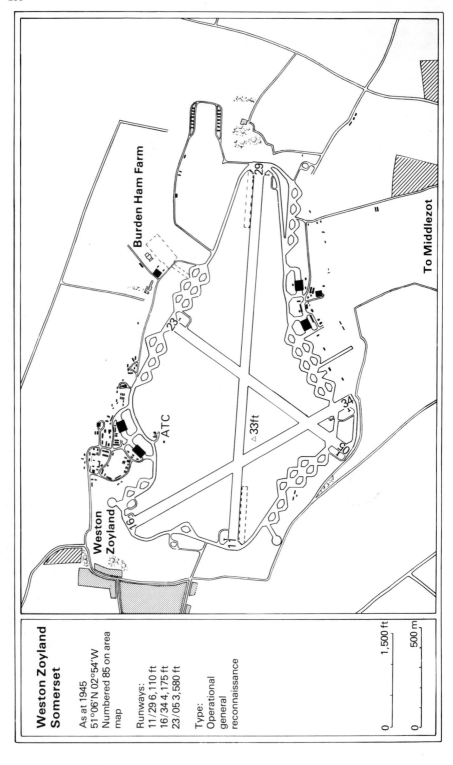

Weston Zoyland
Somerset

As at 1945
51°06'N 02°54'W
Numbered 85 on area
map

Runways:
11/29 6,110 ft
16/34 4,175 ft
23/05 3,580 ft

Type:
Operational
general
reconnaissance

1,500 ft

500 m

Burden Ham Farm

To Middlezot

△ 33ft

ATC

Weston
Zoyland

29

23

34

16

11

Top *Blenheim 1 L1187 of 104 Squadron belly-landed at Weston Zoyland during an armament practice camp in 1939* (D. Clyde-Smith). **Above** *The major unit at Weston Zoyland during the early war years was 1 AACU. Here is one of their Henley target tugs* (D. Clyde-Smith).

equip with Mustangs in May 1942 and took part in operational fighter sweeps, before leaving for Andover at the end of December. During the autumn A and P Flights of 1 AACU had become 1600 and 1601 Flights respectively, but they continued to drone over the Watchet ranges, though now with a mixture of Henleys and Defiants. They were joined by 1625 Flight in January 1943 and plans were made for a general reconnaissance squadron on a site to the south of the airfield. This necessitated tarmac runways and a general upgrading of the airfield, work commencing in the spring of 1943.

With the formation of the Second Tactical Air Force in June 1943, their squadrons started using Weston Zoyland for intensive air-firing practice. Servicing Commando units, formed from members of the Army, Navy and RAF, also practised working under field conditions, and there was a constant turnover in personnel as squadrons came and went. On October 18 1943, No 1492 Flight became 13 APC and in December the

towing Flights became 587 Squadron with Martinets and Henleys for towing, and Hurricanes and Oxfords for simulated attacks on gun positions. 286 Squadron arrived from Weston-super-Mare with similar aircraft at the beginning of December and commenced work alongside 587 Squadron.

In fact the GR squadron never materialised but the site was put to good use by 525 Squadron which formed on September 2 1943 as a transport unit with Warwicks. The work-up of their rather makeshift version of the aircraft proved difficult and though some flights were made to Gibraltar it was a relief when the unit moved to Lyneham in February 1944.

Trials of towed target gliders, manufactured by International Model Aircraft of Merton, Surrey, were undertaken by 286 and 587 Squadrons with success early in 1944. On April 10 they were suddenly moved to Culmhead and Winkleigh and the airfield was prepared for the USAAF.

Two and a half thousand beds were set

up in huts and hangars but, as so often happens, the prospective occupants were delayed and they were not needed for over a month. The first gliders were flown in on May 20 and paratroop exercises followed before some of the C-47s of the 442nd TCG assembled just before D-Day. They formed part of the 50th TCW which took the 101st Airborne Division to Normandy and despite heavy flak most of the troops were put down on their DZ. The whole of the 442nd did not arrive until June 10 and then remained at Weston Zoyland until October.

No 286 Squadron had already returned, followed by 587 in October and the training programme was soon back to normal. In February 1945, 1540 BAT Flight was established with Oxfords to operate with 6 (P) AFU Little Rissington, replaced by 3 (P) AFU Lulsgate Bottom in July. 286 had disbanded at the end of April but 587 Squadron successfully completed the glider target trials using newly delivered Vengeance tugs, and also operated Masters and Harvards. A number of fighter squadrons were spending short periods on the airfield, some prior to disbandment, others while a more permanent base was selected.

No 587 Squadron disbanded in June 1946 and the last squadron, 222, moved its Meteor F3s out during the following October. With the ranges transferred to Middle Wallop and Keevil, Weston Zoyland was reduced to Care & Maintenance and was virtually abandoned.

With the upsurge of training required to service the Korean War, a number of airfields were hurriedly reopened, among them Weston Zoyland. 209 AFS was formed in June 1952 and flew Vampires and Meteors for two years before being renamed 12 FTS. Further changes produced No 3 All Weather Jet Refresher Squadron which left for Strubby in 1955.

Under the command of Group Captain W.B. Menual, the air element of an Atomic Task Force began to form up at Weston Zoyland in November 1955. Seven Canberra B6s of 76 Squadron and three Varsities were the initial equipment, joined in December by the Canberra PR 7s of 542 Squadron. The Varsities left for Pearce, Australia, in March 1956, followed soon afterwards by the Canberras, all to be employed in flying connected with the first British atomic bomb trials in Australia. The last units to use Weston Zoyland were 32 and 73 Squadrons which converted to Canberra

B2 aircraft during January-March 1957 and then left for Cyprus.

Yet again reduced to C&M, the station was closed in January 1958 though retained by the Ministry until 1969. The A372 was re-routed to use part of the main runway and the grass areas quickly returned to agriculture. Numerous derelict buildings still stood in 1980 to the east of the airfield, and there is the standard wartime ATC tower on the nothern perimeter, but a recent change of ownership has put these relics at risk.

Whitchurch, Somerset (now Avon)

ST595686. 2 miles S of Bristol

Turn off the A38 at Barrow Common and you find yourself climbing Dundry Hill. Stay on the narrow road which skirts the brow of the hill and Bristol is laid out like a map. Below you is one open space, now called Hensgrove Park, and the site of the Bristol Sports Centre. Up to 1957 this was Whitchurch airport, and a portion of the single runway and the taxiway up to the old terminal is clearly visible to the east of a large roundabout. There are few airfields with such a convenient viewing platform and therein lies the major reason for its closure.

Whitchurch was born when the Bristol & Wessex Aeroplane Club found Filton too overcrowded for comfort and in 1928 decided to establish a small airfield of their own. With the help of the City Council, a site two miles west of Whitchurch village was chosen Two farms were purchased and during 1929 work commenced on clearing and levelling the ground. Bristol Airport was formally opened by HRH Prince Albert, Duke of York, on May 31 1930 and for the first five years it was operated by the club. From 1932 onwards a number of small airlines ran a variety of summer services through Whitchurch but progress was slow, and in 1935 the City Council took responsibility for the development of the airport.

The Reserve School at Filton used Whitchurch as a RLG throughout the 1930s but in 1938 the Air Ministry negotiated the establishment of 33 E&RFTS on the airport. Operated by Chamier Gilbert Lodge & Co Ltd, it formed in December with 12 Tiger Moths on strength supplemented by Harts and Battles for annual training of reservists during 1939. By this time considerable improvements had been made to the original airport. A large tarmac apron had been laid, runway lighting and a direction finding beacon installed; and with the arrival of the Reserve School additional hangarage was erected.

It was these facilities which attracted Imperial and British Airways when they were told to produce a war dispersal plan requiring the evacuation of Croydon and Heston. Plans became fact at the end of August 1939 and it was not long before 60 large passenger aircraft were assembled at Whitchurch, which became A base.

In the meantime the airport had been requisitioned by the Air Ministry and, with the outbreak of war, all private flying ceased. 33 E&FTS was disbanded, its aircraft being used to supplement other units and leaving Whitchurch free for National Air Communications schedules which gradually got under way during the autumn of 1939, mainly to destinations in France.

The war also brought an increase in aircraft ferrying and the RAF was soon hard-pressed to cope with it. At the same time many experienced civilian pilots were grounded and the Air Ministry reluctantly agreed to experiment with an Air Transport Auxiliary to make use of this unemployed talent. An initial batch of 30 candidates gathered at Bristol and undertook flying tests at Whitchurch on Airspeed Couriers. At the end of the year a number of women pilots were tested and several were accepted for further flying at CFS Upavon before joining the ATA. This task was later transferred to White Waltham and in June 1940 B Section of No 3 Ferry Pilots' Pool (ATA) was formed at Whitchurch for ferrying duties mainly concerned with the products of the Bristol Aeroplane Company.

During 1940 the newly formed BOAC got its landplane schedules organised but suffered a series of setbacks due to weather and domestic problems at Whitchurch. Two HP 42Ws, those enormous biplanes with a built-in headwind, were blown together and wrecked during a gale on March 19, while in October the delivery of DH 91 Albatross G-AEVV/AX903 to 271 Squadron was delayed because it was deliberately set on fire and G-AFDI was destroyed in the same attack. More problems ensued on November 24 when Bristol was heavily bombed and incendiaries dropped on Whitchurch

Whitchurch on August 11 1963. The BOAC base was on the northern side where there is a large apron alongside the hangars (DoE).

destroyed an Ensign and a Douglas DC-3.

Among the more unusual aircraft to fly from the BOAC base were the Curtiss Wright CW-20 G-AGDI and the Fw 200 Condor G-AGAY, but most services were flown by DC-3s to Portugal and Gibraltar, the route across the Bay of Biscay being very hazardous though only one aircraft was actually shot down by enemy fighters—on June 1 1943 with the loss of 17 passengers and crew.

During production of the Beaufighter II at Filton, delays in delivery of the Merlin power plants resulted in many of the airframes being despatched by road to Whitchurch and Colerne to clear the production lines. They were subsequently completed by working parties and for

DC-3s and a DH 91 Albatross at Whitchurch in 1941 (IWM).

once the Ferry Pool had a delivery task on its own doorstep. Bristol University Air Squadron started flying Tiger Moths from Whitchurch in July 1942 and continued until disbanded four years later.

With the improving situation in Europe, the BOAC terminal was moved to Hurn on November 1 1944 and activity at Whitchurch was then confined almost exclusively to the comings and goings of the ATA taxi Ansons and Argus aircraft. The Director General of Civil Aviation took over the airfield from the Air Ministry in June 1945 when BOAC was using Whitchurch for pilot training and conversion of aircraft for passenger or freight transport.

Great Western & Southern Airlines resumed operations through Bristol (Whitchurch) in July 1946 and were followed by a variety of companies attempting to make a success of internal air services. Most quickly faded away but the Bristol & Wessex Aero Club was soon strongly re-established, holding a garden party in May 1947 during which one of four Spitfire LF XVIs of 501 Squadron tipped up on its nose during landing. The club remained until the airfield closed in 1957 on transfer of Bristol Airport to Lulsgate Bottom.

Now two Bellman hangars are in use by industrial firms on a small trading estate on the north side of the original airfield, but houses crowd around the Park and

apart from the remaining piece of runway there are few other signs of the past.

Winkleigh, Devon
SS621094. 1½ miles NW of Winkleigh on B3220

The beautiful but hilly nature of North Devon meant that sites for airfields were few but a satellite for Chivenor was needed and a stretch of moorland just north of Winkleigh was quickly chosen.

Work started in 1940 on a two-runway airfield which took the form of a cross-bow pointing west. The boggy surface proved very difficult, foundations for the runways being hard to stabilise, and it was not until November 1941 that it was first inspected by the parent unit at Exeter. It was a further 12 months before it was anywhere near ready. By this time Coastal Command had lost interest in Winkleigh, and it was Fighter Command that officially accepted the airfield on January 1 1943. It was not an encouraging sight, the whole area a mass of mud, the road still several inches above the level of the runways, and none of the accommodation usable. However, the contractors had managed to erect a single 'T2' hangar and eight Blisters on the north-west side and a standard control tower on higher ground to the south-east, near the administrative site.

During February and March the airmen were moved into the camp from their billets in the village and the first aircraft landed on April 24. But no one had any clear use for Winkleigh and it was reduced to Care & Maintenance on August 20. During October 1943 the airfield was reopened for the USAAF, who used it for pre-invasion exercises with American troops practising beach landings on the North Devon coast. Spitfires of the 12th Recce Squadron, IXth Fighter Command, USAAF, from Keevil and Membury, arrived to provide tactical reconnaissance over the exercise beachhead and remained until December. Various other American detachments followed, a continuous stream of C-47s ferrying American troops from Devon to the south-east of England between February 22 and 24 under the control of the 74th Service Group.

It was April 1944 before Winkleigh received its first resident operational unit when 406 (RCAF) Squadron arrived from Exeter equipped with Beaufighter VIs for night fighting. They were soon in action, Warrant Officer G.F. MacEwen and Flight Sergeant C.S. Headley shooting down a Ju 88 off Start Point on April 23. During the month a number of Mosquito XIIs were received and, during their very first operational night sorties on April 29/30, Squadron Leader 'Blackie' Williams and Flying Officer Kirkpatrick, flying *406/0*, destroyed two Do 217s in the space of 11 minutes.

Part of 286 Squadron also arrived in April equipped with Hurricanes and Defiants, and early in May they were joined by an Albacore detachment from 415 (RCAF) Squadron. These were used nightly for anti-E-Boat patrols aimed at preventing them from penetrating Allied training areas off the south coast and causing chaos amongst the assembled landing craft.

The Luftwaffe attacked ports and pre-invasion assembly areas and during the night of May 14/15 a raid by 30 bombers was made on Bristol. 406 Squadron was up in strength and had their most successful night from Winkleigh, or for that matter in their history. Four enemy aircraft, including an He 177, were destroyed and three probables were claimed. Routine patrols over the English Channel during early June were uneventful but on the 7th the first *Day Ranger* was flown by two Mosquito XIIs and a Do 217 went down in flames off Lannion. Intruder sorties were also flown, resulting in trains and military vehicles being strafed as the Mosquitoes ranged over France.

Released from routine patrols on July 10, they were detailed to guard Allied destroyers off the French coast and at the end of the month 406 started to re-equip with Mosquito XXXs. These went into action on the 21st against seven Do 217s about to attack four destroyers off the Breton coast. Williams and Kirkpatrick,

The crossbow layout of Winkleigh is well illustrated by this vertical taken on June 4 1970 when the road had been re-opened and the runways were in use for the foundations of a trading estate (DoE).

The ATC tower at Winkleigh was perched up on high ground. Still in fairly good condition, it had been used as a house for some years.

flying *MM731*, closed on one, hit an engine which caught fire, and the aircraft crashed into the sea. Williams then noticed that his starboard engine was streaming coolant and feathered the propeller. One Dornier was still ahead and Williams caught up with it and opened fire, causing the port engine to burst into flames. As the bomber started to go down it was hit by another Mosquito and disintegrated.

Meanwhile, 415 Squadron left for Manston on July 12 and Lysanders of 161 Squadron arrived for operations into western France. They dropped and picked up agents, often landing at night by the light of hand torches.

On September 16, 406 Squadron moved to Colerne and at the end of the month Winkleigh was again on C&M. Two months later it transferred to 23 Group in readiness for use as a Norwegian training base. The task was to train recruits in readiness for the rebirth of the Royal Norwegian Air Force. The initial establishment of 12 Harvards was joined later by Cornells shipped from the Norwegian Flying School at Toronto, Canada.

The training base operated for ten months, 22 Harvards and 22 Cornells flying to Gardermoen, near Oslo, in November 1945. Once again Winkleigh was devoid of aircraft, and though it remained a 23 Group airfield no further flying took place and it was transferred to

the Ministry of Agriculture and Fisheries on June 30 1948. On October 15 1956 Winkleigh was again requisitioned by the Air Ministry but remained an inactive site parented by Chivenor until finally disposed of in December 1958.

Now the busy B3320 once again crosses the airfield and the southern perimeter track is used for a minor road. The solitary 'T2' hangar still stands but is very dilapidated, and two of the accommodation sites are largely complete. Near Seckington Cross several standard Maycrete buildings have been neatly converted into houses, and another site is now the Wagon Wheels Holiday Parc. The derelict ATC tower was a private house for some years but now is derelict, and looks over a saw mill and numbers of other industrial enterprises on the airfield.

Winkton, Hampshire

SZ165975. 2½ miles NW of Christchurch

With the formation of the Second Tactical Air Force in June 1943, sites were chosen for a series of ALGs in the south of England for use in the build-up and initial phases of the invasion. Winkton was among these and work started immediately on clearing hedges and filling in ditches to allow two steel mesh runways to be laid. The airfield took in most of Lower Clockhouse Farm but also extended north of the minor road between Sopley and Bransgrove, which was closed. Apart from the runways, facilities were minimal, but by August the Luftwaffe had it marked on target maps. They called it Sopley which was understandable for the LG was very close to the village and important radar station of that name.

The ALG was ready by September 1943 but remained dormant until the following March when it opened as an 11 Group unit. This was nominal only, for on April 4 the 404th FG, IXth Tactical Air Command, USAAF, brought in their P-47 Thunderbolts under the command of Colonel Carroll W. McColpin, a 29-year old veteran who had served in one of the RAF Eagle squadrons. The personnel lived in tents and the aircraft were dispersed around the field in the open.

Operations began on May 1, the aircraft being used as fighter bombers. The first *Crossbow* mission was on the 9th when the three squadrons were briefed to attack separate V-1 sites. The 507th and 508th Squadrons claimed hits with their 500-lb bombs, but the 506th were unable to find their target and dive-bombed the railyard at Serqueux, 20 miles north-east of Rouen instead. They met intense flak and one aircraft was lost. A rare encounter with German fighters occurred on May 18 when the 508th was withdrawing from an unsuccessful attempt to bomb Beaumont-sur-Oise airfield. They were surprised by six Bf 109s and one P-47 was shot down in the confusion.

On D-Day itself the 404th FG flew high level cover over the beachheads, putting up a maximum effort and flying 191 sorties between dawn and dusk. Bad weather during the days following the invasion caused much frustration but on June 10 another major effort was made. 48 P-47s left Winkton during the morning to attack artillery positions, and this was followed by a concentrated assault on bridges. In the evening they turned on the railway system of Normandy and the 506th hit a road bridge, destroyed a rail intersection, 15 trucks and a locomotive, while the 507th cut the tracks either side of two trains and then bombed and strafed the stationary locomotives. Meanwhile, the 508th cut railway lines near Chartres, set rail tanker trucks on fire, destroyed a locomotive and strafed barracks—it was definitely one of the better days.

Similar operations continued until July 6 when the 404th FG moved to the Continent and Winkton was abandoned. The wire mesh runways were lifted and early in 1945 the ALG reverted to farming use after a short but hectic life. There is little evidence now of the existence of Winkton though the line of the runways can be traced by the culverted ditches and the replacement of hedges by concrete posts and wires.

Woodsford (Warmwell), Dorset

See Warmwell

Worth Matravers, Dorset

SY963770. 1 mile W of Worth Matravers village

High up above white cliffs on St Albans Head near Swanage, this small landing ground was shortlived, but in the desperate days of 1940 it served a unique and vital purpose. The Air Ministry Research Establishment, a radar research station, moved from Dundee to Worth Matravers early in 1940 and by June was operating under the control of the Telecommunications Research Establishment

whose HQ was at Leeson House, Langton Matravers.

The sudden deterioration in the situation in France focused attention on invasion, and the possible use of wooden gliders. Little was known about the range at which they could be detected by radar, or indeed whether they could be seen at all, and so the Special Duty Flight at Christchurch was provided with four high-performance gliders which were to be towed out to sea by three ancient Avro 504Ns. The scientists wanted the gliders to leave and return to the radar station itself and fortuitously there was a suitable field just south of the scanners, on Rendscombe Farm.

This became Worth Matravers LG in June 1940 and before each trial the glider trailers were towed up from Christchurch, the glider erected and then the '504Ns flown in. With tow ropes quickly hooked up, the amazingly short take-off of the aircraft and glider combination was used to the full. They then headed out to sea climbing steadily to 10,000 ft (3,048 m), and to about 40 miles (64 km) away from Worth Matravers—only some 20 miles (32 km) from the French coast. Here the glider was released to make its way back to Worth alone. One can imagine how naked the pilots felt during their slow descent towards the invisible English cliffs. As the trials continued they were pressed to make their approches at ever lower levels and on one occasion Philip Wills, the famous glider pilot, only cleared the cliffs by using the up currents produced by the sea breeze.

After a further series of tests with the gliders approaching the scanners from inland, the experiments were terminated in August and the surviving aircraft and gliders went to the Central Landing Establishment at Ringway.

A Magister of 32 MU crashed on the LG on September 14 1940 and Worth Matravers was used occasionally by communications aircraft for a few months before being abandoned in 1941.

Yate, Gloucestershire (now Avon)

ST706830. 10 miles NE of Bristol

A grass airfield with a long but undistinguished career, Yate hit the headlines during the war only once—as an unnamed target in the south-west of England!

The airfield was built in 1916/17 to provide flight test and delivery facilities for No 3 (Western) Aircraft Repair Depot. The depot consisted of four large sheds along the southern edge of the airfield. After the 1914-18 War Yate was abandoned by the Air Ministry, and the buildings remained empty until taken over by George Parnall and Co in 1925. They built a number of experimental aircraft of their own design and in 1931 the prototype of the famous Percival Gull. This was followed by a production batch of 23 Gulls, before the Percival Aircraft Co took over the construction job themselves.

In 1935 Parnall sold out, and a new company was formed by the amalgamation of the firm with Hendy Aircraft Co and Nash & Thompson Ltd as Parnall Aircraft Limited. Although they continued aircraft production on a small scale, the Hendy Heck being their most successful product, the main interest became power-operated gun turrets. A large factory was built alongside the railway line in the south-west corner of the airfield and was in full production by the beginning of the war. The airfield

remained a company facility, four Hendy Hecks being employed on a daily liaison service to RAF units.

Naturally the Germans were interested in all this activity and on September 27 1940 the ground attack Bf 110s of Erpobungsgruppe 210 were briefed for a raid on the Yate factory. They were to be escorted by 42 Bf 110s of ZG26 and preceded by a force of Bf 109s from II/JG2, whose task was to dilute the strength of the defenders by diversionary tactics over the English coast. The ten bomb-laden Bf 110s of Erpr 210 took off from Cherbourg and set course direct for Yate. Over the English coast some of the escorting ZG26 aircraft split away and at first the defending fighters were held while 10 Group controllers tried to decide where the German force was heading. Finally the Hurricanes of 504 Squadron were scrambled and set upon the Bf 110s as they started their dive. The tight formation broke up, Erpr 210 jettisoning their bombs over north Bristol and turning to escape. During their withdrawal they were attacked by Spitfires of 152 and

Yate, seen from the west in June 1941. The Parnall/Fraser Nash factories are already encroaching on the grass airfield (IWM).

609 Squadrons and Hurricanes from 56 and 238, and it rapidly became a rout. When all the claims were sorted out the German losses were ten, including four Bf 110s from Erpr 210. Amongst their casualties was their Gruppenkommandueur, Hauptmann Martin Lutz. British losses were one Spitfire destroyed and a Hurricane badly damaged, the pilot of the Spitfire being killed.

Thus the Yate factory escaped destruction and went on to become the largest sub-contractor of Spitfire components in the country in addition to its work as a major producer of turrets. After the war the airfield was closed and much of it is now covered by buildings.

Yatesbury, Wiltshire

SU055710. 4 miles E of Calne

Thousands of radio operators, both airmen and WAAF, did their basic training at Yatesbury during the Second World War and most will remember their stay in the vast hutted camp alongside the A4 road for its extreme discomfort. During the winters the central heating regularly froze up and in the summer dust storms swirled around the huts in the seemingly interminable wind off the Downs.

To the west of the main camp was the airfield. It had originally been opened in 1916 as a training station and was home to several units, among them 36 and 37 Training Depot Stations which used a variety of training aircraft including the ubiquitous Avro 504K. After the armistice the TDS ceased operations and the airfield was closed in 1919.

In August 1935 the Bristol Aeroplane Company was given a contract for a second RAF Reserve Training School. The company purchased 290 acres of the old 1914-18 Yatesbury airfield and immediately began refurbishing the two 1917-pattern hangars and the landing ground, then built a new administrative block, hospital, MT section and boiler house. The new school opened on January 6 1936 but because of severe autumn weather Yatesbury was not ready and operations started at Filton. The move to Yatesbury commenced the following month, the pupils being billeted in local farmhouses until the beginning of April when the new accommodation was complete.

On February 1 1938 the Bristol School was redesignated 10 E&RFTS and came under the control of 26 (Training) Group. Tiger Moths continued to be used for primary training but now supplemented by Hart variants for advanced work. The success of this training scheme resulted in a further contract for a navigation school at Yatesbury which started flying as 2 Civil Air Navigation School in September. Meanwhile, plans were made for the training of ground radio operators at Yatesbury and construction of the large hutted camp alongside the airfield commenced, 2 Electrical & Wireless School being formed on October 13 1938.

The outbreak of war brought a tremendous expansion in the training task at Yatesbury. 10 E&RFTS became 10 EFTS when the Harts were flown away and the established strength of 18 Tiger Moths increased to 54, largely by the re-allocation of aircraft from disbanded Reserve Schools. The CANS became an AONS and in October the Bristol Wireless School was formed to give air experience in Dragon Rapides to embryo air wireless operators recruited from E & WS courses. The much expanded E & WS was split into four Wings, and two mobile W/T sections were formed in October for the British Expeditionary Force in France.

The severe weather during January and February 1940 halted activity on the airfield and virtually stopped the whole camp. Hangars were iced up and the water system froze. Many weary hours were spent on defence duties by trainee aircrew with little reward or excitement, though in a bizarre accident in April a Sergeant Pilot was killed when struck by a Tiger Moth while he was on duty at a gun post, and during the night of July 28 two sticks of bombs were dropped just north of 10 EFTS headquarters.

The steady expansion of the wireless school and the need for more flying training as the number of W/Op trainees increased, forced out the other units. 10 EFTS moved to Weston-super-Mare in September 1940 and 2 AONS was closed down during December. To reflect its current task more accurately, 2 E&WS became 2 Signals School in September 1940 and a unit which commenced radar training at Yatesbury in January 1941 was renamed 2 Radio School in March. 2 Signals School found themselves with some of the highly unpopular Bothas in October 1940, suffering them for nearly a year, and with the introduction of Proctors in 1942 RAF instructors replaced

Top *Yatesbury on January 15 1956. The hangars and outline of the grass airfield can be seen, and part of the enormous hutted camp to the east* (DoE).

Above *Two 1917 hangars still stand on the northern side of Yatesbury together with a number of more recent WD buildings.*

the Bristol flying personnel. The company continued to maintain the Dominie/Proctor fleet which gradually increased to a peak of 104 aircraft.

To rationalise the confusing variety of names used by wireless-orientated training units, they all become Radio Schools in December 1942. 2 Radio School now became No 9, and the former 2 Signals School took over its title—presumably this was to confound the enemy! In June 1943 the first direct entry W/O A/G courses started, each lasting 20-24 weeks, and ground operator training ceased at Yatesbury the following month.

In fact the output outstripped the anticipated loss rate in the middle of 1943 and a pool was established for trained wireless operators at Yatesbury. Initially 600-strong, it increased to over 1,600 by October 1944, resulting in a further training commitment to keep them current.

The flying element of 2 Radio School was finally closed in July 1945, having trained 18,500 air wireless operators in 224,000 hours flying. It was immediately replaced by 2 EFTS, which arrived from Worcester with the familiar Tiger Moths. The station transferred from 27 to 50 Group with this change, and with the closure of the latter unit, to 23 Group on April 21 1947.

No 2 EFTS closed in September 1947 and the Bristol Aeroplane Company's premises were presented to the RAF Malcolm Club to form a recreational centre for the large number of trainees again undergoing ground radio/radar courses with 2 Radio School. In 1951 they were joined by RAF Regiment personnel, the station being used to form up 2, 5 and 7 Wings and a large number of squadrons. In August 1956 part of the emergency force gathered for the ill-fated Suez campaign formed at Yatesbury. This was 215 Wing which endured a long wait before leaving for Gamil airfield in Egypt to set up air traffic and movement parties.

Guided weapon training transferred to

Typical of the many Proctors used at Yatesbury, this Mk 4 was photographed postwar and was painted silver overall.

Newton in January 1960 and the ground training aircraft left later for various Schools of Technical Training before the station finally closed down in April 1969. Yatesbury came within the proposed North Wessex Downs Area of Outstanding Natural Beauty and the Ministry of Defence was persuaded to remove the whole of the hutted camp. The land was then sold in lots but the Wiltshire County Council then found that the only way to get the unsightly foundations removed was to purchase it from the new owners and dispose of the concrete themselves. This was completed successfully and the camp area returned to farmland, except for one section whose owner refused to sell. Thus, while the airfield itself remains fairly intact, complete with the two 1917-type hangars and the new one built by Bristol for their school (and now used by road haulage contractors), the domestic and ground school site has disappeared except for some access roads and a number of buildings on the unrestored land. They look very incongruous when viewed from the elevated A4 road.

Yeovil, Somerset

ST540158. 1 mile SW of Yeovil

There cannot be many airfields, or for that matter factories, which have resulted directly from a speech in the House of Commons—Yeovil is one. In April 1915 Lloyd George made a speech which caused the directors of Petters Ltd, a Yeovil engineering firm, to offer their services as munition manufacturers to both the War Office and the Admiralty. The latter replied immediately and after a conference offered Petters a contract for building Short 184 seaplanes.

This was hardly what the directors had expected, but fortunately they already had plans to extend their factory and had bought Westland Farm during 1914 for this purpose. One bay of the new factory was already complete and was immediately taken over as the Westland Aircraft Works—and the first aircraft completed by Christmas. This first batch of seaplanes and additional contracts, which included 1½-Strutters, was crated and delivered to Rochester or Hamble for flight testing, but this was clearly unsatisfactory and early in 1917 the firm purchased land for an airfield alongside the factory. Levelling and filling work started immediately and Yeovil aerodrome was ready in April for the first company-built DH4 to be flight-tested.

The airfield was extended during 1918, and after a contract was placed with the firm for the large Vickers Vimy bomber, new factory buildings were prepared. While most contracts were cancelled at the end of the war, the order for Vimys was upheld and the management, aware that

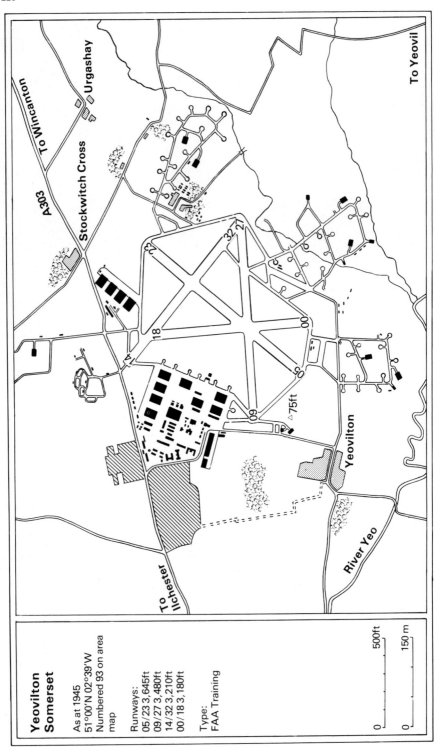

Yeovilton
Somerset

As at 1945
51°00'N 02°39'W
Numbered 93 on area
map

Runways:
05/23 3,645ft
09/27 3,480ft
14/32 3,210ft
00/18 3,180ft

Type:
FAA Training

The Westland factory at Yeovil circa 1944. Both Welkins and Seafires are visible on the airfield (Westland Helicopters Ltd).

they had a well-equipped factory and a good design office, determined to stay in the aeronautical business. It was hard going in the 1920s, however, and at the worst of the slump they were down to 12 men and six foremen.

An order for the Wapiti saved the day and the firm, which became Westland Aircraft Ltd in July 1935, has never looked back. To cope with the increased orders during the late 1930s a new erecting shop was constructed by John Brown & Co Ltd, who now had a controlling interest in the company, and when war was declared in September 1939 the Lysander was in full production and the development of the Whirlwind twin-engined fighter was well advanced.

For several months production was only interrupted by the occasional raid warning, but the first attack on July 15 1940 was completely unheralded, a small number of Ju 88s slipping out of low cloud and dropping 12 bombs on the airfield. They blasted a flight shed and put holes in the grass surface but no damage was done to Whirlwinds parked in front

of the factory. Another attempt was made on September 30 by He 111s of KG55. Forty bombers escorted by Bf 110s crossed the Dorset coast late in the afternoon but were turned away from Yeovil by the combined efforts of the weather, Hurricanes of 56 and 504 Squadrons, and Spitfires of 152 Squadron. On October 7 a more successful attempt was made, this time by 25 Ju 88s of II/KG51 escorted by some 50 Bf 110s of ZG26. Again intercepted by 10 Group fighters, seven of the escorts and two Ju 88s were shot down, but they forced their way through and, although only slight damage was done to the factory, more than 100 casualties resulted, most of them in a shelter which received a direct hit.

Strenuous efforts were made to camouflage the airfield, dummy hedges and ditches being sprayed on the grass using a mixture of paint and sawdust while the factory was disguised as a row of houses. The realism was tested to the satisfaction of the works defence officer when Captain O.P. Jones carefully landed the Short L17 *Syrinx* in about 150 ft (46

The interesting, but unsuccessful, Westminster helicopter on roll-out at Yeovil. The close proximity of the town can be appreciated (Westland Helicopters Ltd).

m) between two of the 'hedges' on a dull November afternoon.

Occasional small-scale raids continued through the winter of 1940/41, a particularly nasty one by a single Do 17, which dropped bombs at lunchtime on March 26 1941, killing one person and wounding several others, including the managing director, Mr Eric Mensforth. The workforce was gradually increased during the war to cope with new tasks given to the company. Westland became parent company for the Curtiss Mohawk, Tomahawk and Kittyhawk series of aircraft and also took part in the manufacture of Spitfires. An initial contract for Mk 1s was soon replaced by a larger one for Mk Vs, a total of 685 being built before switching to Seafires. 1,472 of the latter were constructed using facilities in the Yeovil area. Meanwhile the Welkin was put into production, followed by the impressive-looking Wyvern.

The company had already made the decision to concentrate on helicopters, however, and after a slow and hesitant start they developed into Britain's premier producer of rotary wing aircraft. In March 1957 the Helicopter Flight of 700 Squadron used the manufacturer's facilities for the intensive flying trials of the Whirlwind HAS 7, before transferring to Lee-on-Solent, but overall there has been little service presence at Yeovil over all the years that the airfield has been in existence. Currently Westland Aircraft Ltd is steadily producing Sea King and Lynx helicopters and has new projects under development. Activities can be seen from a minor road along the western boundary of the airfield, but only at a distance.

Yeovilton, Somerset

ST550234. 2 miles E of Ilchester

When the Admiralty regained control of the Fleet Air Arm in 1937 they quickly realised that their plans for new aircraft and carriers would rapidly outgrow their training facilities. They initiated a survey of suitable sites for airfields in the West

Country, and one of their first choices was a stretch of level ground just to the east of Ilchester.

They acquired 417 acres of farmland on July 1 1939 and work started on a typical naval training base with four runways, three of some 3,000 ft (914 m) and a main SW/NE one of 3,645 ft (1,111 m). The land was low-lying and construction was slowed by drainage problems. Named Yeovilton, the airfield was still incomplete when the situation on the south coast became critical, and the Naval Observer School (750, 751 and 752 Squadrons) started to move in from Ford during May 1940. At this time the station could only be described as a shambles, with half-completed buildings and equipment littering the whole camp, but things slowly improved and on June 18 1940 the airfield was commissioned as HMS *Heron* with Captain H.S. Murray Smith, RN, as the commanding officer.

The Observer School was only a temporary deployment for the station as intended was the new Naval Air Fighter School. To this end 794 Squadron formed in August to provide target facilities for the school which arrived from Eastleigh on September 16. The flying components were 759 and 760 Squadrons which started off with a motley collection of Masters, Rocs, Sea Gladiators and Hurricanes, but rapidly got down to the business of producing fighter pilots for the many new first-line squadrons being formed. The aircraft were flown fully armed during the Battle of Britain but the only chance they had to shoot anything down was ruined when one of the He 111s being stalked by two students was hit by flak and blew up, destroying the other bomber as well.

The Observer School moved out in September 1940 and was replaced by the first operational squadron to be based at Yeovilton—an Albacore unit, 827, which remained until March 1941. Meanwhile, the Air Fighting Development Unit (787 Squadron) arrived in January and was joined by 761 operating as the Advanced Flying School using Fulmars and Masters from August 1941.

Yeovilton was also used as a shore base for operational Sea Hurricane squadrons, many of them forming and completing their work-up on the airfield before embarking on carriers; or in the case of 804 Squadron on CAM ships, for their aircraft were used by the Fighter Catapult Unit for convoy protection against Fw 200 Condors.

A decoy airfield was set-up at Kings Moor, some four miles to the west, but in spite of being right in the firing line for bombers penetrating the West Country Yeovilton appeared to lead a charmed life for it was not attacked by the Luftwaffe. By 1941 most of the 12 Bellman hangars had been completed and large portions of the camp had been camouflaged. A hangar was in use on the main technical site and the domestic accommodation, consisting of Nissen and Maycrete huts, was being continually expanded. It was not enough, however, and much property was requisitioned in the surrounding villages, particularly for the WRNS. More dispersal areas were provided by taking over parts of Manor Farm, Specklington Farm and land at Bridgehampton and Podimore. Seven Mains hangars were built in these locations. Despite these extensions the station was reaching saturation point by early 1942, but fortunately satellites at Henstridge and Charlton Horethorne became available and some of Yeovilton's training commitment and units were transferred to these new airfields.

Radar had been introduced on naval ships early in the war and its use in the control of aircraft interception was quickly recognised so a Fighter Controller School started in rudimentary form at Yeovilton during 1941. A Direction Centre was established in Specklington Manor and from glasshouses built on the top the embryo controllers learnt their trade by directing Wrens pedalling radio-equipped ice cream tricycles around Yeovilton's dispersals. With the formation of 790 Squadron at Charlton Horethorne in June 1942 they progressed to the control of real aircraft and the school soon built up an enviable expertise.

Meanwhile arrangements were finalised for Westland Aircraft Ltd to erect a large workshop just to the west of the main technical site and to occupy two of the Bellman hangars (now Station Flight) to enable them to assemble and test-fly the Spitfires and Seafires they were manufacturing under contract.

No 807 Squadron became the first Seafire unit during the summer of 1942 and worked up at Yeovilton, but most of the station effort was devoted to training new fighter pilots. 759 Squadron steadily expanded, having over 60 Sea Hurricanes and some Spitfires and Masters in 1943, and in April it was joined by 748 as another Fighter Pool equipped with

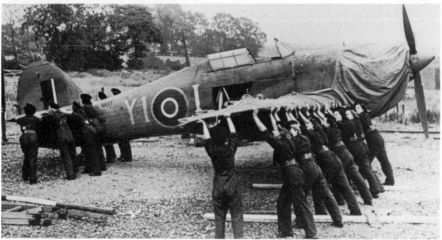

Top *Seafires of 759 Squadron on the Stockwitch Cross site at Yeovilton* (E. Hunt).
Above *Woman-power. Wren mechanics pose with a 759 Squadron Hurricane at Yeovilton in 1943.*

Fulmars and Martlets. The following month 736 re-formed as the School of Air Combat but left for St Merryn in September, and was replaced by a new series of squadrons formed to operate the Firefly. The first, 1770 Squadron, was commissioned on October 1, followed early in 1944 by 1771, but in contrast to most airfields in the south-west Yeovilton had a quiet invasion year with few changes in the training organisation. Work continued on the airfield, however, including a camouflaging programme and more domestic accommodation which allowed some requisitioned property to be given up.

No 748 Squadron moved to Dale in October, leaving 759 and the Fighter Direction School as the residents at Yeovilton. The school went to Kete, South Wales, during 1945, and at the end of the war Yeovilton's fortunes were at a low ebb as the run-down of the Fleet Air

Arm got under way. In November 1945, 700 Squadron arrived from Worthy Down to train maintenance test pilots on Seafires and when 759 (1 Fighter School) finally disbanded in March 1946 they were the only permanent flying unit at Yeovilton.

Disembarked Firefly and Sea Fury squadrons were accommodated during 1948-49, and, with Admiralty policy towards families changing, housing estates on the outskirts of Ilchester were started. In August 1949, 767 Squadron arrived to provide aircraft for the training of Deck Landing Officers (Batsmen) and were joined the following May by 799, which operated as a refresher flying unit until November 1951.

It was at this time that the future of Yeovilton became really secure when it was decided that the station would be the shore base for the Fleet's all-weather fighters. A big rebuilding programme was

Above *Yeovilton in the 1960s after the runway extensions. The Westland repair facility is in the foreground of the main technical/domestic site* (FAA Museum). **Below** *Sea Vixen FAW 1 of 899 Squadron at Yeovilton on the Stockwitch Cross site.*

undertaken by Taylor Woodrow including the lengthening of two runways, the main one to 7,500 ft (2,286 m). This work started in the summer of 1952, resulting in the eventual closure of Pyle Lane, the short cut to the aircrews' favourite pub, the 'Ram and Shark'.

HMS *Heron* became the headquarters of the Flag Officer Flying Training on May 27 1953 and in July also became the parent unit for the Southern Air Division of the RNVR. The airfield was reopened in time for the formation of 764 Squadron in November 1953 as an Operational Flying School, but it was the re-forming of 890 Squadron, the first Sea Venom all-weather fighter unit, which revitalised Yeovilton. Further operational squadrons followed, and on October 18 1956, 766 Squadron re-formed as the All Weather Fighter School.

From 1954 to 1956 Sea Furies of various RNVR squadrons were based at Yeovilton but when the last, 1832, left for Benson in November, the station was virtually an all-jet unit. During the same month all the aircraft were moved to Merryfield for it was again necessary to strengthen the runways and provide new hardstandings for the heavier Sea Vixens about to enter service. The technical site was also revamped and work started on the domestic side of the station. The airfield was reopened in Janury 1958 when 766 Squadron returned, and in November the Sea Vixen IFTU (700Y Squadron) was commissioned—the FAA had entered the big league!

Sea Vixen squadrons formed steadily during the following years and at the beginning of 1961 the Air Direction School returned, complete with the Air-work Services-operated Sea Venoms which flew for them. The control tower was considerably enlarged to accommodate the school, and sprouted a large number of extra aerials for their use.

In June 1962 HMS *Heron* received the Freedom of the Borough of Yeovil in 'recognition of many years of close association with the town' and during the summer 766 Squadron (now officially the Naval Air Fighter School) formed an aerobatic team called 'Fred's Five'. Led by the CO, Lieutenant Commander P. Reynolds, they managed to fly very creditable formation aerobatics, no mean feat in an 18-ton (18,288 kg) aircraft. The Fleet Air Arm Review, commemorating 50 years of naval aviation, took place at Yeovilton on May 28 1964 with HRH

Prince Philip in attendance. He also opened the Fleet Air Arm Museum, which uses one of the Bellman hangars near Stockwich Cross.

Sea Vixens remained the main stock-in-trade at Yeovilton until 1967 when, with the imminent introduction of the Phantom, the runways and hardstandings were again strengthened. 766 Squadron moved to Brawdy to give the contractors a free hand and during the next year many changes were made on both the airfield and camp areas.

The airfield reopened in August 1967 and in the following April 700P Squadron was commissioned to introduce the Phantom to the Fleet. They became 767 in January 1969 as part of the Naval Air Fighter School and on March 31 the operational Phantom unit, 892 Squadron, was formed. They were soon in the news for, during May they achieved the fastest time for the crossing from New York during the Transatlantic Race.

Further confirmation of the importance of Yeovilton was given by the transfer of the headquarters of Flag Officer Naval Air Command from its traditional home at Lee-on-Solent in November 1970 when it took over the tasks of FOFT in addition to its other support roles.

No 766 Squadron was disbanded on December 10 1970 and the run-down of operational Sea Vixen units followed rapidly. By the end of January 1972 only the Airwork Vixens remained in naval service and with the Naval Fighter School reduced to 767 Squadron and 892 dividing its time between Yeovilton and *Ark Royal*, it was obvious that the air station was under-employed. This was soon remedied for, in May, 707 and 846 Squadrons arrived from Culdrose, and Yeovilton became the HQ for the Wessex 5 Commando squadrons and the associated marine units.

The Naval Fighter School closed in August 1972 and Leuchars became the Phantom base, leaving Yeovilton to the choppers and Airwork Services. The latter were joined by the Fleet Requirements Unit from Hurn, the combined unit being renamed the Fleet Requirements and Air Direction Unit on December 1 with Hunters, Canberras and Sea Vixens. During 1975 the FRADU formed a four-Hunter aerobatic team named the 'Blue Herons' and have given shows all over the country. They were unique in being the first civilian pilots to carry out formation aerobatics in jet aircraft, but sadly have now been disbanded.

Joined by 845 and 848 Commando Squadrons when disembarked, the helicopter element remained unchanged until 848 disbanded in March 1976. Later in the year the IFTU for the Lynx was formed, becoming 700L on September 9 and the nucleus of 702 Squadron in 1977.

By 1972 the Fleet Air Arm had sadly resigned itself to losing its fixed-wing component when *Ark Royal* was scrapped in 1978. Circumstances change, however, and after much deliberation and delay an order for Sea Harriers to operate off the through-deck carriers was placed. Spirits rose, especially after it was announced that their home base would be Yeovilton, and that further extensions to the station would be required.

The first Sea Harriers arrived for 700 Squadron in June 1979 and further aircraft followed later in the year, enabling the formation of 800 Squadron on April 23 1980 as the first operational unit, while the trials unit became 899 Squadron. Soon afterwards the Sea King HC 4, a commando version of the anti-submarine helicopter, was introduced into 846 Squadron. Both Sea Harrier and Commando Sea King were publicly displayed very effectively during the 1980 Air Day and doubtless will now be a regular feature at displays throughout the '80s.

Now that the busy A303 has been diverted round Ilchester and HMS *Heron* is on a minor road (B3151), the traffic through the air station is much reduced, making it a pleasanter place for both personnel and visitors to the museum which has gone from strength to strength, and is now one of the major attractions in the area. Much increased in size, having outgrown its accommodation several times, it boasts the largest collection of aircraft in Europe and even has a Concorde under cover. From the large car park and picnic area the activities of the station can be clearly viewed. It is always worth a visit while the annual Yeovilton Air Day, usually held in August, has something to offer the whole family and should not be missed.

Zeals, Wiltshire

ST780327. 1 mile N of Zeals village

There were plenty of targets for 488 (RNZAF) Squadron on the night of May 14/15 1944. Out of a force of 106 German

bombers despatched, 60 were making for Bristol and 488 at Zeals were right in their path. Flight Lieutenant Hall and Flying Officer Cairns in Mosquito XIII *MM551* were vectored on to a bomber by their GCI station. Cairns picked it up on radar and stealthily they closed the gap until the pilot had it visually. A burst from those four 20 mm cannon and the Ju 188 was going down—into the sea. Five minutes earlier Flying Officers Jeffs and Spedding had similarly despatched a Ju 88 and hardly had time to get excited before they were vectored on to another target, which they claimed as a probable. A good start to a score of 34 later gained between D-Day and August 31 1944. Not all of these successes were made from Zeals but the run-up to D-Day and its immediate aftermath was undoubtedly the high point of this airfield's story.

Zeals was opened as a forward operating airfield in the Colerne sector of 10 Group on May 21 1942. 286 Squadron was the first occupant but was soon replaced by the Ibsley Wing (66 and 118 Squadrons), which arrived for four months of *Rhubarbs*, fighter sweeps and bomber escorts. Their first operation took them to Cherbourg docks, escorting 13 Bostons of 2 Group, but during September they were briefly replaced by 402 and 611 Squadrons, and finally returned to Ibsley in December when Zeals became untenable after heavy rain. They left a very miserable 2835 RAF Regiment Squadron at Zeals which was not used again for flying until March 1943 when 132, 174 and 184 Squadrons arrived for *Spartan*, a 15-day close-support exercise with the British Army. The unit became 122 Airfield for the exercise, which involved the squadrons in rapid change of bases and rough living in tents. The already infamous Zeals rain let up during *Spartan* but immediately afterwards 14 Works Area moved in to try and improve the drainage of the 530-acre grass airfield.

Whirlwinds of 263 Squadron appeared briefly during June/July and carried out a number of *Rhubarbs* before returning to Warmwell when Zeals was allotted to the USAAF. After some delay the Americans arrived in August and quickly took over the whole camp, the small RAF contingent retiring to Zeals House on the other side of the A303. Soon afterwards heavy rain again reduced Zeals to a quagmire and the Americans found it

Above *Zeals was a notoriously difficult airfield to fly from, and surely no better photograph could be found to illustrate this. A very bent Corsair of 760 Squadron in August 1945 is recovered by the salvage unit* (FAA Museum). **Below** *The Tower House at Zeals—just recognisable as a conversion of the old air traffic control.*

virtually unusable. 4675 Flight, 5005 Airfield Construction Squadron, laboured to improve it, building hardstandings and other facilities but, apart from the occasional B-17 and the trial of a glider from Stoke Orchard, little happened until December 23 when 26 P-47s landed, followed by 34 more on the 24th. They did not stay long however and neither did the IXth Air Force—they moved to a new airfield in Kent on March 11 1944.

On April 20 the station reopened under the operational control of 10 Group. Again a forward airfield, this time it was for two night fighter squadrons intended to combat nuisance raids by the Luftwaffe which were spreading over the country. 488 Squadron arrived from Bradwell Bay on May 4, and after a brief detachment to Colerne, got down to the business of night flying from this difficult airfield. With a steep-sided valley to the west and the rough grass field itself sloping away to the south-east, it was a tricky place for night flying despite the provision of Drem circuit and funnel lighting. There were a number of Blister hangars, but only one Teeside—hardly adequate for the operation of Mosquitoes with their very temperamental radar. However, the weather remained fairly kind for the next two months and 488, operating with 604 Squadron, Colerne, as 147 Wing, performed nightly over the beachhead in Normandy. On June 18, 410 Squadron moved to Zeals and both squadrons put up an average of eight sorties a night, scoring consistently.

On June 29, 149 Wing arrived from Deanland and took over the two Mosquito squadrons. Squadron Leader March and Flight Lieutenant Eyolfson (410 Squadron) destroyed an Me 410 over the outskirts of Paris on July 8 and reported seeing Flight Lieutenant Huppert and Flying Officer Christie shoot down a Ju 88 before they were forced to bale out of *MM570*. A Flight of 604 Squadron joined 149 Wing at Zeals late in July and had time to destroy a Ju 88 off Granville on the 26/27th before the whole Wing went to Colerne on the 28th. There they

displaced 286 Squadron which returned to Zeals whilst awaiting room at Weston Zoyland.

In October the 3 Glider Training School detachment at Northleach was moved to Zeals and for the next two months the sight of Masters noisily towing Hotspurs into the air became commonplace. They were replaced by the Glider Pick-up Training Flight early in January 1945. Using five Dakotas and 16 Hadrians they practiced snatch techniques using a hook on the towing aircraft to engage the tow-rope which was suspended between two poles. By this means gliders could be recovered from sites inaccessible to aircraft. When Ibsley became available in March the gliders were moved away and the airfield handed over to the Admiralty on April 14 as a replacement for Charlton Horethorne. It became HMS *Humming Bird* on May 18 and 790 (Fighter Direction) Squadron arrived from Horethorne, later joined by 704 and 760 Squadrons, both of which re-formed at Zeals. 704 Squadron operated as a Mosquito OTU while 760 used Corsair, Hellcat and Harvard aircraft for Corsair familiarisation. In July 771 (FRU) Squadron arrived from Twatt and used Wildcats and Corsairs to provide gunnery practice for the Fleet over the Portland ranges.

The Admiralty found Zeals just as unpleasant as all the previous occupants and, with the onset of autumn, discovered other airfields for their squadrons. By November only a closing-down party remained and on January 1 1946 HMS *Humming Bird* was paid off and the site reduced to Care & Maintenance. Soon de-requisitioned, the land was returned to agriculture and the minor road crossing the airfield reopened.

Little is now visible of the airfield. The western perimeter track serves as a farm road and runway for the occasional crop-duster, while parts of the domestic site on the southern boundary are used as hard-standing for farm buildings. The ATC building has been nicely converted into the 'Tower House', easily recognisable by its fine balcony and flat roof.

Index of units referred to in the text